GATHER
THE FRAGMENTS

© Estate of Alan Ecclestone 1993

ISBN 1 870652 17 7 (hardback)
ISBN 1 870652 18 5 (paperback)

First published 1993

Further copies of this book are obtainable from
CAIRNS PUBLICATIONS
47 Firth Park Avenue, Sheffield s5 6HF

Typeset and printed at THE HAND PRESS LIMITED
Westerham Heights Farm
Westerham Hill, Kent TN16 2BD

GATHER
THE FRAGMENTS

A BOOK OF DAYS

Compiled by Alan Ecclestone

Edited by Jim Cotter

SHEFFIELD
CAIRNS PUBLICATIONS
1993

CONTENTS

PREFACE

The contrast could not have been greater. Picture a small table by the window of the living room of a cottage in a hamlet in one of the least accessible areas of northern England. Then listen to the man, Alan Ecclestone, seated at that table, his voice gravelly, his choice of words careful and precise, a passion for truth informing his whole being. The vision in his mind and heart ranges through history – he knows how to remember, how to bring the past alive so that it may bear upon the present; through literature – he knows no better place than the poem and the novel for revealing the intricacies of humankind; through politics and prayer – he refuses to separate the two and longs to see justice and love incarnated in 'persons-in-community' (the phrase of one of his favourite thinkers, John MacMurray). There is nothing mean about him, nothing petty – rather a generosity that is never patronising nor sentimental.

Alan is reading from his 'book of days', quotations of prose and poetry gathered during the years of his retirement, the work of others that has nourished him and to which he continues to pay close attention year by year. We are working steadily through six ring binders, each containing two months of quotations, written out in his own hand. He is telling me why he has chosen each passage for this, his own unique prayer book.

He turns a page, sometimes exclaiming, sometimes falling silent awhile, occasionally passing over a passage that is too private for others' ears and eyes. Then he offers a recollection of an event or a considered yet pithy comment. I find it an effort to concentrate on scribbling down what he is saying: I should prefer to sit back and listen, or stop and reflect, or ask a question or two. From time to time we find ourselves talking on for some minutes, enjoying a roving in mind, before forcing ourselves back to the task in hand.

It takes most of a morning to consider a month of quotations. I feel in need of a break long before Alan seems to, vigorous and alert as he is in his mid-eighties. I suspect that many a pupil has wilted before the unflagging energy of this particular teacher!

Well, all that is in retrospect. Like so many I have been saddened by Alan's death, yet glad that the work we did was more or less complete

vii

and that this labour of love will appear *in memoriam*. There has inevitably been some editing of the manuscript, nearly all of it approved by Alan. He allowed himself two sides of A4 paper for each day: to have reproduced everything would have made an impossibly bulky book. I am sorry that he has not been able to see the final fine tuning, but I hope I have been loyal to his intentions and to the reasons for his choices, thus enabling the most significant extracts to be used.

I owe a debt of gratitude to Edmund de Waal and to Simon Bailey who have read the book aloud with me and suggested several helpful clarifications. They have been as amazed as I have at the range of material offered to us. Between us we did wonder if some half-dozen quotations might be somewhat obscure for most readers – they were to us! So I asked Alan last year if it would be possible to find substitutes for them. (He never regarded the selection as final and would from time to time replace a quotation with something else that had come to his attention.) Characteristically, he allowed one change but insisted that the rest were too important to leave out.

I do have one regret. Together with the written word, Alan also chose photographs and pictures. I wish I could have included them in this volume. But many were too personal, some impossible to trace, and again the book would have been too unwieldy. The visual was as important to Alan as the verbal for stimulating the imagination and prayer. Consequently this collection is one-sided.

I am also grateful to David Scott and Nigel Hancock for ferreting information that has helped to make the references as complete as possible; to Colin Brady who has negotiated the copyright permissions (and fees!) – we have done our best to trace copyright holders but in these days of publishing take-overs and disappearances, some inquiries have run into the sand: (I should be glad to hear of any omissions or errors so that matters can be put right in any reprint); to Alan Dodson, typographer, of Malvern, to Francis Atterbury, printer, of Westerham Heights, and to Rosemary Roberts, artist, of Lastingham, for their skills in producing a book which *invites* perusal; and not least to Alan Webster, formerly Dean of St Paul's, for his foreword.

My main debt is of course to Alan Ecclestone himself. To know him a little was one of the privileges of my life and to be entrusted with gathering these fragments that none of them might be lost has been a singular honour. To be present at his memorial service in Sheffield Cathedral was to witness a panorama of the twentieth century. Alan had lived eighty-eight years, all of them within the bounds of this century. Most of those present were naturally younger than he, but memory spanned the decades. To mention but two people, there was

Phoebe Webb who told us that she had first walked into Darnall Parish Church and met Alan forty-nine years ago, and there was Michael Wilson, son of Jim Wilson, who had been one of the great inspirers of Alan as a young man. And I am grateful to Jim Wilson's grandson, David, who has given permission for his photograph of Alan to be reproduced.

My hope is that readers of this book who did not know this remarkable human being may be enlarged in heart and mind as much as the lives of those who knew him have been enriched.

JIM COTTER
Sheffield, February 1993

FOREWORD

The God with whom this collection is concerned is a God who puts challenging questions and requires of us a response. From Genesis to the Gospels we hear this – God's question to Adam, "Where art thou?"; Cain's question to God, "Am I my brother's keeper?"; the Lord's question to his disciples after washing their feet, "Do you understand what I have done for you?"

For Alan Ecclestone, it was essential that we discover what is 'required' of us. And great literature as well as the Bible could help us. It too puts questions. Are we becoming more or less sensitive to the hopes and joys and sufferings of others? Is our mind getting mildewed, so that ears and eyes, taste and smell, the ability to feel God's people as spirit indwelt, is being lost?

Alan engaged with these questions when, in his retirement he wrote about prayer in *Yes to God*, about Charles Péguy and the way in which prayer and politics are intertwined in *A Staircase for Silence*, about the unresolved questions posed by the Holocaust for both Jews and Christians in *The Night Sky of the Lord*, and about St John's Gospel as poem in *The Scaffolding of Spirit*.

These books were given depth and bite by the experience of forty years of ministry in industrial parishes in the north of England, in Barrow with its shipbuilding, in Frizington with its exhausted iron ore and equally ravaged miners, and in Sheffield with its steel and smoke. His accurate and active passion for justice was forged in no uncertain furnace.

As parish priest he was assiduous in his caring and perceptive visiting and teaching. He was also controversial, prophetic and dramatic. He led protests against inadequate housing, complacency over unemployment, the use of animals and birds for human display, pollution, colonisation, and Europe's treatment of the Jews. I remember at the end of the Second World War he led a march through his parish of Darnall in Sheffield's war-torn east end, protesting against the dropping of atomic bombs by the western allies on Hiroshima and Nagasaki.

He would not allow us to be comfortable with our somewhat shut-in life in an Anglican diocese. He was aware of the global village long before the phrase was coined. To his parish meeting each week he invited visitors from abroad as well as representatives of the city's ethnic minorities. He never felt defensive about his faith. He did not complain that the vicarage he had once lived in had been turned into a mosque. He hung a banner in Holy Trinity Church with the inscription in Chinese characters, *Truth will triumph*. He lectured tirelessly for the Workers' Educational Association and he engaged in Christian-Marxist dialogue in this country and abroad.

He stood five times for Sheffield City Council as a Communist but was never elected. The Church of England never made him a canon. But he was not forgotten: three hundred people came from all over Britain to pay him tribute at his memorial service at Sheffield Cathedral.

After twenty-seven years at Darnall he and his wife Delia retired to Gosforth in Cumbria. His library of 12,000 volumes was housed next door to their white-washed cottage in a converted outhouse. Their talented sons and families and a host of friends continued to visit them, and here Alan wrote his major works. Year in, year out, after Delia had suffered a disabling stroke, he caught the bus into Whitehaven every day to visit her in hospital there. He read, reflected, argued, preached, conducted retreats. He wrote more perceptively than most on spirituality and sexual love. Even in the last week of his life he was discussing Iris Murdoch's latest book, *Metaphysics as a Guide to Morals*.

Alan's friends found him stimulating, surprising, argumentative, and full of humour. His enquiring mind, his laughter and anger and twinkling eyes opened up afresh one's own securely locked heart, shut up through social convention or shyness. Person spoke to person. In his praying at the end of his life he was remembering 190 people who had died, 250 living men and 190 living women, all known to him personally.

He could also rise to the big occasion, such as his Three Hours' Devotion in St Paul's Cathedral in London on Good Friday 1987, where he preached the Cross as the scene of a cosmic struggle for justice. If you went for a walk with him on the shores of Wastwater, opposite those dark and threatening screes, his acute memory for Dickens, Shakespeare, the Bible, and so many contemporary novels and so much poetry would be a delight. He was alert, attentive, disciplined to the end, and his final illness was brought on by his insistence on travelling to the National Gallery to see a favourite Crivelli painting.

Alan saw the artist, authors and poets as God's spies – those who detect hidden energies of divine love and wisdom, understanding and magnanimity in human life, irrespective of membership of any church. He said, "The great antitheses are love and power . . . only by loving people can you establish a secure relationship . . . most Christians do not

believe this . . . God has renounced power over us and approaches us
only with love . . . the greatest and most dramatic scene in all history is
Christ standing before Pontius Pilate."

The extracts in this book come from his lifelong disciplined reflection
as a teacher and learner, and especially as a questioner. He was part of
that crucial 'apostolic succession', those who ask God's questions in the
world today. Often it is not those who are most assured in their orthodoxy, or convinced of their spiritual heredity, who are Spirit-led. So in
this anthology Alan invites us to recognize that men and women
tragically estranged from the life of the churches may lead a resistance
movement against dehumanization, against the oppression of the cash
flow as the only test that matters. He insisted that it was an impoverish-
ment of our faith and spirituality not to see, for instance, the great
Romantic poets – Blake, Coleridge, Wordsworth, Shelley, Keats – as
part of the long succession of spiritual guides who challenge money and
status. He thought the Church of England narrow-minded not to
include them in its official list of saints and teachers.

Alan Ecclestone believed that prayer, if it is to be a personal Yes to
God, needs honesty, passionate engagement and intelligent development. He used to quote from Julian of Norwich, "The one thing that
matters is that we should always say Yes to God whenever we experience Him."

The renewal of the churches and other religious groupings depends
on learning how to think and pray afresh so that corporate action can be
effective for change. It is not new theories of theology, but new corporate
courage and imaginative, scientifically planned adventures of the spirit
that we need and for which Alan Ecclestone worked. If self-centred,
privatised competitiveness, which can be so deadly and lead to crisis and
war, is to be replaced by a worldwide spirit of friendly co-operation,
then the changes within human character have to be deep indeed.

This volume of 'fragments' will help us in that task, and Alan's own
writings and the forthcoming biography will also be searched for
questions and for hints of the way ahead. For here is evidence of a
mature spirituality for contemporary seekers which can feed our
imagination and widen our sympathy. We can be guided, if we will, by
this, one of the twentieth century's most remarkable priests.

ALAN WEBSTER
Norwich, February 1993

This is the day that the Lord hath made;
we will be glad and rejoice in it.

[PSALM 118.24]

All our seeming contradictions arise from the
equation between today that is merely a bridge
to tomorrow and the today that is a spring-board
to eternity. No day has written on its forehead
which of the two todays it is. One can never tell;
every act should be performed as though all
eternity depended on it.

[THEODORE ROSENZWEIG, 1917]

So teach us to number our days:
that we may apply our hearts unto wisdom.

[PSALM 90.12]

That passion may not harm us, let us act as if we
had only eight hours to live.

[PASCAL, *Pensées*, 203]

Come, children, let us shut up the box and the
puppets, for our play is played out.

[WILLIAM THACKERAY, *Vanity Fair*]

JANUARY

1st January

This fragile life between birth and death can nevertheless be a fulfilment – if it is a dialogue. In our life and experience we are addressed; by
thought, speech and action, by producing and influencing we are able to
answer. For the most part we do not listen to the address, or we break
into it with chatter. But if the word comes to us and the answer proceeds
from us then human life exists, though brokenly, in the world. The
kindling of the response in that 'spark' of the soul, the blazing up of the
response, which occurs time and again, we term responsibility. We
practise responsibility for that realm of life allotted and entrusted to us
for which we are able to respond, that is, for which we have a relation of
deeds which may count – in all our inadequacy, as a proper response.

[MARTIN BUBER]

*I was for many years a member of the Communist Party. I used to read this
passage at the beginning of funerals for people with little connection with the
Church, for whom biblical texts had no lived meaning. Yet they were by no
means lacking in religious sensibility.*

2nd January

Well, so that is that. Now we must dismantle the tree,
Putting the decorations back into their cardboard boxes –
Some have got broken – and carrying them up to the attic.
The holly and the mistletoe must be taken down and burnt,
And the children got ready for school. There are enough
Left-overs to do, warmed up, for the rest of the week –
Not that we have much appetite, having drunk such a lot,
Stayed up so late, attempted – quite unsuccessfully –
To love all our relatives, and in general
Grossly overestimated our powers. Once again
As in previous years we have seen the actual Vision and failed

I

To do more than entertain it as an agreeable
Possibility, once again we have sent Him away,
Begging though to remain His disobedient servant,
The promising child who cannot keep His word for long. . .

(Sufferings) will come, all right, don't worry; probably in the
    form
That we do not expect, and certainly with a force
More dreadful than we can imagine. In the meantime
There are bills to be paid, machines to be kept in repair,
Irregular verbs to learn, the Time Being to redeem
From insignificance. The happy morning is over,
The night of agony still to come; the time is noon:
When the Spirit must practise his scales of rejoicing.
God will cheat no one, not even the world, of its triumph.

[W. H. AUDEN, from *For the Time Being*]

This seemed a good poem to share with a group of people at St Bees who met one early January. We need to recognize the special in the ordinary if the special is not to lose its meaning.

3rd January

Prayer is properly not petition, but simply an attention to God which is a form of love. With it goes the idea of grace, of a supernatural assistance to human endeavour which overcomes empirical limitations of personality. What is this attention like, and can those who are not religious believers still conceive of profiting by such an activity? . . .

The chief enemy of excellence in morality (and also in art) is personal fantasy: the tissue of self-aggrandizing and consoling wishes and dreams which prevent one from seeing what there is outside one. Rilke said of Cézanne that he did not paint, 'I like it', he painted, 'There it is'. This is not easy, and requires in art and morals a discipline. One might say here that art is an excellent analogy of morals, or indeed it is in this respect a case of morals. We cease to be in order to attend to the existence of something else, a natural object, a person in need. We can see in mediocre art, where perhaps it is even more clearly seen than in mediocre conduct, the intrusion of fantasy, the assertion of self, the dimming of any reflection of the real world.

[IRIS MURDOCH, from *The Sovereignty of Good*]

I believe this to be one of the most important books of the last twenty years. Is not the 'giving of attention' to the other a form of love and a way into prayer? Is it not the honest attempt to look and not to convert what is attended to into either a consolation or a weapon?

4th January

Often rebuked, yet always back returning
To those first feelings that were born with me,
And leaving busy chase of wealth and learning
For idle dreams of things which cannot be:

Today I will not seek the shadowy region;
Its unsustaining vastness waxes drear,
And visions rising, legion after legion,
Bring the unreal world too strangely near.

I'll walk, but not in old heroic traces,
And not in paths of high morality,
And not among the half-distinguished faces,
The clouded forms of long-past history.

I'll walk where my own nature would be leading:
It vexes me to choose another guide:
Where the grey flocks in ferny glens are feeding,
And the wild wind blows on the mountain side.

What have those lonely mountains worth revealing?
More glory and more grief than I can tell:
The earth that wakes one human heart to feeling
Can centre both the worlds of Heaven and Hell.

[EMILY BRONTË, *Stanzas*]

The searing winds of the bleak gritstone moors in January!

5th January

It has always seemed to me that every conception is immaculate and that this dogma concerning the Mother of God expresses the idea of all motherhood. At the moment of childbirth, every woman has the same aura of isolation, as though she were abandoned, alone. At this vital moment the man's part is as irrelevant as if he had never had anything to do with it, as though the whole thing was gratuitous.

It is the woman, by herself, who brings forth her progeny, and carries it upstairs, to some top storey of life, a quiet, safe place for a cradle. Alone, in silence and humility, she feeds and rears the child.

The Mother of God is asked to "pray zealously to her Son and her God," and the words of the psalm are put into her mouth: "My soul doth magnify the Lord and my spirit hath rejoiced in God my Saviour. For he hath regarded the low estate of his handmaiden: for behold, from henceforth all generations shall call me blessed." It is because of her child that she says this. He will magnify her ("for He that is mighty hath done to me great things"). He is her glory.

Any woman could say it. For every one of them, God is in her child. Mothers of great men must have this feeling particularly, but then, at the beginning, all women are mothers of great men – it isn't their fault if life disappoints them later.

[BORIS PASTERNAK, from *Dr Zhivago*]

This passage came to me as I was preparing a Christmas reflection for Channel 4 television. The birthing is so much the woman and the child – as is that previous formative nine months: the man can merely hold and protect. And can men rejoice that womankind is overturning thousands of years of history and at last claiming a denied meaning? After all, the Magnificat is one of the few Christian hymns that celebrates dragging down tyrants.

6th January

"A cold coming we had of it,
Just the worst time of the year
For a journey, and such a long journey:
The ways deep and the weather sharp,
The very dead of winter."
And the camels galled, sore-footed, refractory,
Lying down in the melting snow.
There were times we regretted
The summer palaces on slopes, the terraces,
And the silken girls bringing sherbet,
Then the camel men cursing and grumbling
And running away, and wanting their liquor and women,
And the night-fires going out, and the lack of shelters,
And the cities hostile and the towns unfriendly

And the villages dirty and charging high prices:
A hard time we had of it.
At the end we preferred to travel all night,
Sleeping in snatches,
With the voices singing in our ears, saying
That this was all folly.

Then at dawn we came down to a temperate valley,
Wet, below the snow line, smelling of vegetation,
With a running stream and a water-mill beating the darkness,
And three trees on the low sky.
And an old white horse galloped away in the meadow.
Then we came to a tavern with vine-leaves over the lintel,
Six hands at an open door dicing for pieces of silver,
And feet kicking the empty wine-skins.
But there was no information, and so we continued
And arrived at evening, not a moment too soon
Finding the place; it was (you may say) satisfactory.

All this was a long time ago, I remember,
And I would do it again, but set down
This set down
This: Were we led all that way for
Birth or Death? There was a Birth, certainly,
We had evidence and no doubt, I had seen birth and death,
But had thought they were different; this Birth was
Hard and bitter agony for us, like Death, our death.
We returned to our places, these kingdoms,
But no longer at ease here, in the old dispensation,
With an alien people clutching their gods.
I should be glad of another death.

[T. S. ELIOT, *The Journey of the Magi*]

*I recall the publication of this poem and am still haunted by the question,
Birth or Death?*

7th January

We do not ask to fold the linen cloth once more
Nor that it should again upon the shelf be placed,
We do not ask that mem'ry's creases be effaced,
To leave this heavy cloak smooth as it was before.

O Mistress of the way and of the reunion,
Mirror of Justice and the spirit's honesty,
Alone you understand, O lovely Majesty,
The meaning of this halt and this communion.

O Mistress of the race and its divisions,
Temple of wisdom, heavenly rectitude,
Alone you understand, divine exactitude,
The judge, his hesitations and decisions.

When we came to sit at the parting of two ways
And had to choose remorse or else regret,
When before a double fate our feet were set,
When forced upon the crossing of two vaults to gaze.

Mistress of the secret, alone you understand
That one of these two paths led fatally below,
You know the way our steps expressly choose to go
As a craftsman chooses wood for the work on hand.

And not at all from virtue, where we have no part,
And not at all from duty which has never charmed,
But like the steady builder with his compass armed,
We needs must take our stand at sorrow's very heart.

And be firmly placed at the axis of distress,
And by that sacred need to bear a heavier load,
And to feel more deeply and go the hardest road,
And receive the evil at its greatest stress.

By that old craftsman's skill, that capability,
Which will no longer serve us happiness to gain,
May we at least be able honour to maintain,
And keep for it alone our fidelity.

[CHARLES PÉGUY, *A Prayer in Confidence*]

Péguy was born on 7 January 1873, a man sufficiently near to being a peasant that he could see in Mary one who understands what this Way is like, with its humiliation and endurance. He tells us of how he foot-slogged his way towards Chartres – the setting for the sequence of poems from which this extract comes.

8th January

When you are old and grey and full of sleep,
And nodding by the fire, take down this book,
And slowly read, and dream of the soft look
Your eyes had once, and of their shadows deep;

How many loved your moments of glad grace,
And loved your beauty with love false or true,
But one man loved the pilgrim soul in you,
And loved the sorrows of your changing face;

And bending down beside the glowing bars,
Murmur a little sadly how Love fled
And paced upon the mountain overhead
And hid his face amid a crowd of stars...

[W. B. YEATS, *When you are old*]

It is the third line of the second stanza that drew me to this poem.

9th January

"All's to come right in the end, Joe, be sure of that!... I don't mean ... that we shall meet corrected and improved editions of each other here-after, in a corrected and improved place, from which all the beasts and the fools, who have not been corrected and improved out of all knowl-edge, are excluded by a Creator who might have had consideration enough for them to let them be – doing no more harm than any other beast or fool who has never come into existence! I believe I describe fairly many people's idea of a selected hereafter. But I don't mean any such thing. I mean when I say all's to come right in the end, that it will do so in some sense absolutely inconceivable by us – so inconceivable that the simple words I use to express it may then have ceased to mean anything, or anything worth recording, to our expanded senses. To a mind that conceives this degree of inconceivability, it seems merely common sense and common prudence to leave it all in God's hands."

"But," said I, "there must be some residuum of the rubbish of our thoughts and perceptions that will hold good throughout for this state and the next. There must be a golden bead at the bottom of the Crucible."

"Of course there is," said the Doctor. "Love is the golden bead at the bottom of the Crucible. But love isn't thought or perception or even passion, in the ordinary sense. It's God knows what! I give it up. But it's a breath of fresh air from the highest Heaven brought somehow into the stuffy cellar of our existence. It's the flash of light that strikes on the wall of the tunnel our train is passing through, and shows us the burst of sunshine that is coming."

[WILLIAM DE MORGAN, from *Joseph Vance*]

The author began this novel while ill in bed. It is far too long and badly shaped, yet it has flashes of authenticity – like the light on the wall of the tunnel . . .

10th January

I wake to sleep, and take my waking slow.
I feel my fate in what I cannot fear.
I learn by going where I have to go.

We think by feeling. What is there to know?
I hear my being dance from ear to ear.
I wake to sleep and take my waking slow.

Of those so close beside me, which are you?
God bless the Ground! I shall walk softly there,
And learn by going where I have to go.

Light takes the tree; but who can tell us how?
The lowly worm climbs up a winding stair;
I wake to sleep, and take my waking slow.

Great Nature has another thing to do
To you and me, so take the lively air
And, lovely, learn by going where to go.

This shaking keeps me steady. I should know
What falls away is always. And is near.
I wake to sleep, and take my waking slow.
I learn by going where I have to go.

[THEODORE ROETHKE, *The Waking*]

Roethke grew up with the sense of the steady growth of plants – his father was a nurseryman. I learn by going where I have to go.

11th January

The miracle wrought by the Holy Spirit is generally referred to as a gift of tongues: is it not equally a gift of ears? . . . The curse of Babel is not the diversity of human tongues – diversity is essential to life – but the pride of each of us which makes us think that those who make different verbal noises from our own are incapable of human speech so that discourse with them is out of the question: a pride which, since speech of no two persons is identical – language is not algebra – must inevitably lead to the conclusion that the gift of human speech is reserved for oneself alone. It is due to this curse that, as Sir William Osler said, "Half of us are blind, few of us feel, and we are all deaf." That we may learn first how to listen and then how to translate are the two gifts of which we stand most urgently in need and for which we should most fervently pray at this time.

[W. H. AUDEN, from the Introduction to *Essay on Protestant Mystics*]

The prayer that we might listen, putting silence around words, is even more urgent now than when Auden wrote this piece in 1964.

12th January

Yes, thou art gone! and round me too the night
 In ever-nearing circle weaves her shade.
 I see her veil draw soft across the day,
I feel her slowly chilling breath invade
 The cheek grown thin, the brown hair spent with grey;
  I feel her finger light
Laid pausefully upon life's headlong train; –
 The foot less prompt to meet the morning dew,
 The heart less bounding at emotion new,
And hope, once crush'd, less quick to spring again.

And long the way appears, which seem'd so short
 To the unpractis'd eye of sanguine youth;
 And high the mountain-tops, in cloudy air,
The mountain-tops where is the throne of Truth,
 Tops in life's morning-sun so bright and bare!

Unbreachable the fort
Of the long-batter'd world uplifts its wall;
And strange and vain the earthly turmoil grows,
And near and real the charm of thy repose,
And night as welcome as a friend would fall.

[MATTHEW ARNOLD, from *Thyrsis*]

Matthew Arnold was aware of the disintegration of European culture and faith, yet glimpsed beauty in the everyday and in human love – the beauty to which we must be sensitive when young, before the tissues begin to harden.

13th January

As they watched (the sun go down), the wind suddenly seemed to drop and the ocean round them became quiet and calm as if the whole Atlantic world was holding its breath at the deathbed of so much light. In that hushed moment the sun itself seemed to gather together the memory of all its days and make one last gesture of full, cumulative stature. It grew enormous, spilt over the rim of itself in a great curve of crimson fire, and then they saw the shadow of the swollen horizon impinging on it like the crest of a dark, Carpathian wood. The sun began to contract . . . until it was a lotus about to close among the lilies in the pool of the sacred crocodile. Finally, and briefly, it was the tip of Apollo's spear thrust for hardening into the fire of the great blacksmith, night. All along the horizon from north and south light came speeding with flashing spurs to join in that fine, pointed, spiked moment of fire. Then the sun disappeared. For a second the sea caught its breath at so great a loss of light, the horizon went dark with anguish – and then it happened. From below the horizon, from the other side of the gulf a tremendous flash of bright, emerald green light shot up across the sky in the most solemn, urgent, majestic and defiant wave of farewell. It came right over the edge of the sea like a flight of burning arrows shot straight at the breast of the advancing night by an army marching not in defeat, but victoriously homewards.

For some minutes the man and woman stood silent, overawed, feeling unimportant in the presence of the miracle. Yet they felt infinitely privileged as if they had just been presented with the fundamental symbol of the master pattern wherein opposites lost themselves in some greater meaning. They'd seen a demonstration of loss which was not loss, together with the heroic thrust which keeps life whole and unending.

[LAURENS VAN DER POST, from *The Face Beside the Fire*]

One of the constant themes of Laurens van der Post is the 'pattern wherein opposites' lose 'themselves in some greater meaning.'

14th January

One of the crowd went up,
And knelt before the Paten and the Cup,
Received the Lord, returned in peace, and prayed
Close to my side. Then in my heart I said:

O Christ, in this man's life –
This stranger who is Thine – in all his strife,
All his felicity, his good and ill,
In the assaulted stronghold of his will,

I do confess Thee here
Alive within this life; I know Thee near
Within this lonely conscience, closed away,
Within this brother's solitary day,

Christ in his unknown heart,
His intellect unknown – this love, this art,
This battle and this peace, this destiny,
That I shall never know, look upon me!

Christ in his numbered breath,
Christ in his beating heart and in his death,
Christ in his mystery! From that secret place
And from that separate dwelling, give me grace.

[ALICE MEYNELL, *The Unknown God*]

On retiring to Gosforth and going to church, I knelt among people who as yet were anonymous. Yet each person there required of me that I say the second stanza of this poem. It is so easy to half-acknowledge and not to notice that the Christ is in them. It is humbling too for the one who has presided at the Holy Communion to look out at the people on leaving the altar, to look on Christ embodied. In which direction should one bow?

15th January

We asked how any deeper, will-moving intercommunication can even be possible among men? For the mere possession of, and appeal to, the elementary forms of abstract thinking, which seem to be our only certain common material, instrument and measure of persuasion, appear never, of themselves, to move the will, or indeed, the feelings . . .

Only a life sufficiently large and alive to take up and return within its own experimental range, at least some of the poignant question and conflict, as well as of the peace-bringing solution and calm . . . only such a life can be largely persuasive, at least for us Westerners and in our times . . . To be truly winning the soul's life must become and must keep itself full and true . . .

Now it is simply false that any man can, even for his own self alone, hold spiritual reality in a simple passive, purely dependent, entirely automatic and painless fashion; or that he can, even at the last, possess it in a full, continuous and effortless harmony and simultaneousness.

[FRIEDRICH VON HÜGEL, from *The Mystical Element in Religion*]

Von Hügel was often convoluted in style, in Germanic fashion, but he well reminds us here of the significant question, What makes things change? Certainly they don't without a generosity and largeness of heart and soul that is the opposite of the crabbed and narrow spirit so often felt in our day.

16th January

"But the earth is wonderful. It is all we have. It has brought me back when, otherwise, I should have died."

The Jew could not hide a look of kindly cunning.

"And at the end? When the earth can no longer raise you up?"

"I shall sink into it," she said, "and the grass will grow out of me."

But she sounded sadder than she should have.

"And the Chariot," he asked, "that you wished to discuss at one stage? Will you not admit the possibility of redemption?"

"Oh, words, words!" she cried, brushing them off her freckled hands. "I do not know what they mean."

"But the Chariot", she conceded, "does exist. I have seen it. Even if a certain person likes to hint that it was only because I happened to be sick. I have seen it. And Mrs Godbold has, whom I believe and trust. Even my poor father, whom I did not, and who was bad, bad, suspected some such secret was being kept hidden from him. And you, a very learned man, have found the Chariot in books, and understand more than you will tell."

"But not the riders! I cannot visualize, I do not understand the riders!"

"Do you see everything at once? My own house is full of things waiting to be seen. Even quite common objects are shown to us when it is time for them to be."

The Jew was so pleased he wriggled slightly inside his clothes. "It is you who are the hidden zaddik!"

"The what?" she asked.

"In each generation, we say, there are thirty-six hidden zaddikim, holy men who go secretly about the world, healing, interpreting, doing their good deeds."

[PATRICK WHITE, from *Riders in the Chariot*]

Do you notice? So often we don't notice enough, we are not enough awake or aware. In Elizabethan English 'nothing' was pronounced in the same way as 'noting'. Did Shakespeare write Much Ado about Nothing *to ask what we have actually noticed?*

17th January

O golden tongued Romance, with serene lute!
Fair plumed Syren, Queen of far-away!
Leave melodizing on this wintry day,
Shut up thine olden pages, and be mute:
Adieu! for, once again, the fierce dispute
    Betwixt damnation and impassion'd clay
    Must I burn through; once more humbly assay
The bitter-sweet of this Shakespearean fruit:
Chief Poet! and ye clouds of Albion,
    Begetters of our deep eternal theme!
When through the old oak Forest I am gone,
    Let me not wander in a barren dream,
But, when I am consumed in the fire,
Give me new Phoenix wings to fly at my desire.

[JOHN KEATS, *On sitting down to read* King Lear *once again*]

That oh so narrow line between 'damnation' and 'impassion'd clay'. As T. S. Eliot put it in Four Quartets, *we can be redeemed only 'by fire or fire'.*

18th January

> When in disgrace with fortune and men's eyes
> I all alone beweep my outcast state,
> And trouble deaf heaven with my bootless cries,
> And look upon myself, and curse my fate,
> Wishing me like to one more rich in hope,
> Featur'd like him, like him with friends possess'd
> Desiring this man's art, and that man's scope,
> With what I most enjoy contented least;
> Yet in these thoughts myself almost despising,
> Haply I think on thee, – and then my state,
> Like to the lark at break of day arising
> From sullen earth, sings hymns at heaven's gate;
> For thy sweet love remember'd such wealth brings
> That then I scorn to change my state with Kings.

[WILLIAM SHAKESPEARE, *Sonnet XXIX*]

Our lives are impoverished if we do not cherish friendship. And this sonnet resonates for those who can catch the note, with the One who turned from relationships of powerful domination and submission and breathtakingly called his followers his friends.

19th January

She made no effort to get things round her . . . She didn't struggle and strain to buy things and then care for them more than life itself.

She didn't go all out after fine clothes, clothes that beautify what is ugly and evil.

She was misunderstood and abandoned even by her husband. She had lost six children, but not her sociable ways. She was a stranger to her sisters and sisters-in-law, a ridiculous creature who stupidly worked for others without pay. She didn't accumulate property against the day she died. A dirty-white goat, a gammy-legged cat, some rubber plants . . .

We had all lived side by side with her and never understood that she was that righteous one without whom, as the proverb says, no village can stand.

Nor any city. Nor our whole land.

[ALEXANDER SOLZHENITSYN, from *Matryona's House*]

On whom does the continuing life of the world depend?

20th January

An exalted mode of living is not special to romantic experiences in its restricted, amorous sense, and one speaks (even if in a modern patronizing fashion) of the romance of many other spheres of human action as well. Romance, in the Shakespearean context, has indeed such breadth; it is the defining character of every human way that is 'engaged', that has faith. From out of such faith (where 'faith' must be understood as a binding in relation, and not simply as belief) meaning comes. For the one who is so bound, a certain structure of values is given or, rather, discloses itself as meaning, and this meaning not only supports but is the mode of his being; the breaking of his faith breaks him.

Religion, which in this sense is quintessential romance, is necessarily closed to attack from the outside, because its revelation and its faith (the relation from which all meaning springs) stream forth from a Being beyond the reality at hand. But in romantic love, revelation extended itself from a being whose outward form is apprehensible to all. The foundations of belief in romantic love do not involve factors beyond what seem to be accessible in the actual lived reality that all men know (although the term 'know' and the reality that is tied to it are themselves ultimately problematic). Romantic love, therefore, is at once open to criticism, by a disengaged view on the ground that it raises structures of extravagant faith on foundations of mere earth, that meanings which are absolute cannot be derived from phenomena which are relative, which are situated within a temporal world order. Such criticism in Shakespearean comedy can be witty and, at the same time, profound.

[DAVID HOROWITZ, from *Shakespeare, An Existential View*]

Don't be so romantic! Why not?

21st January

I see you, a child
In a garden sheltered for buds and playtime,
Listening as if beguiled
By a fancy beyond your years and the flowering maytime.
The print is faded: soon there will be
No trace of those who pose enthralling,
Nor visible echo of my voice distantly calling
"Wait! Wait for me!"

Then I turn the page
To a girl who stands like a questioning iris
By the waterside, at an age
That asks every mirror to tell what the heart's desire is.
The answer she finds in that oracle stream
Only time could affirm or disprove,
Yet I wish I was there to venture a warning. "Love
Is not what you dream."

Next you appear
As if garlands of wild felicity crowned you –
Courted, caressed, you wear
Like immortelles the lovers and friends around you.
'They will not last you, rain or shine,
They are but straws and shadows,'
I cry: "Give not to those charming desperadoes
What was made to be mine."

One picture is missing –
The last. It would show me a tree stripped bare
By intemperate gales, her amazing
Noonday of blossom spoilt which promised so fair.
Yet, scanning those scenes at your heyday taken,
I tremble, as one who must view
In the crystal a doom he could never deflect – yes, I too
Am fruitlessly shaken.

I close the book;
But the past slides out of its leaves to haunt me
And it seems, wherever I look,
Phantoms of irreclaimable happiness taunt me.
Then I see her, petalled in new-blown hours,
Beside me – "All you love most there
Has blossomed again," she murmurs, "all that you missed there
Has grown to be yours."

[CECIL DAY LEWIS, The Album]

*Snapshots of memories have extraordinary power, not least in their clarity as
we get older. Are we claiming our inner resources anew, gathering our energies
for the next leap forward? Do we indeed remember or do we rather inhabit memory as a dimension like space and time?*

22nd January

He is the Way.
Follow Him through the Land of Unlikeness;
You will see rare beasts, and have unique adventures.

He is the Truth.
Seek Him in the Kingdom of Anxiety;
You will come to a great city that has expected your return for years.

He is the Life.
Love Him in the world of the Flesh;
And at your marriage all its occasions shall dance for joy.

[W. H. AUDEN, from *For the Time Being*]

Do we try to escape from or enter more deeply into our strangeness, our anxieties, our bodiliness? Can we, can the city, bear and contain all that has been building up and pressing upon us this century?

23rd January

One foot in Eden still, I stand
And look across the other land.
The world's great day is growing late,
Yet strange these fields that we have planted
So long with crops of love and hate.
Time's handiworks by time are haunted,
And nothing now can separate
The corn and tares compactly grown.
The armorial weed in stillness bound
About the stalk; these are our own.
Evil and good stand thick around
In fields of charity and sin
Where we shall lead our harvest in.

Yet still from Eden springs the root
As clean as on the starting day.
Time takes the foliage and the fruit
And burns the archetypal leaf
To shapes of terror and of grief
Scattered along the winter way.

But famished field and blackened tree
Bear flowers in Eden never known.
Blossoms of grief and charity
Bloom in these darkened fields alone.
What had Eden ever to say
Of hope and faith and pity and love
Until was buried all its day
And memory found its treasure trove?
Strange blessings never in Paradise
Fall from these beclouded skies.

[EDWIN MUIR, *One Foot in Eden*]

*What an imaginative charge there is in Edwin Muir's poetry of Orkney. That
'blossoms of grief and charity bloom in these darkened fields alone', is this not a
sign of hope in these days? We are infinitely richer than our ancestors!*

24th January

The architects of the twelfth and thirteenth centuries took the Church
and the universe for truths, and tried to express them in a structure
which should be final . . . the result was an art marked by a singular
unity, which endured and served its purpose until man changed his
attitude toward the universe. The trouble was not in the art or the
method or the structure, but in the universe itself which presented
different aspects as man moved. Granted a church, St Thomas's Church
was the most expressive that man has made and the great Gothic
cathedrals were its most complete expression.

Perhaps the best proof of it is their apparent instability. Of all the
elaborate symbolism which has been suggested for the Gothic cathedral,
the most vital and most perfect may be that the slender nervure, the
springing motion of the broken arch, the leap downwards of the flying
buttress – the visible effort to throw off a visible strain – never let us
forget that Faith alone supports it, and that, if Faith fails, Heaven is lost.
The equilibrium is visibly delicate beyond the line of safety; danger
lurks in every stone. The peril of the heavy tower, of the restless vault,
of the vagrant buttress; the uncertainty of logic, the inequalities of the
syllogism, the irregularities of the mental mirror – all these haunting
nightmares of the church are expressed as strongly by the Gothic
cathedral as though it had been the cry of human suffering, and as no

emotion had ever been expressed before or is likely to find expression again. The delight of its aspiration is flung up to the sky. The pathos of its self-distrust and anguish of doubt is buried in the earth as its last secret.

[HENRY ADAMS, from *Mont-St-Michel and Chartres*]

To see the Gothic cathedral, really to 'notice' it is to recognize that 'danger lurks in every stone' and to know the tension between delight of aspiration and anguish of doubt.

25th January

> O wily painter, limiting the scene
> From a cacophony of dusty forms
> To the one convulsion, what is it you mean
> In that wide gesture of the lifting arms?
>
> I turn, hardly enlightened, from the chapel
> To the dim interior of the church instead,
> In which there kneel already several people,
> Mostly old women: each head closeted
> In tiny fists holds comfort as it can.
> Their poor arms are too tired for more than this
> – For the large gesture of solitary man,
> Resisting, by embracing, nothingness.

[THOM GUNN, from *In Santa Maria del Popolo, Rome*]

It is the light alone that reveals the mystery, not light streaming down from the sky or radiating from the figure of Christ (*Ecstasy of St Francis*). The mature Caravaggio drew the last consequences. In his *Conversion of St Paul*, he rendered vision solely on the level of inner humiliation. Light, without heavenly reassurance, has the power to strike Saul down and transform him into Paul . . .

[S. J. FREEDBURG, from *Painting in Italy, 1500–1600*]

Thom Gunn's poem refers to Caravaggio's painting of the Conversion of St Paul. Paul was a religious genius. But did Christ like religious geniuses? Did the Gentile Church lose touch with its Jewish roots? Did it become high and exalted above the poor women in the pews in Gunn's poem?

26th January

Whether to sally and see thee, girl of my dreams,
    Or whether to stay
And see thee not! How vast the difference seems
    Of Yea from Nay
Just now. Yet this same sun will slant its beams
    At no far day
On our two mounds, and then what will the difference weigh!

Yet I will see thee, maiden dear, and make
    The most I can
  Of what remains to us amid this brake
    Cimmerian
Through which we grope, and from whose thorns we ache,
    While still we scan
Round our frail faltering progress for some path or plan.

By briefest meeting something sure is won;
    It will have been:
Nor God nor Demon can undo the done,
    Unsight the seen,
Make muted music be as unbegun,
    Though things terrene
 Groan in their bondage till oblivion supervene.

So, to the one long-sweeping symphony
    From times remote
Till now, of human tenderness, shall we
    Supply one note,
Small and untraced, yet that will ever be
    Somewhat afloat
Amid the spheres, as part of sick Life's antidote.

[THOMAS HARDY, *To meet, or otherwise*]

A poem that can be read on a number of levels. No other poet of the nineteenth century so faced that which is loved and lost. No matter how small a love, when it is lost there is a heart-tug which you have to live with for the rest of your life. In Hardy there is a tenderness suffusing this ache. He understood the pain which is the underside of love – which is also St John's Gospel and much of Browning and of Blake.

27th January

(Mozart) had heard, and caused those who have ears to hear, even today, what we shall not see until the end of time – the whole context of providence. As though in the light of this end he heard the harmony of creation to which the shadow also belongs, but it is a shadow which is not darkness, deficiency is not defeat, sadness cannot become despair, trouble cannot degenerate into tragedy, and infinite melancholy is not ultimately forced to claim undisputed sway. Thus the cheerfulness in this harmony is not without its limits. But the light shines all the more brightly because it breaks forth from the shadow ... Mozart saw this light more than we do, but heard the whole creation enveloped by the light. Hence it was fundamentally in order that he should not hear a middle or neutral note, but the positive far more strongly than the negative. He heard the negative only in and with the positive. Yet in their inequality he heard them both together, for example in the Symphony in G minor of 1788. He never heard only the one in abstraction. He heard concretely, and therefore his compositions were and are total music. Hearing creation unresentfully and impartially, he did not produce merely his own music but that of creation, its twofold and yet harmonious praise of God.

[KARL BARTH, from *Church Dogmatics*]

Music is not my field, and this is the only extract about music to appear in this book. But here are words about music (which moves me) that I can follow!

28th January

O pastoral heart of England! Like a psalm
   Of green days telling with a quiet beat –
O wave into the sunset flowing calm!
   O tired lark descending on the wheat!
Lies it all peace beyond that western fold
   Where now the lingering shepherd sees his star
Rise upon Malvern? Paints an Age of Gold
   Yon cloud with prophecies of linked ease –
Lulling this land, with hills drawn up like knees,
   To drowze beside her implements of war?

Man shall outlast his battles. They have swept
   Avon from Naseby Field to Savern Ham;
And Evesham's dedicated stones have stepp'd
   Down to the dust with Montfort's oriflamme.
Nor the red tear nor the reflected tower
   Abide; but yet these eloquent grooves remain,
Worn in the sandstone parapet hour by hour
   By labouring bargemen when they shifted ropes.
Even so shall man turn back from violent hopes
   To Adam's cheer, and toil with spade again.

Ay, and his mother Nature, to whose lap
   Like a repentant child at length he lies,
Not in the whirlwind or the thunder-clap
   Proclaims her more tremendous mysteries:
But when in winter's grave, bereft of light,
   With still small voice of divinelier whispering
– Lifting the green head of the aconite,
   Feeding with sap of hope the hazel-shoot –
She feels God's finger active at the root,
   Turns in her sleep, and murmurs of the Spring.

   [ARTHUR QUILLER-COUCH, *Upon Eckington Bridge*]

*It is the details of the grooves in the sandstone parapet of the bridge that struck
me here. So often poets light up a tiny bit of the environment and charge it with
light.*

29th January

At the bottom of the heart of every human being, from earliest infancy
until the tomb, there is something that goes on indomitably expecting,
in the teeth of all experience of crimes committed, suffered, and witnessed, that good and not evil will be done to him. It is that above all
that is sacred in every human being. The good is the only source of the
sacred. There is nothing sacred except the good and what pertains
to it . . .
   In those who have suffered too many blows, in slaves, for example,
that place in the heart from which the infliction of evil evokes a cry of
surprise may seem to be dead. But it is never quite dead; it is simply
unable to cry out any more. It is sunk into a state of dumb and ceaseless
lamentation. And even in those who still have the power to cry out, the

cry hardly ever expresses itself, either inwardly or outwardly, in co-
herent language. Usually, the words through which it seeks expression
are quite irrelevant.

That is all the more inevitable because those who most often have
occasion to feel that evil is being done to them are those who are least
trained in the art of speech. Nothing, for example, is more frightful than
to see some poor wretch in the police court stammering before a
magistrate who keeps up an elegant flow of witticisms.

Apart from the intelligence, the only human faculty which has an
interest in public freedom of expression is that point in the heart which
cries out against evil. But if it cannot express itself, freedom is of little
use to it. What is first needed is a system of public education capable of
providing it, so far as possible, with means of expression; and next, a
regime in which the public freedom of expression is characterized not
so much by freedom as by an attentive silence in which this faint and
inept cry can make itself heard . . .

[SIMONE WEIL, from *Waiting on God*]

*A scorching flame of a personality, a woman of utter integrity yet fascinated
by destructive power.*

30th January

How fever'd is the man, who cannot look
    Upon his mortal days with temperate blood,
Who vexes all the leaves of his life's book,
    And robs his fair name of its maidenhood:
It is as if the rose should pluck herself,
    Or the ripe plum finger its misty bloom,
As if a Naiad, like a meddling elf,
    Should darken her pure grot with muddy gloom.
But the rose leaves herself upon the briar,
    For winds to kiss and grateful bees to feed.
And the ripe plum still wears its dim attire,
    The undisturbed lake has crystal space,
Why then should man, testing the world for grace,
    Spoil his salvation for a fierce miscreed?

[JOHN KEATS, *Sonnet on Fame*]

*We do so try to be something other than what we are. That which is – love
that. Do not strain after the illusory.*

31st January

There lives in Hamburg, in a one-roomed lodging in the Baker's Broad Walk, a man whose name is Moses Lump; all the week he goes about in wind and rain, with his pack on his back, to earn his few shillings; but when òn Friday evening he comes home, he finds the candlestick with seven candles lighted, and the table covered with a fair white cloth, and he puts away from him his pack and his cares, and he sits down to table with his squinting wife and yet more squinting daughter, and eats fish with them, fish which has been dressed in beautiful white garlic sauce, sings therewith the grandest psalms of King David, rejoices with his whole heart over the deliverance of the children of Israel out of Egypt, rejoices, too, that all the wicked ones who have done the children of Israel hurt, have ended by taking themselves off; that King Pharaoh, Nebuchadnezzar, Haman, Antiochus, Titus, and all such people, are well dead, while he, Moses Lump, is yet alive and eating fish with his wife and daughter; and I can tell you, Doctor, the fish is delicate and the man is happy, he has no call to torment himself about culture, he sits contented in his religion and in his green bedgown, like Diogenes in his tub, he contemplates with satisfaction his candles, which he on no account will snuff out for himself; and I can tell you, if the candles burn a little dim, and the snuffer-woman, whose business it is to snuff them, is not at hand, and Rothschild the Great were at that moment to come in, with all his brokers, discounters, agents, and chief clerks, with whom he conquers the world, and Rothschild were to say: "Moses Lump, ask of me what favour you will, and it shall be granted you." Doctor, I am convinced, Moses Lump would quietly answer, "Snuff me those candles!" and Rothschild the Great would exclaim with admiration, "If I were not Rothschild, I would be Moses Lump."

[MATTHEW ARNOLD, from *Essay on Heinrich Heine*]

The skies have darkened since Matthew Arnold wrote, and yet . . . Is hope extinguished or is it still rising above the waters? So much of this century has not yet been digested. *Our imagination has baulked. We still do not know if there can be poetry after Auschwitz.*

FEBRUARY

1st February

Listen, and when thy hand this paper presses,
O time-worn woman, think of her who blesses
What thy thin fingers touch, with her caresses.

O mother, for the weight of years that break thee,
O daughter, for slow Time must yet awake thee,
And from the changes of my heart must make thee.

O fainting traveller, morn is grey in heaven.
Dost thou remember how the clouds were driven?
And are they calm about the fall of even?

Pause near the ending of thy long migration,
For this one sudden hour of desolation
Appeals to one hour of thy meditation.

Suffer, O silent one, that I remind thee
Of the great hills that stormed the sky behind thee.
Of the wild winds of power that have resigned thee.

Know that the mournful plain where thou must wander
Is but a grey and silent world, but ponder
The misty mountains of the morning yonder.

Listen: – the mountain winds with rain were fretting,
And sudden gleams the mountain tops besetting,
I cannot let thee fade to death, forgetting

What part of this wild heart of mine I know not
Will follow thee where the great winds blow not
And where the young flowers of the mountain grow not,

Yet let my letter with thy lost thoughts in it
Tell what the way was when thou didst begin it,
And win with thee the goal when thou shalt win it...

[ALICE MEYNELL, *Letter from a girl to her own old age*]

25

The attempt to see your life from youth to old age haunts me, facing the sadness of so much waste and failure and yet coming to terms with the landscape our lives have produced, accepting it all with tenderness and blessing.

2nd February

(John Lewis in a book called *Christianity and the Social Revolution* wrote:) "It now becomes possible to enmesh the ideal in the material world without loss. So long as the social and economic organization was of such a character that it could not permit the realisation of his ideals, the idealist was steadily forced to accommodate his principles to its inexorable demands in so far as he decided to live and work in society and not to dream . . . But when social development reaches the stage when ideals are realisable, the struggle becomes capable of a successful issue. It is not settled, but it is no longer condemned to futility by the very nature of the conditions . . . The prophet should be able to welcome the new age. Now at last it will be possible to manifest the will of God in social relations, and show forth the glory of His purpose in the common ways of life . . .

"The sacred is far from being the 'wholly other'; it is the quality of the secular raised to its highest power and consecrated to the noblest purposes. As each part of life is integrated into the social organism, it finds itself, and takes on the special quality that belongs to a part of a new whole . . ."

I make no apology for quoting this splendid passage at length, since it . . . embodies the profoundly Christian doctrine that the world is redeemable. There is nothing holy but flesh and blood. The essence of our purpose should not be so much, as M. Polyani would have it, to keep science 'holy', but to make the whole of human society holy.

[JOSEPH NEEDHAM, from *Time: The Refreshing River*]

One of the best statements I know of the way in which the whole universe is sacramental. Human beings have a part to play in creating community, honouring the life and work of each involved in it. The unseen and the unsayable have their part in the whole but are not separable from the material: they no longer compensate for the intractable structures of the day. Those structures are now moveable. They may be imperfect, but that is no reason to opt out. And if the mystical is now a dimension of one reality rather than a separate reality, institutional religion has no value as a separate entity in secular society, for it is then merely a bulwark to the current ideology.

3rd February

This is God's hive; the bees
  of Hybla never stored
ripe honey, such as these
  rich walls afford.

Thought swarmed here once; the stark
  Thebaid brake its comb,
and poured out of the dark
  wild honey to Rome.

Then, as of old
  the skies of Patmos dipt:
very gold of very gold
  glowed in the crypt.

And flawless, lit with green
  cool light as from a wave,
the sea-veined cipolline
  pillared the nave.

What sweetness ventured thus
  to tempt Theology
to build her such a house?
  or set the darling bee.

So wide to rove that men
  have never wholly lost
the gold that clustered then
  about the Host?

[R. N. D. WILSON, *St Apollinare in Classe*]

*This church is a Byzantine foothold in Ravenna. The poem is strange and pro-
vokes the question, Did the beauty become frozen? The bees swarmed here, yes,
but now?*

4th February

Self-transcendence is the essence of existence. Being human is directed
to something other than itself...
  One must recognize that being human profoundly means being
engaged and entangled in a situation, and confronted with a world

whose objectivity and reality is in no way detracted from by the sub-
jectivity of that 'being' who is in the world.

Preserving the 'otherness', the objectiveness, of the object means
preserving that tension which is established between object and subject.
This tension is the same as the tension between the 'I am' and the
'I ought', between reality and ideal, between being and meaning. And if
this tension is to be preserved, meaning has to be prevented from co-
inciding with being. I should say that it is the meaning of meaning to set
the pace of being...

When Israel wandered through the wilderness, God's glory preceded
in the form of a cloud: only in this way was it possible that Israel was
guided by God. Imagine, on the other hand, what would have happened
if God's presence, symbolized by the cloud, had dwelt in the midst of
Israel: instead of leading them, this cloud would have clouded everything, and Israel would have gone astray.

[VICTOR FRANKL, from *The Will to Meaning*]

*We are always wanting to tame the divine, to claim God for ourselves, to
imprison God in our midst.*

5th February

When Byron's eyes were shut in death,
We bowed our head and held our breath.
He taught us little: but our soul
Had felt him like the thunder's roll...

When Goethe's death was told, we said –
Sunk, then, is Europe's sagest head.
Physician of the Iron Age,
Goethe has done his pilgrimage...
He said – The end is everywhere:
Art still has truth, take refuge there.
And he was happy, if to know
Causes of things and far below
His feet to see the lurid flow
Of terror, and insane distress,
And headlong fate, be happiness.

And Wordsworth! – Ah, pale ghosts, rejoice!...
He found us when the age had bound

> Our souls in its benumbing round;
> He spoke, and loos'd our heart in tears.
> He laid us as we lay at birth
> On the cool flowery lap of earth;
> Smiles broke from us and we had ease.

[MATTHEW ARNOLD, from *Memorial Verses*]

Goethe was aware that we were on the edge of a revolution in thought and that science was about to give us an awesome power. He struggled with this in Faust but could not come to terms with it. Byron believed passionate romantic love to be the key to existence, and that nothing else was significant. Wordsworth looked at and responded to a small patch of earth, from which he drew for inspiration as from a well.

6th February

As I am about to exhort you, reverend fathers, to endeavour to reform the condition of the Church, because nothing has so disfigured the face of the Church as the secular and worldly way of living on the part of the clergy, I know not how I can commence my discourse more fitly than with the Apostle Paul, in whose cathedral ye are now assembled – "Be ye not conformed to this world, but be ye reformed in the newness of your minds, that ye may prove what is the good, and well-pleasing, and perfect will of God"...

You desire civil liberty, and not to be drawn before civil courts . . . But if ye desire this liberty, loose yourselves first from worldly bondage, and from the cringing service of men, and claim for yourselves that true liberty of Christ, that spiritual liberty through grace from sin, and serve God and reign in Him, and then (believe me) the people will not touch the anointed of the Lord their God.

You desire security, quiet and peace. And this is fitting. But desiring peace, return to the God of love and peace; return to Christ, in whom is the true peace of the Spirit which passeth all understanding; return to the true priestly life . . .

These, reverend fathers and most distinguished men, are the things that I thought should be spoken concerning the reformation of the clergy. I trust that, in your clemency, you will take them in good part . . . Consider the miserable state and condition of the church, and bend your whole minds to its reformation. Suffer not, fathers, suffer not this so

illustrious assembly to break up without result. Suffer not this your
congregation to slip by for nothing...

[DEAN COLET, quoted by F. SEEBOHM, *The Oxford Reformers*]

*Colet, Dean of St Paul's, addressed the clergy of both Houses of Convocation on
6 February 1512. It was a critical moment for the Church. Reformation was in
the air, but could the Church reform itself? Here Colet speaks to the treason of
all clerks – the desire for security and power.*

7th February

Behind His lolling head the sky
Glares like a fiery cataract
Red with the murders of two thousand years
Committed in His name and by
Crusaders, Christian warriors
Defending faith and property.

Amid the plain beneath His transfixed hands,
Exuding darkness as indelible
As guilty stains, fanned by funereal
And lurid airs, besieged by drifting sands
And clefted hillsides our about-to-be
Bombed and abandoned cities stand.

He who wept for Jerusalem
Now sees His prophecy extend
Across the greatest cities of the world,
A guilty panic reason cannot stem
Rising to raze them all as He foretold;
And He must watch this drama to the end.

Though often named, He is unknown
To the dark Kingdom at His feet
Where everything disparages His words,
And each man bears the common guilt alone
And goes blindfold to his fate
And fear and greed are sovereign Lords...

Not from a monstrance silver-wrought
But from the tree of human pain
Redeem our sterile misery,

Christ of Revolution and of Poetry,
That man's long journey through this night
May not have been in vain.

[DAVID GASCOYNE, from *Ecce Homo*]

The cities and people of the world are under judgment. We have not yet said,
despite Coventry and Dresden and Hiroshima, that these things must never
never be again. Even though cities would flop like packs of cards at the first
breath of explosion now, we are still slaves to the sovereign lords of fear and
greed.

8th February

Let us go hence, my songs; she will not hear.
Let us go hence together without fear.
Keep silence now, for singing-time is over,
And over all old things and all things dear.
She loves not you nor me as all we love her.
Yea, though we sang as angels in her ear,
  She would not hear.

Let us rise up and part; she will not know,
Let us go seaward as the great winds go,
Full of blown sand and foam. What help is there?
There is no help, for all these things are so,
And all the world is bitter as a tear.
And how these things are, tho' ye strive to show,
  She would not know. . .

Let us go hence, go hence, she will not see.
Sing all once more together. Surely she,
She too, remembering days and words that were,
Will turn a little towards us, sighing. But we,
We are hence, we are gone, as though we had not been there.
Nay, and though all men seeing had pity on me,
  She would not see.

[A. C. SWINBURNE, from *A Leave-Taking*]

If left to ourselves, do we human beings always croon a song under our breath?
It is like listening to the sea – Swinburne was brought up on the Northumber-
land coast – giving a gentle shape to sadness lest grief tear us apart.

9th February

All Art re-presents. I have hyphenated re-presents for a good reason.
but must now show the reason. If I wrote, for example, of Hogarth's
highly realistic painting called 'The Shrimp Girl' that it 'represented
such and such', I should not convey at all what that work in fact is. If I
wrote 're-presented such and such' there is a slight gain, and 're-presented
such and such under other forms' is still more a gain, but much more
amplification is required to cover fully what is indicated under the
shorthand hyphenated term 're-present'. I shall therefore attempt a
fuller statement sticking to Hogarth's 'Shrimp Girl' as my example
partly because it is a picture of which I am fond, also because no one can
cavil as to its merits; but more because it is highly visual, and, as they
say, 'faithful to the appearance of nature'. It is a charming record of an
apparently charming subject, so all that could be desired by the most
popular and sophisticated standards. My fuller statement of what that
painting is and does might read somewhat as follows: It is a 'thing', an
object contrived of various materials and so ordered by Hogarth's muse
as to show forth, recall and re-present strictly within the conditions of a
given art and under another mode, such and such a reality. It is a
signum of that reality and it makes a kind of anamnesis of that reality.

[DAVID JONES, from *Epoch and Artist*]

*Gather up all the fragments of the past that nothing be lost. All is infinitely
precious even if mauled and soiled and broken.*

10th February

Silent listening was only the beginning of community. It instituted
community, and, as always, here too there had to be continual return to
the original institution, so that by this summoning to concentration new
strength could again and again be drawn from the depths of the beginning. But the inner life of the community does not begin and end with
this initial silent listening. This life is born only in an act which is
essentially a renewal. Not in a mere repetition of a beginning once
created, but in the re-creating of what has grown effete. The re-creating
of bodily life, the transforming of matter grown old, occurs in the
course of a meal. Even for the individual, eating and drinking constitute
rebirth for the body. For the community, the meal taken in common is
the action through which it is reborn to conscious life.

The silent community of hearing and heeding establishes even the smallest community, that of the household. The household is based on the circumstance that the word of the father of the family is heard and heeded. Still, the common life of the household does not become manifest in the common heeding but in the meal at which all the members of the house gather round the table. Here each is the equal of every other; each lives for himself, and yet is joined with all the others. It is not table talk that establishes this community, for in many rural districts it is not customary to speak during the meal, it is even contrary to custom. Talking at table does not, at any rate, establish community; at most it expresses it. One can talk in the street and in the square wherever people meet haphazardly. The common meal with its silent community, represents actual community alive in the midst of life.

[FRANZ ROSENZWEIG, from *The Star of Redemption*]

Have we lost the 'full' silence of a silent meal – especially in retreat houses? The silence has become utilitarian – that we may better speak – rather than remaining silent even when it feels a complete waste of time.

11th February

Batter my heart, three-person'd God; for you
As yet but knock; breathe, shine, and seek to mend;
That I may rise, and stand, o'er throw me, and bend
Your force, to break, blow, burn, and make me new.
I, like a usurp'd town, to another due,
Labour to admit you, but O, to no end.
Reason, your viceroy in me, me should defend,
But is captived, and proves weak or untrue.
Yet dearly I love you, and would be loved fain,
But am betroth'd unto your enemy;
Divorce me, untie, or break that knot again,
Take me to you, imprison me, for I,
Except you enthrall me, never shall be free,
Nor ever chaste, except you ravish me.

[JOHN DONNE, *Holy Sonnet XIV*]

On first reading Donne at Cambridge, he seemed to me to sum up so much, even if he is a bit feverish and the polar opposite to gentle Shakespeare.

12th February

Words are the most subtle symbols which we possess and our human fabric depends upon them. The living and radical nature of language is something which we forget at our peril. It is totally misleading to speak, for instance, of 'two cultures', one literary-humane, and the other scientific, as if these were of equal status. There is only one culture, of which science, so interesting and so dangerous, is now an important part. But the most essential and fundamental aspect of culture is the study of literature, since this is an education in how to picture and understand human situations. We are men and we are moral agents before we are scientists, and the place of science in human life must be discussed in words. This is why it is and always will be more important to know about Shakespeare than to know about any scientist; and if there is a 'Shakespeare of science' his name is Aristotle.

I have used the word 'attention', which I borrow from Simone Weil, to express the idea of a just and loving gaze directed upon an individual reality. I believe this to be the characteristic and proper mark of the active moral agent.

[IRIS MURDOCH, from *The Sovereignty of Good*]

The remark about the two cultures is so important. The attempted split is false. And Shakespeare is important because human relationships, established in language and silence, are so fundamental.

13th February

Picture-forming seems crucial. The physicist Max Planck believed his quest could not be carried on without some concept of a real world we shall never know, but must perpetually strive to map and discover . . .

We cannot perhaps picture our picture-making. Even with all our windows we shall only catch glimpses of the real world . . . We shall not answer the question, What is man?, nor the harder question, What is real?, What is true?, but our plurality of windows should surely protect us against, rather than inducing, solipsist despair . . .

What Kepler discovered about optics Vermeer applied and exemplified in the light and colour of the *View of Delft*. And from that painting Marcel Proust picked out the patch of yellow wall and associated it for all time – or all imaginable time – with an exact irreducible vision of truth, order, and likeness. Great intuition – in all fields – perceives order and likeness in the differences and multitudinous movements of the universe. Intuitions of order fail, and are succeeded by others, but we persist in seeking.

[A. S. BYATT, from *Still Life*]

This passage comes from a novel around the life of Van Gogh. We want to know where we are, but the world-picture is now so vast and complex that we cannot answer the questions we want to answer. So we retreat into the private and buy the packaged articles of the advertised. Yet we also 'persist in seeking'. Can the arts, then, come in to provide symbols that can at least in part connect us, join us, to that complex world which science has revealed?

14th February

> Remember me when I am gone away,
> Gone far away into the silent land;
> When you can no more hold me by the hand,
> Nor I half turn to go yet turning stay.
> Remember me when no more day by day
> You tell me of our future that you plann'd:
> Only remember me; you understand
> It will be late to counsel then or pray.
> Yet if you should forget me for a while
> And afterwards remember, do not grieve:
> For if the darkness and corruption leave
> A vestige of the thoughts that once I had,
> Better by far you should forget and smile
> Than that you should remember and be sad.

[CHRISTINA ROSSETTI, *Remember*]

I have enjoyed saying this poem by heart many times.

15th February

Writing poetry educates one into the nature of the game – which is humanity's profoundest activity. In their star-dances the savages try to unite their lives to those of the heavenly bodies – to mix their quotidian rhythms into those great currents which keep the wheels of the universe turning. Poetry attempts to provide much the same sort of link between the muddled inner man with his temporal preoccupations and the uniform flow of the universe outside. Of course everyone is conscious of these impulses; but poets are the only people who do not drive them off.

[LAWRENCE DURRELL, from *Reflections on a Marine Venus*]

Because of all that we are aware of now, we are bounden to discover the poet in each of us and to cherish the vocation of poets.

16th February

When to the sessions of sweet silent thought
I summon up remembrance of things past,
I sigh the lack of many a thing I sought,
And with old woes new wail my dear times' waste:
Then can I drown an eye, unus'd to flow,
For precious friends hid in death's dateless night,
And weep afresh Love's long since cancell'd woe,
And moan the expense of many a vanished sight:
Then can I grieve at grievances foregone,
And heavily from woe to woe tell o'er
The sad account of fore-bemoaned moan,
Which I new pay as if not paid before.
    But if the while I think on thee, dear friend,
    All losses are restor'd and sorrows end.

[WILLIAM SHAKESPEARE, *Sonnet XXX*]

'Remembrance of times past' – Proust used it as the title for his book about childhood. A small memory, perhaps of the smell and taste of tea and biscuits taken with a relative long ago, can unlock and let loose a vanished world. In the sacramental act you let loose the energy within the memory – and 'all losses are restor'd and sorrows end.'

17th February

It was time to go. The three friends had begun life together; and the last of the three had no motive – no attraction – to carry (their education) on after the others had gone. (It) had ended for all three, and only beyond some remoter horizon could its values be fixed or renewed. Perhaps some day . . . say 1938, their centenary, they might be allowed to return together for a holiday, to see the mistakes of their own lives made clear in the light of the mistakes of their successors; and perhaps then, for the first time since man begun his education among the carnivores, they would find a world that sensitive and timid natures could regard without a shudder.

[HENRY ADAMS, from *The Education of Henry Adams*]

In the first decade of this century, Henry Adams writes of how education always lags behind what a person is experiencing in the present. It doesn't fit you for the situation you are in. How much more true this has been as the century has gone on. And is the hope expressed in the last sentence forlorn?

18th February

The soul has many motions, body one.
An old wind-tattered butterfly flew down
And pulsed its wings upon the dusty ground –
Such stretchings of the spirit make no sound.
By lust alone we keep the mind alive,
And grieve into the certainty of love.

Love begets love. This torment is my joy.
I watch a river wind itself away;
To meet the world, I rise up in my mind;
I hear a cry and lose it on the wind.
What we put down, must we take up again?
I dare embrace. By striding, I remain.

Who but the loved know love's a faring-forth?
Who's old enough to live? – a thing of earth
Knowing how all things alter in the seed
Until they reach this final certitude,
This reach beyond this death, this act of love
In which all creatures share, and thereby live.

Wings without feathers creaking in the sun,
The close dirt dancing on a sunless stone
God's night and day: down this space He has smiled,
Hope has its hush: we move through its broad day –
O who would take the vision from the child? –
O, motion O, our chance is still to be!

[THEODORE ROETHKE, *The Motion*]

As good a poem as you get about the movement of the human spirit, which is
always in danger of becoming frozen and brutalized. Picasso was the first to
depict that danger, painting in 1907. It is all too familiar now.

19th February

If history is a dialogue between Deity and mankind, we can understand
its meaning only when we are the ones who are addressed, and only to
the degree to which we render ourselves receptive. We are, then, simply
denied the capacity to judge current history and arrive at the conclusion
that 'This or that is its true meaning,' or 'This is what God intends, and
that is contrary to God's will.' But what we are permitted to know of
history comes to this: 'This, in one way or another, is history's challenge
to me; this is its claim on me; and so this is its meaning as far as I am
concerned.' This meaning, however, is not 'subjective' in the sense that
it originates in my emotion or cerebration, and then is transferred to
objective happenings. Rather, it is the meaning I perceive, experience
and hear in reality. The meaning of history is not an idea that I can
formulate independent of my personal life. It is only with my personal
life that I am able to catch the meaning of history for it is a dialogical
meaning.

[MARTIN BUBER, from *Israel and the World*]

I have always felt that, compared with the Jews, Christians do not take history
seriously. The Jewish people live by history. And history is about being addressed
personally, about our response, about a continuous dialogue. Where are you?
What have you done? Face what you have done in history. There is no Christian
sense of this. And there is no sense that the British story and the Christian
story are connected.

20th February

And as the moon rose higher the inessential houses began to melt away
until gradually I became aware of the old island here that flowered once
for the dutch sailor's eyes – a fresh green breast of the new world. Its
vanished trees, the trees that had made way for Gatsby's house, had
once pandered in whispers to the last and greatest of all human dreams;
for a transitory enchanted moment man must have held his breath in
the presence of this continent, compelled into an aesthetic contempla-

tion he neither understood nor desired, face to face for the last time in history with something commensurate with his capacity for wonder.

[SCOTT FITZGERALD, from *The Great Gatsby*]

Not, fortunately, 'the last time in history', for we have now held our breath in the presence not of a continent on earth alone, but of the planets and the galaxies, perhaps exceeding our earthbound capacity of wonder and stretching it to undreamt of proportions, commensurate with the Universe itself.

21st February

No civilisation but has its version of Babel, its mythology of the primal scattering of languages. There are two main conjectures, two great attempts at solving the riddle via metaphor. Some awful error was committed, an accidental release of linguistic chaos, in the mode of Pandora's box. Or, more commonly, man's language condition, the incommunicados that so absurdly divide him are a punishment...

Why did certain languages effect a lasting grip on reality? Did Hebrew, Aramaic, Greek, and Chinese (in a way that may also relate to the history of writing) have distinctive resources? Or are we, in fact, asking about the history of particular civilisations, a history reflected in and energized by language in ways so diverse and interdependent that we cannot give a credible answer? I suspect that the receptivity of a given language to metaphor is a crucial factor. That receptivity varies widely: ethno-linguists tells us, for example, that Tarascan, a Mexican tongue, is inhospitable to new metaphors, whereas Cuna, a Panamanian language, is avid for them. An Attic delight in words, in the play of rhetoric, was noticed and often mocked throughout the Mediterranean world... By contrast other civilisations seem 'speechless', or at least, as may have been the case in ancient Egypt, not entirely cognizant of the creative and transformational powers of language. In numerous cultures blindness is a supreme infirmity and abdication from life: in Greek mythology the poet and seer are blind, so that they may, by the antennae of speech, see further.

[GEORGE STEINER, from *After Babel*]

Language is marvellous and, especially when receptive to metaphor, can stretch our imagination. Do we need blind poets – and actors like Shakespeare – who can speak to those who come to be entertained? What indeed can be said

about the life we are faced with? Can I say something more than my con-
temporaries who are also writing? Did Shakespeare ponder thus?

22nd February

Proud Maisie is in the wood,
  Walking so early;
Sweet Robin sits on the bush,
  Singing so rarely.

"Tell me, thou bonny bird,
  When shall I marry me?"
–"When six braw gentlemen
  Kirkwards shall carry ye."

"Who makes the bridal bed,
  Birdie, say truly?"
–"The gray-headed sexton
  That delves the grave duly.

"The glowworm o'er grave and stone
  Shall light thee steady;
The owl from the steeple sing,
  Welcome, proud lady!"

[WALTER SCOTT, *Madge Wildfire's Song*]

*Walter Scott was one of the few writers in English who was aware of and tried
to convey the sense of the history to which we belong as people – quite apart
from political achievements and structures. The ballads expressed this, providing people with a tune to hum and words to sing. They are like the Psalms in
this: think of Psalm 23 set to Crimond.*

23rd February

Ebbs from soiled fields the last drab vestige of snow,
Through February's veils the hazy distance looms.
In sunken woods no melancholy horn is blown,
Only an invisible process of decay consumes.

I have sat at this window and watched the day
Consumed, as though its substance were a powdering wood

In whose grey embers the origin of all decay
Smouldered, as it patiently smoulders within my blood.

Rotting vegetation, a leaf like a leather glove,
A glove or a fleshless hand, of a corpse or a tree;
Excrement; a dead dog buried in a garden grave;
I am all these, and all these moulder in me.

I am the limestone in the cave, the putrefying bone,
The seashell mashed and splintered by the mechanical surf,
The green, soft-fallen tree-trunk, the crumbling stone,
The waterlogged carrion under the thatch of turf.

The odour of mortality rises from the death of the day,
Earth's subtle chemistry proceeds; water drips from the
    boughs;
Nourished on black corruption, warmed in the breath of decay
The seeds of Spring lie swelling in their soaking house.

[D. S. SAVAGE, *February*]

*Not a great poem, but I know no other which gets hold of the sudden decay that
the tag end of the year produces – yet not without hope. A February thought
indeed that we can do without diamonds but not without dung.*

24th February

It is always dangerous to draw too precise parallels between one
historical period and another; and among the most misleading of such
parallels are those which have been drawn between our own age in
Europe and North America and the epoch in which the Roman Empire
declined into the Dark Ages. Nonetheless certain parallels there are.
A crucial turning point in that earlier history occurred when men and
women of good will turned aside from the task of shoring up the Roman
imperium and ceased to identify the continuation of civility and moral
community with the maintenance of that imperium. What they set
themselves to achieve instead – often not recognizing fully what they
were doing – was the construction of new forms of community within
which the moral life could be sustained so that both morality and
civility might survive the coming ages of barbarism and darkness. If my
account of our moral condition is correct, we ought also to conclude
that for some time now we too have reached that turning point. What

matters at this stage is the construction of local forms of community within which civility and the intellectual and moral life can be sustained through the new dark ages which are already upon us. And if the tradition of the virtues was able to survive the horrors of the last dark ages, we are not entirely without grounds for hope. This time however the barbarians are not waiting beyond the frontiers; they have already been governing us for quite some time. And it is our lack of consciousness of this that constitutes part of our predicament. We are waiting not for a Godot but for another – doubtless very different – St Benedict.

[ALASDAIR MACINTYRE, from *After Virtue*]

I usually disagree with Alasdair MacIntyre on Marxism and Christianity. Here, in the light of a book that treats of social and personal virtue, he offers, as a moral philosopher, this comment on our historical situation. I too am baffled by our inertia in the face of the dismantling of our morality. Money rules – and the power to do things. Do we need, then, an assembling of a few men and women who will listen to the Spirit in what is going on, in the midst of everything (not in heaven or hell), taking time seriously, in an ordered way which can be done by both learned and ignorant?

25th February

        . . . As for you, my love, it's harder,
        Though neither prisoner nor warder,
        Not to desire you both: for love
        Illudes us we can lightly move
        Into a new dimension, where
        The bounds of being disappear
        And we make one impassioned cell.
        So wanting to be all in all
        Each for each, a man and a woman
        Defy the limits of what's human.

        But when we cease to play explorers
        And become settlers, clear before us
        Lies the next need – to re-define
        The boundary between yours and mine;
        Else, one stays prisoner, one goes free.
        Each to his own identity
        Grown back, shall prove our love's expression
        Purer for this limitation.

Love's essence, like a poem's, shall spring
From the not saying everything.

[CECIL DAY-LEWIS, from *On not saying everything*]

How hard it is to recognize our limitations for each other, especially as couples and in families. On the one hand we do not want the structure of the patriarchal household with the power of life and death held by the father. On the other hand, is the inner realization of the need for limitation enough to sustain us through the years? We may try to deny the need for limitations and leave one partner for another. And it is flattering if you are selected in the dance of changing partners – but not if you are cast aside. And even if you are 'successful', the law of diminishing returns will operate to despair.

26th February

Caleb could not have finished even this quiet Sunday afternoon conversation, in the course of which we had risen to lofty matters, without a return to his old favourite subjects of sheep and his shepherding life on the downs. He was miles away from his beloved home now, lying on his back, a disabled man who would never again follow a flock on the hills nor listen to the sounds he loved best to hear – the multitudinous tremulous bleatings of the sheep, the tinklings of numerous bells, and the crisp ringing bark of his dog. But his heart was still there, and the images of past scenes were more vivid in him than they can ever be in the minds of those who live in towns and read books. 'I can see it now,' was a favourite expression of his when relating some incident in his past life. Whenever a sudden light, a kind of smile, came into his eyes, I knew that it was some ancient memory, a touch of quaintness or humour in some farmer or shepherd he had known in the vanished time – his father, perhaps, or old John, or Mark Dick, or Liddy, or Dan'l Burdon, the solemn seeker after buried treasure.

After our long Sunday talk we were silent for a time, and then he uttered these impressive words: 'I don't say that I want to have my life again, because 'twould be sinful. We must take what is sent. But if 'twas offered to me and I was told to choose my work, I'd say, Give me my Wiltsheer downs again and let me be a shepherd there all my life long.'

[W. H. HUDSON, from *A Shepherd's Life*]

Would we say that as a factory hand?

27th February

These barrows of the century-darkened dead, –
Memorials of oblivion, these turfed tombs
Of muttering ancestries whose fires, once red,
Now burn for me beyond mysterious glooms;
  I pass them day by day while daylight fills
  My sense of sight on these time-haunted hills.

Could I but watch those burials that began
Whole history – flint and bronze and iron beginnings,
When under this wide Wiltshire sky crude man
Warred with his world and augured our world-winnings!
Could I but enter that unholpen brain,
Cabined and comfortless and insecure,
That ruled some settlement on Salisbury Plain
And offered blood to blind primeval powers, –
Dim Caliban whose doom was to endure
Earth's ignorant nullity made strange with flowers.

[SIEGFRIED SASSOON, *Prehistoric Burials*]

*Edwin Muir also has this sense of belonging to what has gone on through birth
and burial through the centuries. Not far behind us in the generations are the
medieval peasant and Caliban, with but a rare streak of the imagination in a
few individuals. Such imagination is hard to cherish: it is much easier to plot
the stars or direct the affairs of nations.*

28th February

Now in these mountain grasses beneath a winter sky
I watch the valleys lighted, I hear the curlew cry,
I hear the sorrowful echoes borne from the Severn Sea,
And the dirge of desolation, the sigh of history.

O mountain grasses ignorant of man and all his pain,
Sing in this freezing twilight, murmur to me again
Of the prehistoric aeons, the landscapes pure and bare,
The centuries of silence, the unpolluted air.

O northern winds, my lovers, roar round me where I stand,
A naked creature lonely in a brown and barren land,

And scatter from my memory the weeds of human lore
And make me as cold, as careless, as a wave on a desolate shore.

[IDRIS DAVIES, *One February Evening*]

*February again! We do not want this, but it is important to know it, to be
exposed to the blasted heath.*

29th February

Moments of great calm
Kneeling before an altar
Of wood in a stone church
In summer, waiting for God
To speak; the air a staircase
For silence; the sun's light
Ringing me, as though I acted
A great role. And the audience
Still; all that close throng
Of spirits waiting, as I,
For the message.
                        Prompt me, God
But not yet. When I speak
Though it be you who speak
Through me, something is lost.
The meaning is in the waiting.

[R. S. THOMAS, *Kneeling*]

We are a people so impatient . . .

MARCH

1st March

Not having you in my life is like going back to time, after once living in Eternity. Your awkwardness and gaucheness were the outer covering of a perfect understanding so great that your very ugliness aroused my desire. With all your unlike-me ways, I always felt that you were nevertheless me. I shall always want you. Nothing is real to me that is not Hilda-me.

[STANLEY SPENCER]

Stanley Spencer wrote this when he wanted to go back to his first wife.

2nd March

> What were life
> Did soul stand still therein, forego her strife
> Through the ambiguous present to the goal
> Of some all reconciling future? . . .
> Earth's young significance is all to learn! . . .
> What once lives never dies – What here attains
> To a beginning, has no end, still gains . . .
> With so much knowledge is it hard to bear
> Brief interposing ignorance?

[ROBERT BROWNING, from *Parleying with Gerard de Lauresse*]

An extraordinary description of what really matters. From a late poem not readily available.

3rd March

There are times when I think that hopes of spiritual freedom are the saddest delusion that can torture the human brain. For I see only too

well that I am not one of those who are able to do the necessary violence
to their feelings and wonder that others can make such an effort. All
that I can obtain from myself is not to give up the Idea that, when all is
said and done, spirit is bound to prevail, but I am afraid that in my case
its prey will be no more than a corpse. Perhaps the important thing
does not lie in conquering but in fighting on to the end.

[JULIAN GREEN, from *Diaries*]

*This has never been more true for me than it is now. It is not easier nearer the
end. Julian Green's diaries, kept from the age of twenty, long and explicit,
reveal a man who tried to be honest, through great travail.*

4th March

On arriving at the extremity of the plain, I looked towards the dingle.
Isopel Berners stood at the mouth, the beams of the early morning
shone full on her noble face and figure. I waved my hand towards her.
She slowly lifted her right arm. I turned away; and never saw Isopel
Berners again.

[GEORGE BORROW, from *Romany Rye*]

*As you read George Borrow's story, this is an unexpected moment. But there
are faces we see for the last time and will do never again.*

5th March

Not, I'll not carrion-comfort, Despair, not feast on thee;
Not untwist-slack they may be – these last strands of man
In me or, most weary, cry I can no more. I can;
Can something, hope, wish day come, not choose not to be.
But ah, but O thou terrible, why wouldst thou rude on me
Thy wring-world right foot rock? Lay a limb against me? Scan
With darksome devouring eyes my bruised bones? and fan
O in turns of tempest, me heaped there; me frantic to avoid thee,
    and flee?
Why? That my chaff might fly; my grain lie, sheer and clear.
Nay in all that toil, that coil, since (it seems) I kissed the rod,
Hand rather, my heart lo! sapped strength, stole joy, would laugh,
    cheer.

Cheer whom though? the hero whose heaven-handling flung me, foot
    trod
Me? or me that fought him? O which one? is it each one? that night,
    that year.
O now done darkness I wretch lay wrestling with (my God!) my God.

                                    [G. M. HOPKINS, *Carrion Comfort*]

A man who struggled with despair but refused to give in. I can, can hope . . .

6th March

Meeting with God does not come to man in order that he may concern
himself with God, but in order that he may realize meaning in the
world. All revelation is summons and sending. But again and again man
brings about, instead of realization, a reflection of Him who reveals: he
wishes to concern himself with God instead of with the world. Only, in
such a reflection, he is no longer confronted with a Thou, he can do
nothing but establish an It-God in the realm of things, believe that he
knows of God as an It, and so speak about Him. Just as the 'self'-seeking
man, instead of directly living something or other, a perception or an
affection, reflects about his perceptive or reflective I, and thereby misses
the truth of an event, so the man who seeks God (though for the rest he
gets on very well with the self-seeker in the one soul), instead of allowing
the gift to work itself out, reflects about the Giver – and misses both.

                                    [MARTIN BUBER, from *I and Thou*]

*Martin Buber knows deeply what Judaism is saying, turning upside down what
most people think religion is about. Has Christianity moved too far from its
Jewish stock? We allowed the world to get on with itself (as long as we had a
substantial part in it!), allowing problems of slavery, migrants, and invasion to
take at best second place to discussions about the nature of God.*

7th March

        Labour is blossoming or dancing where
        The body is not bruised to pleasure soul,
        Nor beauty born out of its own despair,
        Nor blear-eyed wisdom out of midnight oil.
        O chestnut-tree, great-rooted blossomer,

Are you the leaf, the blossom or the bole?
O body swayed to music, O brightening glance,
How can we know the dancer from the dance?

[W. B. YEATS, from *Among School Children*]

*A sensitive person, bringing to poetry the whole history of Ireland, breaking out
of his straitjacket under Rome, falling prey to his own visionary exploration,
and only touching his Celtic roots in fragments, seeing the cosmos as dance.*

8th March

All knowledge by union; all knowledge by incorporation . . . ; all knowledge through love has its natural fundament in our primary bond with
the mother. The skeptic warns the believer not to 'swallow' things and
not 'to be taken in'. And from his point of view he is right. Faith, the
most sublime form of non-scientific knowledge, is (if we consider its
natural history, independent of all questions of grace) a form of swallow-
ing or being taken in. It goes back to an infantile, oral form of union.
This is also true about Wisdom. 'Sapientia' is derived from 'sapere', to
taste, and Sophia is the she-soul of Eastern Christendom.

[KARL STERN, from *The Flight from Woman*

*We eat certain foods because of generations of trial and error. We tried some-
thing and concluded that we could or could not eat it. What are we prepared to
take in, taste, and see what nourishes and what causes pain? The organism has
to taste even ideas. This is not by head knowledge; rather is it by the wisdom
which comes from so digesting knowledge that it has become part of us.*

9th March

This bread I break was once the oat,
This wine upon a foreign tree
Plunged in its fruit;
Man in the day or wine at night
Laid the crops low, broke the grape's joy.

Once in this wind the summer blood
Knocked in the flesh that decked the vine,
Once in this bread

The oat was merry in the wind;
Man broke the sun, pulled the wind down.

This flesh you break, this blood you let
Make desolation in the vein,
Were oat and grape
Born of the sensual root and say;
My wine you drink, my bread you snap.

[DYLAN THOMAS, *This Bread I Break*]

The pulsing life in oat and grape turning into bread and wine: Is the humanity broken just ours or Christ's in which we are all involved? We are so often not aware of the oat and grape and the swirl of life which we believe focused in the Holy Communion. There is something wild *about this ritual. 'Knocked in the flesh' . . .*

10th March

Steeply the stars are scattered, and the cold in the settlement of the
    heavens.
This moon is on the wing – hold on, don't let your grip slacken!
It closes your eyes – and beyond the limits of tired vision
A skater, like a pair of compasses, draws measured circles –
In winter's black and white engravings nuances disappear,
The stern poverty of phases mumbles like an oration.
Five paces to the window and four from wall to wall,
And the mounted eye blinks through the iron.
The monotonous guile of an interrogation trails past,
The young escort is guilelessly coarse in soldierly fashion . . .
Oh, what calmness – to wander silently through the winter,
Not even allowing the word 'no' to fall from cracked, sewn-up lips!
The snowy pendulum has worn away: how many weeks have
    passed?
Oh the eye is darker above the poem, the forehead hotter,
Through heat and cold – I will reach, I will reach April!
I am already on the road. And God's hand is on my shoulder.

[IRINA RATUSHINSKAYA, *October 1982*]

Irina Ratushinskaya was released from prison in Kiev in October 1986.

11th March

Above all matter is not just the weight that drags us down, the mire
that sucks us in, the bramble that bars our way. In itself, and before we
find ourselves where we are, and before we choose, it is simply the slope
on which we can go up just as well as go down, the medium that can
uphold or give way, the wind that can overthrow or lift up. Of its nature,
and as a result of original sin, it is true that it represents a perpetual
impulse towards failure. But by nature too, and as a result of the
Incarnation, it contains the spur or the allurement to be our accomplice
towards heightened being, and this counter-balances and even domin-
ates the 'fomes peccati'. The full truth of our situation is that, here below, and by virtue of our immersion in the universe, we are each one of
us placed within its layers or on its slopes, at a specific point defined by
the present moment in the history of the world, the place of our birth,
and our individual vocation. And from that starting-point, variously
situated at different levels, the task assigned to us is the climb towards
the light, passing through, as to attain to God, a given series of created
things which are not exactly obstacles but rather footholds, inter-
mediaries to be made use of, nourishment to be taken, sap to be purified
and elements to be associated with us and borne along with us.

[PIERRE TEILHARD DE CHARDIN, from *Le Milieu Divin*]

*The debate on the relationship between science and religion has moved on, but
this passage is suggestive of the way in which we live in one world and not two
and yet there is no one vision of the one world which will be adequate.*

12th March

You know, you needn't feel bad because you lack the power to 'tell
yourself the whole truth', for once, for your own good. Believe me, no
man has this power; no man can help himself. Though the world is full
of people who try to make themselves believe that they can, they
succeed no better than Münchhausen did when he tried to pull himself
out of the mire by the scruff of his neck. Each of us can only seize by the
scruff whoever happens to be closest to him in the mire. This is the
'neighbour' the Bible speaks of. And the miraculous thing is that,
although each of us stands in the mire himself, we can each pull out our
neighbour, or at least keep him from drowning. None of us has solid
ground under his feet; each of us is only held up by the neighbourly

hands grasping him by the scruff, with the result that we are each held up by the next man, and often, indeed most of the time (quite naturally, since we are neighbours mutually), hold each other up mutually. All this mutual upholding (a physical impossibility) becomes possible only because the great hand from above supports all these holding hands by their wrists. It is this, and not some non-existent 'solid ground under one's feet', that enables all the human hands to hold and to help. There is no such thing as standing, there is only being held up.

[FRANZ ROSENZWEIG, from *Letter to Ilse Hahn*]

A friend of Martin Buber, Franz Rosenzweig was born of non-practising Jewish parents in the Rhineland. He decided to go to a synagogue for the last time at Yom Kippur, and stayed!

13th March

She took a last and simple meal when there were none to see her steal –
A jug of cream upon the shelf, a fish prepared for dinner;
And now she walks a distant street with delicately sandalled feet
And no-one gives her much to eat, or weeps to see her thinner.

O my beloved, come again, come back in joy, come back in pain,
To end our searching with a mew, or with a purr our grieving;
And you shall have for lunch or tea whatever fish swim in the sea,
And all the cream that's meant for me – and not a word of thieving!

[E. V. RIEU, *The Lost Cat*]

A little light relief. I love cats.

14th March

We need one another to be ourselves. This complete and unlimited dependence of each of us upon the others is the central and crucial fact of personal existence. Individual independence is an illusion; and the independent individual, the isolated self, is a nonentity. In ourselves we are nothing, we have no value in ourselves, and are of no importance whatever, wholly without meaning or significance. It is only in relation to others that we exist as persons; we are invested with significance by others who have need of us; and borrow our reality from those who care for us. We live and move and have our being not in ourselves but in one another; and what rights or powers or freedom we possess are ours by the grace and favour of our fellows. Here is the basic fact of our human condition; which all of us can know if we stop pretending, and do know in moments when the veil of self-deception is stripped from us and we are forced to look upon our own nakedness.

[JOHN MACMURRAY, from *Persons in Relation*]

A writer central to my life and thinking. His Search for Reality in Religion *is the best small book about religion that I know. George Macleod once commented to me that we haven't made much of MacMurray because we haven't yet caught up with him. Surely he is right to say that the individual is a non-entity. Perhaps the word should be used only as an adjective. Certainly the passage is comment indeed on the eighties. The pupil brought up on facts in Dickens'* Hard Times *says to Mr Gradgrind, 'But surely you must know that self-interest is the law of life.'*

15th March

Left by his friend to breakfast alone on the white
Italian shore, his Terrible Dream arose
Over his shoulder; he wept to himself in the night,
A dirty landscape-painter who hated his nose.

The legions of cruel inquisitive They
Were so many and big like dogs: he was upset
By Germans and boats; affection was miles away:
But guided by tears he successfully reached his Regret.

How prodigious the welcome was. Flowers took his hat
And bore him off to introduce him to the tongs;
The demon's false nose made the table laugh; a cat
Soon had him waltzing madly, let him squeeze her hand;
Words pushed him to the piano to sing comic songs;

And children swarmed to him like settlers. He became a land.

[W. H. AUDEN, *Edward Lear*]

When you dislocate the structures you have a chance of seeing something new: this is the function of nonsense. And Edward Lear is poignant because he had been hurt by life and needed the reassurance of the madder element of things.

As a pioneer he trod the path between the madness of isolation and the mire of conformity. (Jesus of course was thought to be mad.)

16th March

We perfect our souls 'towards God'. 'Being like' God is then not some-thing which is unconnected with our earthly life; it is the goal of our life, provided that our life is really a perfecting of our soul 'toward' God. And this being so, we may well add that the perfection of a soul is called into being like God, which yet does not mean any equality, but means that this soul has translated into reality that likeness to God which was granted it. We perfect our souls 'toward' God: this means that each of us who does this makes perfect his likeness to God, his 'yehida', his soul, his 'only one', his uniqueness as God's image.

'For in the image of God made he man.' It is on this that the imitation of God is founded. We are destined to be like Him: this means we are destined to bring to perfection out of ourselves, in actual life, the image in which we were created, and which we carry in us, that we may - no longer in this life - experience its consummation.

[MARTIN BUBER, from *Imitatio Deo*]

This 'imitatio' is not in the fashion of Thomas à Kempis. We are not spectators of creation but take our part, with all risk and cost, with the likelihood of failure, in the creating. We are not to remain in Eden. The Fall was a step forwards, not backwards! Judaism starts with Genesis 12 not with Genesis 1. The wandering begins because we are constantly discovering the way, not because we have lost it. And our own age knows well enough about the universe in motion. We shouldn't be surprised that we have to get up and move on.

17th March

How the world is made for each of us!
   How all we perceive and know in it
Tends to some moment's product thus,
   When a soul declares itself – to wit,
By its fruit – the thing it does!

Be Hate that fruit or Love that fruit,
   It forwards the General Deed of Man,
And each of the Many helps to recruit

The life of the race by a general plan,
Each living his own, to boot

I am named and known by that hour's feat,
  There took my station and degree.
So grew my own small life complete
  As Nature obtained her best in me –
One born to love you, sweet!

[ROBERT BROWNING, from *By the Fireside*]

When I make a decision – like marriage – I find that in that moment 'I am named'. Life turns on these choices, these earthly choices, which nevertheless can open a gate for our loving and our creativity. (There is quite a bit of doggerel in this poem – 'to boot' – but it is after all a love poem!)

18th March

Socialism will come to Europe and the world in a different way from that imagined by the nineteenth century revolutionaries, but it will come all the same, in the shape of Welfare States, making capitalism in its ancient form and laissez-faire a savage vestige of the past.

Is this a dream? 'But are not the dreams of one generation the realities of the next?'

Now that all passion is spent in me, I know that what finally prevails is not what one was aiming at – the absolute – but something akin to it. But for the young, passions, struggle and illusion are a vital necessity. It is only by errors, by disappointments, by lost battles, that men learn, and start afresh. I believe that a new synthesis will emerge out of the present conflict of ideas and opposing social forces, if there is time.

I often wonder whether, if I had to start again, I would act in the same way, cherish the same hopes, follow the same urge for bettering the world. I believe I would. For we all have our particular destiny to fulfil, our part to play, and it is for history to judge how far we succeed in contributing something of value.

[MICHAEL KAROLYI, from *Memoirs*]

From an aristocratic family of the Austro-Hungarian Empire, Michael Karolyi became a leader of the socialist party in the Diet. Later, exiled in Britain, as the old empire fell to pieces, he kept on paying sensitive attention simply to what had to be done.

19th March

There are works, few in number and not necessarily well known, that can be made only in a given cultural phase, but which, once made, have a unique validity for all the subsequent phases of that culture. I think this could be argued for the Anglo-Saxon *Dream of the Rood*. I am certain it is true of the *Vexilla Regis*, and that is why we have an instinctive sense of its belonging to us, that we must not lose it . . .

The advancing vexilla, which provides not only a concrete image but the poem's initial thrust, is even more poignant when we recall the actual vexilla Fortunatus saw with his physical eyes were standards, imitative of the past imperium but in fact now carried before petty Merovingian dynasts at fratricidal wars of loot. Such was the sordid violence from which the poet gave the Liturgy this enduring image of banners. It is the sort of thing that poets are for; to redeem is part of their job.

[DAVID JONES, from *Epoch and Artist*]

The reference is to Fortunatus, poet of the dying Roman world, composing what is known to us as the hymn, Ye royal banners forward go, *and seeing an image of the cross in something which was almost a parody, a mockery, of the standard of the Roman legions.*

20th March

All along the valley, stream that flashest white,
Deepening thy voice with the deepening of the night,
All along the valley, where thy waters flow,
I walked with one I loved two and thirty years ago.
All along the valley while I walked today,
The two and thirty years were a mist that rolled away;
For all along the valley, down thy rocky bed,
Thy living voice to me was as the voice of the dead,
And all along the valley, by rock and cave and tree,
The voice of the dead was a living voice to me.

[ALFRED TENNYSON, *In the Valley of Cauteretz*]

On June 5th 1970 I walked up this valley through Cauteretz to Porte d'Espagne and stayed there the night. The voice of the waters was as impressive as Tennyson had known it.

21st March

... what we have to face today is a divorce of natural theology from the mind and imagination of the most sensitive segment of our society. The disengagement of theology from imagination, . . . from the deepest sources of intellectual and artistic creativity, . . . is all but complete. The loss is sustained on both sides . . . The dilemma is this: theologians cannot redraw the picture until they regain contact with those ranges of thought, feeling and imagination which now live – even for the Christian believer – quite independently of theology . . . The best text-books for contemporary natural theologians are not the second-hand theological treatises but the living works of artists who are in touch with the springs of creative imagination. The starting-point of natural theology is not argument but sharpened awareness. For the moment it is better for us that arguments have fallen to pieces.

[HOWARD ROOT, from *Beginning All Over Again*]

Having lost touch with the imagination of the times, theology has become dessicated and prayer a closed-in pietism. There is hardly any evidence of the imagination in modern liturgies. (Nor is there of our bodiliness. If 'gesture is language', then what is expressed is either formal or berserk, both without meaning.)

22nd March

All great drawing is drawing by memory. That is why it takes so long to learn. If drawing were transcription, a kind of script writing, it could be taught in a few years. Even before a model, you draw from memory. The model is a reminder. Not of a stereotype you know by heart. Not even of anything you can consciously remember. The model is a reminder of experience you can only formulate and therefore only remember by drawing. And those experiences add up to the sum total of your awareness of the tangible, three-dimensional, structural world . . . Make a mark on (a blank white page) . . . and the edges of the page . . . have become the borders of a microcosm. Make two marks of uneven pressure and the whiteness . . . becomes opaque three-dimensional space that must be made less opaque and more and more lucid by every succeeding mark. That microcosm is filled with the potentiality of every proportion you have ever perceived or sensed. That space is filled with the potentiality of every form, sliding plane, hollow, point of contact, passage of separation you have ever set eye or hand on. And it does not stop even there. For, after a few more marks, there is air, there is pressure, and therefore there is bulk and weight. And this scale is then filled with the potentiality of every degree of hardness, yieldingness, force of movement, activeness or passiveness that you have ever buried your head in or knocked it against. And from all this you must select in a few minutes, as nature did through millennia, in order to create a human ankle, a human arm-pit with the pectoral muscle burying itself like an underground stream, or the bough of a tree. From all this you must select the one lock and one key.

[JOHN BERGER, from *A Painter of Our Time*]

A novel about an artist who is a refugee from Hungary. Drawing is not copying, but the line sums up all that you can remember, all your past.

23rd March

Thus piteously Love closed what he begat:
The union of this ever-diverse pair!
These two were rapid falcons in a snare,
Condemned to do the flitting of the bat.
Lovers beneath the singing sky of May,
They wandered once; clear as the dew on flowers.
But they fed not on the advancing hours:
Their hearts held cravings for the buried day.
Then each applied to each that fatal knife,
Deep questioning, which probes to endless dole,
Ah, what a dusty answer gets the soul
When hot for certainties in this our life! –
In tragic hints here see what evermore
Moves dark as yonder midnight ocean's force,
Thundering like ramping hosts of warrior horse,
To throw that faint thin line upon the shore!

[GEORGE MEREDITH, *Modern Love*]

The one poem where he said something important. There is so much heat for certainties in our day. Despite its noise and clamour, all it produces is a momentary wave-line which soon vanishes.

24th March

A silence fell upon the three of them now, a silence through which they could hear all manner of faint sounds. The silence seemed to mount up from the sea and sink down from the sky. It flowed around and around; buoying up the sounds that floated upon it, as if they'd been relaxed swimmers on a smooth tide; and the silence mingled with the sun-sparkles too, that were rocking on the incoming waves, and with the rare sea-scents that kept entering that turret window. But the sounds were what the silence loved best of all; and they rose from all manner of different directions.

They were casual sounds, drifting sounds, accidental sounds, without order and without cohesion. But they were the music of life. Some came from fishermen drying their nets on the rocks, some from seagulls along the walls of the jetty, some from cattle and sheep in the castle-meadows; some from horses and hounds in the castle yard. They were fainter, more volatile, more ethereal than the living things that uttered them . . . Fused together, these isolated sounds evoked a sense of continuity of life by sea and land, a continuity simple, tranquil, universal, detached from individual hunger or desire or pain or joy.

[JOHN COWPER POWYS, from *Owen Glendower*]

I remember the comment of a man taken into the countryside at night on military training. The company were asked to listen. Only one man said he heard a stream, and he was a countryman. The others were lost because they could not hear anything familiar to them. Who hears the sounds others do not hear?

25th March

Look at the stars! Look up at the skies!
  O look at all the fire-folk sitting in the air!
  The bright boroughs, the circle-citadels there!
Down in dim woods the diamond delves! the elves' eyes!
The grey lawns cold where gold, where quickgold lies!
  Wind-beat whitebeam! airy abeles set on a flare!
  Flake-doves sent floating forth at a farmyard scare! –
Ah well, it is all a purchase, all is a prize.

Buy then! bid then! – What? – Prayer, patience, alms, vows,
Look, look: a May-mess, like on orchard boughs!
  Look! March-bloom, like on mealed-with-yellow sallows!

These are indeed the barn; withindoors house
The shocks. This piece-bright paling shuts the spouse
   Christ home, Christ and his mother and all his hallows.

[G. M. HOPKINS, *The Starlight Night*]

*Hopkins with his rush of exclamations is overwhelmed by the all-ness of things,
by a cosmic Annunciation.*

26th March

Being means striving to go on, to go along, to extend, to continue. Yet
being human means to go beyond sheer continuity. Being human
occurs, comes about in moments. Being human consists of outbursts of
singularity. Singularity is a dimension easily forgotten, always threatened by the continuous assaults of wholesaleness. Sheer continuity leads
to the suspension of singularity, drudgery, inner devastation, demolition
of all moments. To discover the hospitality of being, one must cultivate
the art of reaching beyond oneself. A life rising in outbursts into meaning
is a way of sensing the beneficence of time.

[ABRAHAM HESCHEL, from *Who is Man?*]

*Heschel points to the way in which God requires of us singularity within the
texture of the whole. This is what makes us human. Only a person can exhibit
singularity, for it adds to the total life. But you don't enjoy it by yourself. If our
lives were merely a collection of individual experiences, unshared, we would all
be mad. Individualism is a dead end; singularity enriches the whole.*

27th March

Th'expense of Spirit in a waste of shame
Is lust in action; and till action, lust
Is perjured, murderous, bloody, full of blame,
Savage, extreme, rude, cruel, not to trust;
Enjoy'd no sooner but despised straight;
Past reason hunted; and, no sooner had,
Past reason hated, as a swallow'd bait
On purpose laid to make the taker mad;
Mad in pursuit, and in possession so;

Had, having, and in quest to have, extreme;
A bliss in proof, and proved, a very woe;
Before a joy proposed; behind, a dream.
  All this the world well knows; yet none knows well
  To shun the heaven that leads men to this hell.

[WILLIAM SHAKESPEARE, *Sonnet CXXIX*]

A late sonnet which sums up much of what Shakespeare was getting at all the time. No one else has ever described the difference between lust and love so emphatically, and also admitted that we all fail to act upon our knowledge. He saw that words, God's greatest gift for expressing the truth, can be deceptive, destructive, degrading, and defiling. Love is of God and yet it is always at risk of being subverted, at every moment, to its opposite.

28th March

Read the Introduction to Kierkegaard by Jolivet. Few books have upset me so much since I came into this world. It is horrifying at times to discover oneself in another man, and this has happened to me when I read this book . . . In the flashes of Kierkegaardian thought one has glimpses of great depths that are singularly like a revelation. 'Christianity has not materialised,' he writes.

As long as something inside us protests against ourselves, there is room for hope. It is when one accepts oneself as one is and gives up, that the game is in danger of being lost. In other words (if I wanted to be funny), one can set one's mind at rest so long as one feels uneasy!

[JULIAN GREEN, from *Diaries*]

Julian Green was always struggling with this sense of dissatisfaction.

29th March

To Mercy, Pity, Peace, and Love
All pray in their distress;
And to these virtues of delight
Return their thankfulness.

For Mercy, Pity, Peace, and Love
Is God, our father dear,

And Mercy, Pity, Peace, and Love
Is Man, his child and care.

For Mercy has a human heart,
Pity a human face,
And Love, the human form divine,
And Peace the human dress.

Then every man, of every clime,
That prays in his distress,
Prays to the human form divine,
Love, Mercy, Pity, Peace.

And all must love the human form,
In heathen, Turk or Jew;
Where Mercy, Love and Pity dwell
There God is dwelling too.

[WILLIAM BLAKE, *The Divine Image*]

My first vicar didn't like this hymn – not quite the fulness of Christian faith. But there is precious little of the human form of God in the hymn book. After all, the ascription to God the All-Merciful goes right across Judaism, Christianity, and Islam. But mercy has not been characteristic of the last two and the first now faces the problem of what happens when the powerless achieve power. Power corrupts because we all have the desire to treat others as vermin. This is the source of all justifications for the atrocities of racism and religious hatred.

30th March

Poetry is the record of the best and happiest moments of the happiest and best minds. We are aware of evanescent visitations of thought and feeling sometimes associated with place or person, sometimes regarding our own mind alone, and always arising unforeseen and departing unbidden, but elevating and delightful beyond all expression: so that even in the desire and regret they leave, there cannot but be pleasure, participating as it does in the nature of its object. It is as it were the interpenetration of a diviner nature through our own; but its footsteps are like those of a wind over the sea which the coming calm erases, and whose traces remain only, as on the wrinkled sand which paves it. These and corresponding conditions of being are experienced principally by those of the most delicate sensibility and the most enlarged imagination

and the state of mind produced by them is at war with every base desire.
The enthusiasm of virtue, love, patriotism, and friendship is essentially
linked with such emotions; and whilst they last, itself appears as what it
is, an atom to the universe. Poets are not only subject to the experiences
as spirits of the most refined organization, but they can colour all that
they combine with the evanescent hues of this ethereal world; a word, a
trait in the representation of a scene or a passion, will touch the enchanted cord, and reanimate, in those who have ever experienced these
emotions, the sleeping, the cold, the buried image of the past. Poetry
thus makes immortal all that is best and most beautiful in the world; it
arrests the vanishing apparitions which haunt the interlunations of life,
and veiling them, or in language or in form, sends them forth among
mankind, bearing sweet news of kindred joy to those with whom their
sisters abide – abide, because there is no portal of expression from the
caverns of the spirit which they inhabit into the universe of things.
Poetry redeems from decay the visitations of divinity in man.

[PERCY BYSSHE SHELLEY, from *Defence of Poetry*]

Perhaps overblown, yet an eloquent and evocative passage about the nature of
poetry.

31st March

>   Is that it, woman? Does it strike you so?
>   The Great Breath blowing a tiny seed of fire
>   Fans out your petals for excess of flame,
>   Till all your being smokes with fine desire?
>
>   Or are we kindled, you and I, to be
>   One rose of wonderment upon the tree
>   Of perfect life, and is our possible seed
>   But the residuum of the ecstasy?
>
>   How will you have it? – the rose is all in all,
>   Or the ripe rose-fruits of the luscious fall?
>   The sharp begetting or the child begot?
>   Our consummation matters, or does it not?
>
>   To me it seems the seed is just left over
>   From the red rose-flowers' fiery transcience;

Just orts and slarts; berries that smoulder in the bush
Which burnt just now with marvellous immanence.

Blossom, my darling, blossom, be a rose
Of roses unchidden and purposeless; a rose
For rosiness only, without an ulterior motive;
For me it is more than enough if the flower unclose.

[D. H. LAWRENCE, from *Rose of All the World*]

One of Lawrence's most expressive poems in understanding the sexual in life.
Perhaps one of the greatest love poems in English.

APRIL

1st April

(*On the Mona Lisa*) ... Perhaps of all ancient pictures time has chilled 'La Gioconda' least. As often happens with works in which invention seems to reach its limit, there is an element in it not given to, not invented by, the master ...

The presence that rose thus so strangely beside the waters is expressive of what in the ways of a thousand years men had come to desire. Here is the head upon which all 'the ends of the world are come' and, the eye-lids are a little weary. It is a beauty wrought out from within upon the flesh, the deposit, cell by cell, of strange thoughts and fantastic reveries and exquisite passions ... the animalism of Greece, the lust of Rome, the mysticism of the middle age with its spiritual ambition and imaginative loves, the return of the Pagan world, the sins of the Borgias. She is older than the rocks among which she sits; like the vampire, she has been dead many times, and learned the secrets of the grave; and has been a diver in deep seas, and keeps their fallen day about her; and trafficked for strange webs with Eastern merchants; and, as Leda, was the mother of Helen of Troy, and, as St Anne, the mother of Mary; and all this has been to her but as the sound of lyres and flutes, and lives only in the delicacy with which it has moulded the changing lineaments, and tinged the eye-lids and the hands. The fancy of a perpetual life, sweeping together ten thousand experiences, is an old one; and modern philosophy has conceived the idea of humanity as wrought upon, by, and summoning up in itself all modes of thought and life. Certainly Lady Lisa might stand as the embodiment of the old fancy, the symbol of the modern idea.

[WALTER PATER, from *The Renaissance*]

The painting stands for itself. The writing is haunting if florid. But perhaps it takes us further into the picture. Certain faces do seem to contain more than either their years or their generation would indicate.

2nd April

Fair Daffodils, we weep to see
    You haste away so soon;
As yet the early-rising sun
    Has not attained his noon.
            Stay, stay,
        Until the hasting day
            Has run
        But to the even-song;
And having prayed together, we
    Will go with you along.

We have short time to stay, as you
    We have as short a spring;
As quick a growth to meet decay,
    As you or anything.
            We die
        As your hours do, and dry
            Away,
        Like to the summer's rain;
Or as pearls of morning-dew,
    Ne'er to be found again.

[ROBERT HERRICK, *Fair Daffodils*]

*There was a moment in the early seventeenth century when this kind of lyric
came as naturally as speech. It is all there on the surface, like the ripples of
water on a brook. There is something important about catching the moment –
and Herrick does it with such a light touch. Dare we say that these lines dance
where Wordsworth's plod?*

3rd April

. . . Catholic Christendom thought that there was only one visible
Church on earth and that was doctrinally inerrant. This for explicable
historical reasons broadened into the notion that the Church of Rome
with all her dogmas, devotions, and ecclesiastical structure was the more
or less perfected incarnation of God's revelation. This gave it driving
force. Without this illusion it would have lacked propulsion. For we
start as nursery people and a child's whole development depends on
stability, on what is true at the time for him. Historic Catholic Christian-

ity has, from this aspect, the spiritual equivalent of geocentric ideas in the scientific field. Christianity escaped from the national-spiritual exclusiveness of Israel to the international-spiritual exclusiveness of medieval Catholicism, as little squeamish about the missa damnata as about the economic servitude of the bulk of mankind. We forget how dependent we have been on the imperfect, the unpleasant, and even the loathsome, what an enormous debt civilisation owes to slavery, appalling poverty, religious intolerance, credulity, and even fraud. At a certain stage in its history Catholic Christianity depended on the existence of spiritual serfs, on the silent multitudes who believed what they were told, lived as they were told, and died as they were told. It was that or nothing. Religion, as much as anything else, is the art of the possible. In the history of Christianity we can see the Franciscan failure writ large.

[MAGDALEN GOFFIN, from *The Broken Pitcher*]

Is the waste inevitable? It is like this at the moment. We have to admit that this has been so for two thousand years. We can't expect to change it overnight. But we are in duty bound to change what we can, even if we are damnably slow about it. We must not be defeated. And it is a waste of energy to rail against God or our ancestors.

4th April

There are some heights in Wessex, shaped as if by a kindly hand
For thinking, dreaming, dying on, and at crises when I stand,
Say, on Ingpen Beacon eastward, or on Wylls-Neck westwardly,
I seem where I was before my birth, and after death may be.

In the lowlands I have no comrade, not even the lone man's friend –
Her who suffereth long and is kind, accepts what he is too weak to
   mend:
Down there they are dubious and askance; there nobody thinks as I,
But mind-chains do not clank where one's neighbour is the sky. . .

As for the one rare fair woman, I am now but a thought of hers,
I enter her mind and another thought succeeds me that she prefers;
Yet my love for her in its fullness she herself even did not know;
Well, time cures hearts of tenderness, and now I can let her go.

So I am found on Ingpen Beacon, or on Wylls-Neck to the west,
Or else on homely Bulbarrow, or little Pilsdon Crest,

Where men have never cared to haunt, nor women have walked with
   me;
And ghosts then keep their distance; and I know some liberty.

[THOMAS HARDY, *Wessex Heights*]

There are some awkward lines in this poem, but there is a tenderness in the two
middle stanzas quoted here. For Hardy, the brief glimpses of love are real. You
hold to them. But the persons responsible you have to let go.

5th April

The concept of miracle which is permissible from the historical approach
can be defined at its starting-point as an abiding astonishment. The
philosophizing and the religious person both wonder at the phenomenon, but the one neutralizes his wonder in ideal knowledge, while the
other abides in that wonder; no knowledge, no cognition, can weaken
his astonishment. Any causal explanation only deepens the wonder for
him. The great turning-points in religious history are based on the fact
that again and ever again an individual and a group attached to him
wonder and keep on wondering; at a natural phenomenon, at a historical event, or at both together, always at something which intervenes
fatefully in the life of this individual and this group. They sense and
experience it as wonder. This, to be sure, is only the starting-point of the
historical concept of wonder, but it cannot be explained away. Miracle
is not something 'supernatural' or 'superhistorical', but an incident, an
event which can be fully included in the objective, scientific nexus of
nature and history; the vital meaning of which, however, for the person
to whom it occurs, destroys the security of the whole nexus of knowledge for him, and explodes the fixity of the fields of experience of
'Nature' and 'History'. Miracle is simply what happens; in so far as it
meets people who are capable of receiving it, or prepared to receive it,
as miracle. The extraordinary element favours this coming together,
but it is not characteristic of it; the normal and ordinary can also undergo a transfiguration into miracle in the light of the suitable hour.

[MARTIN BUBER, from *Moses*]

Buber was horrified by the claim that the miraculous proves God. It is the fact of
my life that is a miracle to me! And the disclosures of that life continue all the
time.

6th April

And what do they talk about in that momentary halt in the tavern? Of the eternal questions, of the existence of God and immortality. And those who do not believe in God talk of socialism or anarchism, of the transformation of all humanity on a new pattern, so that it all comes to the same, they're the same questions turned inside out. Isn't it so? . . . What would be marvellous, is not that God should really exist; the marvel is that such an idea, the idea of the necessity of God, could enter the head of such a savage, vicious beast as man. So holy it is, so touching, so wise and so great a credit it does to man. As for me, I've long resolved not to think whether man created God or God man . . . and therefore I tell you that I accept God simply. And you must note this: if God exists and if He really did create the world, then, as we all know, He created it according to the geometry of Euclid and the human mind with the conception of only three dimensions in space. . .

[FYODR DOSTOEVSKY, from *The Brothers Karamazov*]

We are left to think this one out! No other European literature churns over the questions about God as much as the Russian. Jewish literature does. Is it that the vastness and mystery of God impinges inevitably in the desert and on the steppes?

7th April

Who would have thought my shrivell'd heart
   Could have recover'd greenness? It was gone
Quite underground, as flowers depart
   To feed their mother-root when they have blown;
      Where they together
      All the hard weather,
Dead to the world, keep house unknown.

These are thy wonders, Lord of Power,
   Killing and quickening, bringing down to hell
And up to heaven in an hour;
   Making a chiming of a passing bell.
      We say amiss,
      This or that is;
Thy word is all, if we could spell.

And now in age I bud again;
After so many deaths I live and write;
I once more smell the dew and rain,
And relish versing: O my only Light,
It cannot be
That I am he
On whom thy tempest fell all night.

[GEORGE HERBERT, from *The Flower*]

This poem is in similar vein to yesterday's quotation, but in seventeenth century England: 'I once more smell the dew and rain.'

8th April

To the Augustans, as to Dr Johnson, the gods were 'images of which time has tarnished the splendour.' But to the twelfth and thirteenth centuries, they have been dead and are alive again; they are part of the resurrection miracle of the Northern Spring.

For this is the amazing discovery of medieval lyric. Spring comes slowly up that way, but when it comes it is an ecstasy. In the North far more than in the South, Persephone comes actually from the dead. It is a new thing, and their own.

Of all things the beginning
Was on an April morn:
In spring the earth remembereth
The day that she was born.

And so the feast of Venus,
Wherever Love holds sway,
By mortal and immortal
Is kept as holiday.

[From a play on the Nativity by BENEDIKTBEURN]

The scholars were strong in faith when they challenged Mary Virgin with that enchantment.

Nor is it the full-blown spring, the May morning of Provence . . . These . . . are the poets of February, when this year's birds begin calling in the twilight trees, of January itself, those days of incredible sweetness, the first stirring of the blood, the first mounting of the sap, so much

more poignant than the full burgeoning . . . It is the background of the
wild earth, of rain-washed April, that gives their earthiest passion its
amazing cleanness.

[HELEN WADDELL, from *The Wandering Scholars*]

*In the northern lyricism of the twelfth and thirteenth centuries there was a
new feature, a fresh enjoyment of the gifts God has given us.*

9th April

What lovely things
Thy hand hath made:
The smooth-plumed bird
In its emerald shade,
The seed of the grass,
The speck of stone
Which the wayfaring ant
Stirs – and hastes on!

Though I should sit
By some tarn in thy hills
Using its ink
As the spirit wills
To write of Earth's wonders
Its live, willed things,
Flit would the ages
On soundless wings
Ere unto Z
My pen drew nigh;
Leviathan told,
And the honey-fly;
And still would remain
My wit to try –
My worn reeds broken,
The dark tarn dry,
All words forgotten –
Thou, Lord, and I.

[WALTER DE LA MARE, *The Scribe*]

*A moving simplicity in this poem, the poet himself a sensitive man, aware of
details and fragments.*

10th April

For, indeed, a change was coming upon the world, the meaning and direction of which even still is hidden from us, a change from era to era. The paths trodden by the footsteps of ages were broken up; old things were passing away, and the faith and the life of ten centuries were dissolving like a dream. Chivalry was dying; the abbey and the castle were soon together to crumble into ruins; and all the forms, desires, beliefs, convictions of the old world were passing away, never to return. A new continent had risen up beyond the western sea. The floor of heaven, inlaid with stars, had sunk back into an infinite abyss of immeasurable space; and the firm earth itself, unfixed from its foundations, was seen to be but a small atom in the awful vastness of the universe. In the fabric of habit in which they had so laboriously built for themselves, mankind were to remain no longer.

And now it is all gone – like an unsubstantial pageant faded; and between us and the old English there lies a gulf of mystery which the prose of the historian will never adequately bridge. They cannot come to us, and our imagination can but feebly penetrate to them. Only among the aisles of our cathedrals, only as we gaze upon their silent figures sleeping on their tombs, some faint conceptions float before us of what these men were when they were alive; and perhaps in the sound of church bells, that peculiar creation of the medieval age, which falls upon the ear like the echo of a vanished world.

[JAMES ANTHONY FROUDE, from *History of England*]

No other historian wrote of this change so movingly. And what was London like when all the church bells rang and there were no machines to compete with their sound?

11th April

Mr H. was an austere man, and had the reputation of being singularly unworldly, for a river man. Among other things, he said that Arkansas had been injured and kept back by generations of exaggerations concerning the mosquitoes here. One may smile, he said, and turn the matter off as being a small thing; but when you come to look at the effects produced, in the way of discouragement of immigration and diminished values of property, it was quite the opposite of a small thing, or thing in any wise to be coughed down or sneered at. These mosquitoes had been persistently represented as being formidable and lawless, whereas 'the truth is, they are feeble, insignificant in size, diffident to a fault, sensitive' – and so on, and so on . . . But if he was soft on the Arkansas mosquitoes, he was hard enough on the mosquitoes of Lake Providence to make up for it . . . He said that two of them could whip a dog, and four of them could hold a man down . . . referred in a sort of casual way – and yet significant way – to the fact that the life policy in its simplest form is unknown in Lake Providence – they take out a mosquito policy beside . . .

[MARK TWAIN, from *Life on the Mississippi*]

Nothing else quite like Mark Twain has come out of America.

12th April

Augustine has lessons for Christians, and the first is to beware of lust for power. He had condemned this in pagans, had seen it as distinctive of the Devil, and the Redemption as a rejection of it. But once his side was gaining on schismatics in North Africa, he deployed in the cause of cruelty all the metaphors that are religion's curse . . .

Augustine . . . turned words into playthings, and the second lesson is that they are not. Thus, he read Romans 14.23 as 'Whatever is not from faith is sin', failed to see that 'faith' here is 'good faith', and so held pagan's apparently virtuous actions to be sinful . . .

. . . the third lesson is that religious insights suffer from *la maladie de la chaise*: they want to keep on going, and they must be halted. Otherwise the depth of an insight becomes the lunacy of a system – as Augustine may have learned when, as an old man, he was intellectually trounced by the Pelagian, Julian of Eclanum.

Julian can be charged with shallowness, but the sheer simplicity of his questions was devastating. You say that all inherit guilt: so babies are guilty? You reply they are oppressed by another's sin: who then judges them guilty, and condemns them to eternal punishment? God? What barbarian would talk of God as you do?

[P. J. FITZPATRICK, from *Turkish Delight Laced with Incense*]

Augustine? I detest him! His treatment of women was so appalling that it over-shadows all his theologising. He refuses to allow that you can no longer separate Word and Flesh. Once separated, once you refuse the reality of the Incarnation, you are left with a theology that is merely a heap of words.

13th April

Oh, Aberedw, Aberedw. Would God I might dwell and die by thee.
Memory enters in and brings back the old time in a clear vision and
waking dream, and again I descend from the high moor's half-encircling
sweep and listen to the distant murmur of the river as it foams down the
ravine from its home in the Green Cwm and its cradle in the hills. Once
more I stand by the riverside and look up at the cliff castle towers and
mark the wild roses swinging from the crag and watch the green woods
waving and shimmering with a twinkling dazzle as they rustle in the
breeze and shining of the summer afternoon, while here and there a
grey crag peeps from among the tufted trees. And once again I hear the
merry voices and laughter of the children as they clamber down the
cliff path among the bushes or along the rock ledges of the riverside or
climb the Castle Mount, or saunter along the narrow green meadow
tree-fringed and rock-bordered and pass in and out of Llewellyn's cave,
or gather wood and light the fire amongst the rocks upon the moor, or
loiter down the valley to Cavan Twm Bach and cross the shining ferry
at sunset, when the evening shadows lie long and still across the broad
reaches of the river. Oh, Aberedw, Aberedw.

[FRANCIS KILVERT, from *Diary*, 1870–79]

It speaks for itself. Such lyrical writing.

14th April

For believers, history is always related to a God whom we know as the
ground and the dynamic of creation and salvation. *Extra mundum nulla
salus*: outside the world there is no salvation. Ordinary, everyday
history is the sphere of God's liberating action! For believers, it is meaningful to ask about the soteriological significance of everything that
happens in human history. Does it bear a perspective of meaning or
not? Is it saving or not? Believers cannot be content with a discussion of
the political and social sphere which expresses only the political and
social components. So theologians cannot be silent on non-theological
problems . . . If talk about the Kingdom of God is to continue to offer
any basis (for discussion of meaningfulness) it is an absolutely necessary
task for Christians to examine developments which may or may not be
saving and analyse them as salvation (or not) which is (or is not) in line
with the Kingdom of God. Talk about eschatological salvation loses any

rational ground when there is no positive relationship between this claim to salvation and what is experienced by human beings in making them whole . . .

Human beings can realize the promise of their own being only as grace. Its basis and support lies in the fact that believers experience every small bit of salvation as a foretaste of the promise of the perfect salvation that God will give. The longing for liberation also takes on the connotation of being freed or redeemed from suffering and injustice.

[JOHAN DE TAVERNIER, from *Human or 'secular' as a medium for the history of salvation or its opposite.*]

The magazine Concilium *from which this piece comes represents the movement which challenges the old order of the Church, taking the Second Vatican Council and going further, putting the world at the centre of the stage.*

15th April

That which we call the 'work' of Christ did not consist in the execution of a programme of material construction (though he was a carpenter). But neither did that 'work' consists in the elaboration of a programme for the transformation of the world (though he was a prophet). The 'work' of Christ consisted in his obedience to, his unswerving trust in the silence he called 'Father'. If he had time to make his revelation, it was because the revelation he was occurred, definitively, in that act of 'mortal wounding'. Good Friday was not the unfortunate disruption of his preaching. It was the execution of that which his preaching proclaimed: God's transformative fidelity to his creation.

Christians have always been tempted to transform the tragedy of Jesus into comedy by supposing that resurrection gives to his story a 'happy ending'. But no story has an ending until it is fully told. The context that gives meaning (or fails to do so) to the history of each individual (including Jesus) is the history of the human race. And because that history continues, the story has, as yet, no ending. The question of the meaning of history . . . remains an open question. It is not closed by faith in Jesus' resurrection. Which is why the grammar of the language in which faith seeks expression is less the language of assertion and prediction than of prayer and trust, The Christian may have grounds for hope, but he has no grounds for 'metaphysical optimism'.

[NICHOLAS LASH, from *A Matter of Hope*]

Exuberant religious claims need to hear this accent of restraint. The end of the story has not yet come: so one cannot know all its meaning . . . And Jesus trusted "in the silence he called 'Father'."

16th April

I never exhaust the beauty of trees and woods. Careless of their species, I observe them as patterns against the sky, perhaps most beautiful when leafless. But though leafless they are never lifeless. The leaves are scarcely fallen when the new buds begin shyly to press through the tender bark, like dark blebs of blood. There are 365 days in a year and a tree has the same number of faces, or rather facets, for it is a composite picture of many minute changes . . . Perhaps only once or twice a year there is a chance to wander in these woods when sunlight has succeeded hoar frost or a light fall of snow, and the whole scene scintillates in electric brilliance. Very rarely such an event takes place in April, when the first pale green leaves have already unfolded, and the undergrowth is starred with primroses and violets. I am then reminded of something very unnatural but still poetic, those crystallised fruits we sometimes eat at Christmas; but these are clumsy compared with a frosted veil of snowflakes on a bed of violets.

[HERBERT READ, from *The Contrary Experience*]

I once painted the same woodland scene each month for a year, in Blengdale near Gosforth. It made me look long and ask how the scene had changed since the previous month.

17th April

Because we two can never again come back
On life's one forward track –
Never again first-happily explore
This valley of rocks and vines and orange trees
Half Biblical and half Hesperides,
With dark blue seas calling from a shell-strewn shore;
By the strange power of the Spring's resistless green,
Let us be true to what we have shared and seen,
And as our amulet this idyll save.
And since the unreturning day must die,

Let it for ever be lit by an evening sky
And the wild myrtle grow upon its grave.

[SIEGFRIED SASSOON, *Because we two can never again come back*]

My wife and I used to read this poem to each other a good deal. We do indeed regret that we must let go and die, and yet the 'resistless green' is the counterpart, the spring an intimation of the new life that takes over. You suffer the attrition and corruption of what you hold in common, and you cannot go back, but you can still 'be true to what we have shared and seen'.

18th April

I do not consider the individual to be either the starting point or the goal of the human world. But I consider the human person to be the irremovable central place of the struggle between the world's movement away from God and its movement toward God. This struggle takes place today to an uncannily large extent in the realm of public life, of course not between group and group but within each group. Yet the decisive battles of this realm as well are fought in the depth, in the ground or the groundlessness of the person.

[MARTIN BUBER, from *Between Man and Man*]

Why hasn't this registered enough in our Christian discourse? We are supposed to be Trinitarian, with the reality of 'inter-animation' (John Donne) at the heart of creation. In you I am alive . . . And echoing the Book of Common Prayer, *'that you may dwell in me, and I in you.'*

19th April

Joyce has caught the psychology of sleep as no one else has ever caught it, laying hold on states of mind which it is difficult for the waking intellect to recreate, and distinguishing with marvellous delicacy between the different levels of dormant consciousness. There are the relative vividness of events reflected from the day before; the nightmare viscidity and stammering of the heavy slumbers of midnight; the buoyancy and self-assertive vitality which gradually emerge from this; the half-waking of the early morning, which lapses back into the rigmarole of dreams; the awareness, later, of the light outside, with its effects as of the curtain of the eye-lids standing between the mind and the day.

Through all this, the falling of twilight, the striking of the hours by the clock, the morning fog and its clearing, the bell for early mass, and the rising sun at the window, make themselves felt by the sleeper. With what brilliance they are rendered by Joyce! And the voices that echo in Earwicker's dream – the beings that seize upon him and speak through him . . . Joyce has only to strike the rhythm and the timbre, and we know which of the spirits is with us.

[EDMUND WILSON, from *On* Finnegan's Wake]

I can spend half an hour with a page of Joyce. It leaves me breathless, with hundreds of abstruse and complex compounds rushing along.

20th April

When the ecstatic body grips
Its heaven, with little sobbing cries,
And lips are crushed on hot blind lips,
I read strange pity in your eyes.

For that in you which is not mine
And that in you which I love best,
And that which my day-thoughts divine
Masterless still, still unpossessed,

Sits in the blue eyes frightened stare,
A naked, lonely-dwelling thing,
A frail thing from its body lair
Drawn at my body's summoning;

Whispering low, 'O unknown man
Whose hunger on my hunger wrought,
Body shall give thee what body can,
Shall give you all, save what you sought.'

Whispering, 'O secret one, forgive,
Forgive and be content though still
Beyond the blood's surrender live
The darkness of the separate will.

'Enough, if in the veins we know
Body's delirium, body's peace –
Ask not that ghost to ghost shall go,
Essence in essence merge and cease.'

But swiftly, as in sudden sleep,
That you in you is veiled and dead;
And the world's shrunken to a heap
Of hot flesh straining on a bed.

[E. R. DODDS, *When the ecstatic body grips*]

One of the few poems to express the consummation of physical love. Most poets either draw back (Milton) or get lost in wordiness (Lawrence).

21st April

On Aikenshaw the sun blinks braw,
The burn rins blithe and fain:
There's nought wi' me I wadna give
To looke thereon again.

On Keilder-side the wind blaws wide;
There sounds no hunting-horn
That rings sae sweet as the winds that beat
Round banks where Tyne is born.

The Wansbeck sings with all her springs,
The bents and braes give ear;
But the wood that rings wi' the song she sings
I may not see nor hear;
For far and far thae blithe burns are,
And strange is a'thing near,

The light there lightens, the day there brightens,
The loud wind there lives free:
Nae light come nigh me or wind blows by me
That I wad hear or see.

We'll see nae mair the sea-banks fair,
And the sweet grey gleaming sky,
And the lordly strand of Northumberland,
And the goodly towers thereby:
And none shall know but the winds that blow
The graves wherein we lie.

[A. C. SWINBURNE, from *A Jacobite's Exile*]

*Northumberland and the Border, where I have walked a lot, evoke most strongly
my feeling of fleshly participation in a particular landscape. Seen with the
inner eye of exile, you know you will never see it again – and we all reach that
point – yet it has become part of you. You were nourished there, and it is a part
of the stuff of your life. And it's worth singing about.*

22nd April

"I must own to you that I shall never give up looking forward to the day
when all discord shall be silenced. Try to imagine its dawn. The tempest
of blows and execrations is over; all is still; the new sun is rising, and the
weary men united at last, taking count in their conscience of the ended
contest, feel saddened by their victory, because so many ideas have
perished for the triumph of one, so many beliefs have abandoned them
without support. They feel alone on the earth and gather close together.
Yes, there must be many bitter hours! But at last the anguish of hearts
shall be extinguished in love."

And on this last word of wisdom, a word so sweet, so bitter, so cruel
sometimes, I said goodbye to Natalia Haldin. It is hard to think I shall
never look any more into the trustful eyes of that girl – wedded to
an invincible belief in the advent of loving concord springing like a
heavenly flower from the soil of men's earth, soaked in blood, torn by
struggles, watered with tears.

[JOSEPH CONRAD, from *Under Western Eyes*]

*Conrad was near enough to this Slavonic sensibility, with all its pain, to be able
to translate it into English. It is Poland speaking still.*

23rd April

'*Hamlet* is words and so is Hamlet. He is as witty as Jesus Christ, but
whereas Christ speaks Hamlet is speech. He is the tormented empty
sinful consciousness of man seared by the bright light of art, the god's
flayed victim dancing the dance of creation. The cry of anguish is obscure
because it is overheard. It is the eloquence of direct speech . . . But it is
not addressed to us. Shakespeare is passionately exposing himself to the
ground and author of his being. He is speaking as few artists can speak,
in the first person yet at the pinnacle of artifice. How veiled that deity,
how dangerous to approach, how almost impossible with impunity to

address, Shakespeare knew better than any man. *Hamlet* is a wild act of audacity, a self-purging, a complete self-castigation in the presence of the god. Is Shakespeare a masochist? Of course. He is the king of masochists. His writing thrills with that secret. But because his god is a real god and not an eidolon of private fantasy, and because love has here invented language as if for the first time, he can change pain into poetry and orgasms into pure thought.'

. . . Shakespeare here makes the crisis of his own identity into the very central stuff of art. He transmutes his private obsessions into a rhetoric so public that it can be mumbled by any child. He enacts the purification of speech, and yet also this is something comic, a sort of trick, like a huge pun, like a long almost pointless joke. Shakespeare cries out in agony, he writhes, he dances, he laughs, he shrieks, and he makes us laugh and shriek ourselves out of hell. Being is acting. We are tissues and tissues of different persons and yet we are nothing at all. What redeems us is that speech is ultimately divine. What part does every actor want to play? Hamlet.

[IRIS MURDOCH, from The Black Prince]

Shakespeare's birthday. So today's quotation has to be about Hamlet. *In this play we discover Shakspeare as nowhere else. The word written and acted – and overtaken by the deceptiveness of words.*

24th April

> I have met them at the close of day
> Coming with vivid faces
> From counter or desk among grey
> Eighteenth-century houses.
> I have passed with a nod of the head
> Or polite meaningless words,
> Or have lingered before I had done
> Of a mocking tale or gibe
> To please a companion
> Around the fire at the club,
> Being certain that they and I
> But lived where motley is worn:
> All changed, changed utterly:
> A terrible beauty is born . . .

[W. B. YEATS, from Easter 1916]

*April 24th was the date of the Easter Rising. Yeats knew the people involved,
one of whom commented to me, who was brought up on Home Rule, 'Ireland
became alive.' It is something the English cannot understand because they have
never been conquered.*

25th April

"And he, casting away his garment, rose and came to Jesus."

And he cast it down, down, on the green grass,
Over the young crocuses, where the dew was –
He cast the garment of his flesh that was full of death,
And like a sword his spirit showed out of the cold sheath.

He went a pace or two, he went to meet his Lord,
And, as I said, his spirit looked like a clean sword,
And seeing him the naked trees began shivering,
And all the birds cried out aloud as it were late spring.

And the Lord came on, He came down and saw
That a soul was waiting for Him, one without flaw,
And they embraced in the churchyard where the robins play,
And the daffodils hang down their heads, as they burn away.

The Lord held his head fast, and you could see
That he kissed the unsheathed ghost that was gone free –
As a hot sun, on a March day, kisses the cold ground;
And the spirit answered, for he knew well that his peace was found.

The spirit trembled, and sprang up at the Lord's word –
As on a wild, April day, springs a small bird –
So the ghost's feel lighting him up, he kissed the Lord's cheek,
And for the greatness of their Love neither of them could speak.

But the Lord went then, to show him the way
Over the young crocuses, under the green may,
That was not quite in flower yet – to a far distant land.
And the ghost followed, like a naked cloud, holding the sun's hand.

[FREDEGOND SHOVE, from *The New Ghost*]

*An archaic form, perhaps aligned to the New Testament. The evangelist might
have written it thus. It is nearly too precious but there is a curious innocence
about it.*

26th April

A loud clang of iron makes them both jump. The sergeant has sounded
the first stroke of eight on the railway iron. They sit silent till the last.
Then Johnson says in an uncertain voice, "Is that the time now? I tink
perhaps you give me time make small small prayer."

"As much time as you like." . . .

Johnson goes down on his knees beside Rudbeck's chair, joins his
palms in front of his nose, and shuts his eyes. He does not pray. He thinks
of forms of words which he might have used, still more expressive of his
own indifference to Fate and his devotion to Rudbeck . . . he thinks of
further consolation and encouragement which he might offer him . . .

Johnson feels extraordinary lightness and cheerfulness . . He hears
Rudbeck's chair creak, and, peeping, sees him getting up slowly. He says
to himself, "I no 'fraid of nutting – Johnson no 'fraid of nutting in de
world." But he sinks a little lower. His body is almost fainting. But
Rudbeck does not say, "It is time now." He goes stealthily out of the hut.
A moment later, Johnson, peeping, sees him returning across the bright
sunlight with the sentry's carbine in his hand. He stops in the porch to
glance into the breech.

Johnson knows then that he won't have to get up again from his
knees. He feels the relief like a reprieve, unexpected, and he thanks
Rudbeck for it. He triumphs in the greatness, the goodness, and the
daring inventiveness of Rudbeck . . . He bursts out aloud, "Oh Lawd, I
tank you for my frien' Mister Rudbeck – de biggest heart in de world."

Rudbeck leans through the door, aims the carbine at the back of the
boy's head and blows his brains out. Then he turns and hands it back to
the sentry. "Don't forget to pull it through."

[JOYCE CARY, from *Mister Johnson*]

The pain and irony and awfulness of colonisation!

27th April

> The moving sun-shapes on the spray,
> The sparkles where the brook was flowing,
> Pink faces, plightings, moonlit May,
> These were the things we wished would stay;
>   But they were going.

Seasons of blankness as of snow,
The silent bleed of a world decaying,
The moan of multitudes in woe,
These were the things we wished would go;
  But they were staying.

Then we looked closelier at Time,
And saw his ghostly arms revolving
To sweep off woeful things with prime,
Things sinister with things sublime
  Alike dissolving.

[THOMAS HARDY, *Going and Staying*]

Hardy is a poet who can look at Nature and see both sides – unlike Words-
worth? Rarely does Wordsworth achieve this simplicity of versifying.

28th April

In seed time learn, in harvest teach, in winter enjoy.
Drive your cart and your plow over the bones of the dead.
The road of excess leads to the place of wisdom.
Prudence is a rich ugly old maid courted by Incapacity.
He who desires but acts not breeds pestilence.
The cut worm forgives the plough.
Dip him in the river who loves water.
A fool sees not the same tree that a wise man sees.
He whose face gives no light shall never become a star.
Eternity is in love with the productions of time.
The busy bee has no time for sorrow.
The hours of folly are measur'd by the clock, but of wisdom
  no clock can measure.
All wholesome food is caught without a net or trap.
Bring out number, weight and measure in a year of dearth.
No bird soars too high, if he soars with his own wings.
A dead body revenges not injuries.
The most sublime act is to set another before you.
If the fool would persist in his folly, he would be wise.

[WILLIAM BLAKE, from *Proverbs of Hell*]

A flood of aphorisms!

29th April

Good art teaching (and creativity itself) is dependent on a greater than
usual tolerance of anxiety because of the need to work through one's
total personality. This requires a more than average strength of the ego.
It is wrongly thought that creative people thrive on neurotic illness.
This is not so. The philistine can ignore his illness by living with only a
part of his personality and can keep his illness from showing. The
creative person faces his illness and its attendant anxieties so that they
noisily dominate his behaviour. And he is not more neurotic for this
reason: rather the reverse is true. If satisfactory human relationships
are proof of mental health, as is universally accepted, then the creative
mind is healthy through establishing at least one good object relationship: with his own work acting as an independent being. He is able to
accept what Adrian Stokes has called the 'otherness' of the work of art.
This acceptance requires the whole apparatus of projection, integration
and introjection, which is part of any good relationship. The link between
creativity and good object relations also works in the reverse direction.
The continuous growth and nursing of a human bond requires a modi-
cum of creative imagination, the receptive watchfulness needed in
creative work ... If he allows his work to talk back to him as an independent being, his work will also be capable of talking to others with the
same eloquence. But the communication between the artist and his
work comes first.

[ANTON EHRENZWEIG, from *The Hidden Order of Art*]

*This passage draws out the parallels between creativity in art and in human
relationship. The artist is aware of a true order, broken up in our everyday
awareness, of which art itself catches glimpses and which it reveals.*

30th April

Forget six counties overhung with smoke,
Forget the snorting steam and piston stroke,
Forget the spreading of the hideous town;
Think rather of the pack-horse on the down,
And dream of London, small, and white, and clean,
The clear Thames bordered by its gardens green;
Think, that below the bridge green lapping waves
Smite some few keels that bear Levantine staves,

Cut from the yew wood on the burn-top hill,
And pointed jars that Greek hands toiled to fill,
And treasured scantly spice from some far sea,
Florence gold cloth, and Ypres napery,
And cloth of Bruges, and hogsheads of Guienne;
While nigh the thronged wharf Geoffrey Chaucer's pen
Moves over bills of lading – mid such times
Shall dwell the hollow puppets of my rhymes.

[WILLIAM MORRIS, from *The Earthly Paradise: 1*]

You will need an eye for the vision, and to see beyond what obscures. But is there even a hint left of the earthly paradise around Kelmscot in Oxfordshire?

MAY

1st May

Hear a word, a word in season,
    for the day is drawing nigh,
When the cause shall call upon us,
    some to live, and some to die!

He that dies shall not die lonely,
    many an one hath gone before;
He that lives shall bear no burden
    heavier than the life they bore.

Nothing ancient is their story,
    e'en but yesterday they bled,
Youngest they of earth's beloved,
    last of all the valiant dead.

E'en the tidings we are telling
    was the tale they had to tell,
E'en the hope that our hearts cherish
    was the hope for which they fell.

In the grave where tyrants thrust them
    lies their labour and their pain,
But undying from their sorrow
    springeth up the hope again.

Mourn not therefore, nor lament it
    that the world outlives their life;
Voice and vision yet they give us,
    making strong our hands for strife.

Some had name, and fame, and honour,
    learn'd they were, and wise and strong,
Some were nameless, poor, unlettered,
    weak in all but grief and wrong . . .

      [WILLIAM MORRIS, from *Poems by the Way*]

Jack Putterill taught us to sing this hymn at Sneyd Church at meetings of the Catholic Crusade in the late 1920s. We sang it to the tune of 'Ode to Joy'! We were trying to keep in touch with our roots in English Catholicism, in the English radical tradition. Sadly the Communist Party never tapped this deep, and the Labour Party has forgotten its history. Rootless, we have been delivered to Disneyland.

2nd May

I found the whole path throbbing with the fragrance of hawthorn-blossom. The hedge resembled a series of chapels, whose walls were no longer visible under the mountains of flowers that were heaped upon their altars; while underneath, the sun cast a square of light upon the ground, as though it had shone in upon them through a window; the scent that swept out over me from them was as rich, and as circum-scribed in its range, as if I had been standing before the Lady-altar . . .

And it was indeed a hawthorn, but one whose flowers were pink, and lovelier even than the white. It too was in holiday attire, for one of those days which are the only true holidays, the holy days of religion, because they are not appointed by any capricious accident, as secular holidays are appointed, upon days which are not specially ordained for such observances, which have nothing about them that is essentially festal – but it was attired even more richly than the rest . . . High up on the branches, like so many of those tiny rose-trees, their pots concealed in jackets of paper lace, whose slender stems rise in a forest from the altar on the greater festivals, a thousand buds were swelling and opening, paler in colour but each disclosing as it burst, as at the bottom of a cup of pink marble its blood-red stain, and suggesting even more strongly than the full-blown flowers, the special, irresistible quality of the hawthorn-tree, which, wherever it budded, wherever it was about to blossom, could bud and blossom in pink flowers alone. Taking its place in the hedge, but no different from the rest as a young girl in holiday attire among a crowd of dowdy women in everyday clothes, who are staying at home, equipped and ready for the 'Month of Mary', of which it seemed already to form a part, it shone and smiled on the cool, rosy garments, a Catholic bush indeed, and altogether delightful.

[MARCEL PROUST, from *Swann's Way*]

Like the young Proust who knew two childhood walks near Cambrai (Swann's Way was one of them). I remember going for walks with my father and asking,

*Which path shall we go? By the top fields or by the bridge where we saw the dog
fall in? . . . And this: Can only country churches be decorated with an abun-*
dance *of local gathered flowers and branches?*

3rd May

Since the wise men have not spoken, I speak that I am a fool;
A fool that hath loved his folly,
Yea, more than the wise men their books or their counting houses or
    their quiet homes,
Or their fame in men's mouths;
A fool that in all his days hath done never a prudent thing,
Never hath counted the cost, nor recked if another reaped
The fruit of his mighty sowing, content to scatter the seed,
A fool that is unrepentant, and that soon at the end of all
Shall laugh in his lonely heart as the ripe ears fall to the reaping-
    hooks
And the poor are filled that were empty,
Tho' he go hungry.

I have squandered the splendid years that the Lord God gave to my
    youth
In attempting impossible things, deeming them alone worth the toil.
Was it folly or grace? Not men shall judge me, but God.
I have squandered the splendid years:
Lord, if I had the years I would squander them over again,
Aye, fling them from me!
For this I have heard in my heart, that a man shall scatter, not
    hoard,
Shall do the deed of today, nor take thought of tomorrow's teen,
Shall not bargain nor huxter with God; or was it a jest of Christ's?
And is this my sin before men, to have taken Him at His word? . . .

[PADRAIC PEARSE, from *The Fool*]

*Padraic Pearse, the poet of the Republican Movement in Ireland, was executed
on this day in 1916, The Catholic Crusade became involved because of its fight
against imperialism. I hung a copy of this poem on the wall of Darnall Church,
to the delight of a neighbouring Roman Catholic priest. I also recall talking to
the man who shared Pearse's cell after the Easter Rising: he was no. 17 and was
pardoned.*

4th May

> 'Tis time, I think, by Wenlock town
>   The golden broom should blow:
> The hawthorn sprinkled up and down
>   Should charge the land with snow.
>
> Spring will not wait the loiterer's time
>   Who keeps so long away;
> So others wear the broom and climb
>   The hedgerows heaped with may.
>
> Oh tarnish late on Wenlock Edge,
>   Gold that I never see;
> Lie long, high snowdrifts in the hedge
>   That will not shower on me.

[A. E. Housman, from *A Shropshire Lad*]

A poem you simply murmur . . . And I love Wenlock Edge. As a Mercian I perceive in Shropshire and Staffordshire something of the depth and continuity of English history, not least in the balanced countryside. (By contrast, there is little sense of this in West Cumbria: nearly all the old buildings here have been completely rebuilt).

5th May

There are only two radical alternatives open to human faith. Both are hypotheses. To accept either is to run a risk, to lay a wager; but the gamble is forced upon us by life itself. To live is to bet, because the conduct of life pledges all our poor assets, and pledges our soul, to the one side or the other. You may choose the broad and obvious path of heathen philosophy, fancifully decorated, if you like, with some heathen religion . . . Your life will be a tragic or a comic episode in a universal hurly-burly of atoms or laws or energies or illusions. I don't say you may not find such a life bearable or even entertaining; all the animals take to it with gusto, and why shouldn't man, if he is nothing but a talking, laughing, machine-making animal?

But there is an alternative, which is to believe in the human heart, to believe in the supernatural, and to refuse to follow the great heathen procession except perfunctorily and provisionally . . . We impose on all natural facts and on all natural desires a supernatural interpretation.

A miracle, we say, has occurred, both in the manger of Bethlehem and in our own souls . . . there is one and only one thorough, consistent, realistic, encyclopaedic expression of faith in the human heart. It is Catholic dogma: the dogma that God has become man, actually and historically and for ever, with all that is involved in that mystery. Any revisions and reforms of Catholic faith are backsliding into heathenism; they deny, in some measure, the supremacy of the human heart, and of the supernatural: and in that measure they lead back, covertly but inevitably to the heathen highway of a feigned conformity and a real despair. And while I admit that heathen philosophers may judge a supernatural reinstatement of the human heart to be a pathetic fallacy, yet the believer in a divine heart is not without many a confirmation of his faith by his own experience and by the fruits which this faith has always borne among the faithful.

[GEORGE SANTAYANA, from *The Last Puritan*]

His mother a Scot, his father Spanish, Santayana was a dry sceptic yet appreciative of all that faith had done.

6th May

Human being as being-challenged-in-the-world can be understood only in terms of requiredness, demand, and expectation. Significant living is an attempt to adjust to what is expected and required of a human being.

The sense of requiredness is as essential to being human as his capacity for reasoning. It is an error to equate the two as it is a distortion to derive the sense of requiredness from the capacity for reasoning.

The sense of requiredness is not an afterthought; it is given with being human, not added to it but rooted in it.

What is involved in authentic living is not only an intuition of meaning but a sensitivity to demand, not a purpose but an expectation. Sensitivity to demands is as inherent in being human as physiological functions are in human being.

A person is he of whom demands can be made, who has the capacity to respond to what is required, not only to satisfy his needs and desires. Only a human being is said to be responsible. Responsibility is not something man imputes to himself; he is a self by virtue of his capacity for responsibility, and he would cease to be a self if he were to be deprived of responsibility . . .

Here is a basic difference between the Greek and the biblical conception of man. To the Greek mind, man is above all a rational being;

rationality makes him compatible with the cosmos. To the biblical
mind man is above all a commanded being; a being of whom demands
may be made. The central problem is not: What is being? but rather:
What is required of me?

[ABRAHAM HESCHEL, from *Who is Man?*]

*'Require' is a word I hold to. If God says, 'I need you', you are given a place in
the scheme of things. But this is not the authoritarian command of the army. It
is a personal demand which gives you a dignity and a place and a meaning.*

7th May

> Love still has something of the sea
>   From whence his mother rose;
> No time, his slaves from Doubt can free
>   Nor give their thoughts repose.
>
> They are becalmed in clearest days
>   And in rough weather tost,
> They wither under cold delays,
>   Or are in tempests lost.
>
> One while, they seem to touch the port:
>   Then straight into the main!
> Some angry wind in cruel sport
>   The vessel drives again.
>
> At first disdain and pride they fear
>   Which if they chance to 'scape,
> Rival and falsehood soon appear
>   In a more dreadful shape.
>
> By such degrees to joy they come
>   And one so long withstood
> So slowly they receive the sum
>   It hardly does them good.
>
> 'Tis cruel to prolong a pain
>   And to defer a joy
> (Believe me, gentle Celemene)
>   Offends the wingèd Boy.

> A hundred thousand oaths, your fears
> Perhaps would not remove
> And if I gazed a thousand years
> I could no deeper love.

[SIR CHARLES SEDLEY, *Song*]

*Perhaps only the first two lines of this poem count (not unusual in poetry!)
I used to quote it at weddings. Love lets you in for tempests and only the
occasional calm. But without the depths and the time it takes to come to fruition,
love is counterfeit, and the one who thinks he loves is actually adrift.*

8th May

Neither of them spoke. He was regaining his sense in a slight tremor
that ran upwards along his rigid body and hung about his trembling
lips. She drew back her head and fastened her eyes on his in one of those
long looks that are a woman's most terrible weapon; a look that is more
stirring than the closest touch, and more dangerous than the thrust of a
dagger, because it also whips the soul out of the body, but leaves the
body alive and helpless, to be swayed here and there by the capricious
tempest of passion and desire; a look that enwraps the whole body, and
that penetrates into the innermost recesses of the being, bringing
terrible defeat in the delirious uplifting of accomplished conquest. . .

. . . Her mother was right. The man was her slave. As she glanced
down at his kneeling form she felt a great pitying tenderness for that
man she has used to call – even in her thoughts – the master of life.

She lifted her eyes and looked steadily at the southern heavens under
which lay the path of their lives – her own and that man's at her feet.
Did he not say to himself that she was the light of his life? She would be
his light and his wisdom; the world be his greatness and his strength;
yet hidden from the eyes of all men she would be, above all, his only
lasting weakness. A very woman.

In the sublime vanity of her kind she was thinking already of moulding a god from the clay at her feet. A god for others to worship. She was
content to see him as he was now and to feel him quiver at the slightest
touch of her light fingers. And while her eyes looked sadly at the southern stars a faint smile seemed to be playing about her firm lips. Who
can tell in the fitful light of a camp fire? It might have been a smile of
triumph, or of conscious power, or of tender pity, or perhaps, of love.

[JOSEPH CONRAD, from *Almayer's Folly*]

This is Conrad at his most intense. I think this is the nearest any male novelist gets to understanding what this confrontation between men and women is really about. But I may be mistaken. And the last sentence reminds me of the Mona Lisa. Can art say more?

9th May

To her
I am a coloured blur,
    A just-heard voice,
    As she sits there –
She hasn't any choice.

Life fades
Like on-off hearing aids,
    And in her sleep
    The realler world
Is dreaming, long and deep.

This now
Needs living through somehow,
    Patience is all
    And the time left,
Though slow, is surely all.

I touch
The body changed so much,
    She understands
    Some tenderness
Through bony arms and hands.

Contact
Is joining and a fact,
    We once were one
    And touching's how
All love-making gets done.

[GAVIN EWART, *The Late Eighties*]

No other poem I know quite captures the physical aspect of sick old age. So much is puzzling as we watch and wait and touch. Teilhard wrote that our diminishments and decay are not to be moaned about but to be lived positively: dying is something that we do.

10th May

In Xanadu did Kubla Khan
  A stately pleasure-dome decree:
Where Alph, the sacred river ran
Through caverns measureless to man
  Down to a sunless sea.
So twice five miles of fertile ground
With walls and towers were girdled round:
And there were gardens bright with sinuous rills
Where blossomed many an incense-bearing tree;
And here were forests ancient as the hills
Enfolding sunny spots of greenery.

But O, that deep romantic chasm which slanted
Down the green hill athwart a cedarn cover!
A savage place! as holy and enchanted
As e'er beneath a waning-moon was haunted
By woman wailing for her demon-lover!
And from this chasm, with ceaseless turmoil seething,
As if this earth in fast thick pants were breathing,
A mighty fountain momently was forced;
Amid whose swift half-intermitted burst
Huge fragments vaulted like rebounding hail,
Or chaffy grain beneath the thresher's flail:
And 'mid these dancing rocks at once and ever
It flung up momently the sacred river.
Five miles meandering with a mazy motion
Through wood and dale the sacred river ran,
Then reach'd the caverns measureless to man,
And sank in tumult to a lifeless ocean:
And 'mid this tumult Kubla heard from far
Ancestral voices prophesying war!

[S. T. COLERIDGE, from *Kubla Khan*]

It is the function of the imagination to bring together the discordant into a unity that leaves you contemplating an achievement. With Kubla Khan *and* The Rime of the Ancient Mariner *you can but listen and enter the experience if you will. For the imagination brings the whole soul into activity – unlike fantasy, which is one-dimensional: it plays with things without paying anything for them. Fantasy is not costly whereas the imagination is strenuous. Holding things together is hard work.*

11th May

Perdita   Now my fairest friend, (*to Florizel*)
I would I had some flowers o' th' spring, that might
Become your time of day; and yours and yours,
                              (*to Mopsa & other girls*)
That wear upon your virgin branches yet
Your maidenheads growing: O Proserpina,
For the flowers now that, frighted, thou let'st fall
From Dis's waggon! daffodils,
That come before the swallow dares, and take
The winds of March with beauty; violets, dim,
But sweeter than the lids of Juno's eyes
Or Cytherea's breath; pale primroses,
That die unmarried, ere they can behold
Bright Phoebus in his strength (a malady
Most incident to maids); bold oxlips and
The crown imperial; lilies of all kinds,
The flower-de-luce being one. O these I lack
To make you garlands of; and my sweet friend
To strew him o'er and o'er!

Florizel   What, like a corpse?
Perdita   No, like a bank, for love to lie and play on:
Not like a corpse; or if – not to be buried,
But quick, and in mine arms. Come, take your flowers;
Methinks I play as I have seen them do
In Whitsun pastorals: sure this robe of mine
Does change my disposition.

Florizel   What you do,
Still betters what is done. When you speak, sweet,
I'll have you ever do it: when you sing,
I'd have you buy and sell so, so give alms,
Pray so, and, for the ord'ring your affairs.
To sing them too: when you do dance I wish you
A wave o'the sea, that you might ever do
Nothing but that, more still, still so,
And own no other function.

[WILLIAM SHAKESPEARE, from *The Winter's Tale*]

This is Shakespearean verse at its most lyrical and lilting. He is now in the sun-light, not in the moonlight of A Midsummer Night's Dream. *And a woman has taken charge! Here too are the flowers of rural Warwickshire. Perhaps I should have lived there. My parents were both keen on flowers and taught me their names. And they grew unusual plants in our small garden.*

12th May

"... To transform the world, to recreate it afresh, men must turn into another path psychologically. Until you have become really, in actual fact, a brother to everyone, brotherhood will not come to pass. No sort of scientific teaching, no kind of common interest, will ever teach men to share property and privileges with equal consideration for all. Everyone will think his share too small and they will be always envying, complaining, and attacking one another. You ask when it will come to pass; it will come to pass, but first we have to go through the period of isolation."

"What do you mean by isolation?" I asked him.

"Why, the isolation that prevails everywhere, above all in our age – it has not fully developed, it has not reached its limit yet. For everyone strives to keep his individuality as apart as possible, wishes to secure the greatest possible fulness of life for himself; but meantime all his efforts result not in attaining fulness of life but self-destruction, for instead of self-realization he ends by arriving at complete isolation. All mankind in our age have split into units, they all keep apart, each in his own groove; each one holds aloof, hides himself and hides what he has from the rest, and he ends by being repelled by others and repelling them. He heaps up riches by himself and thinks, 'How strong I am now and how secure,' and in his madness he does not understand that the more he heaps up, the more he sinks into self-destructive impotence. For he is accustomed to rely upon himself alone and to cut himself off from the whole; he has trained himself not to believe in the help of others, in men and in humanity, and only trembles for fear he should lose his money and the privileges he has won for himself. Everywhere in these days men have, in their mockery, ceased to understand that the true security is to be found in social solidarity rather than in isolated individual effort. But this terrible individualism must inevitably have an end, and all will suddenly understand how unnaturally they are separated from one another. It will be the spirit of the time, and people will marvel that they have sat so long in darkness without seeing the light. And then the sign of the Son of Man will be seen in the heavens."

[FYODOR DOSTOEVSKY, from *The Brothers Karamazov*]

*This is so prophetic of our own century. We should stop using the word
'individual'. If you use the Devil's words, you will soon think the Devil's
thoughts.*

13th May

There is one particular day in Western history about which neither
historical record nor myth nor sculpture can make report. It is a Saturday. And it has become the longest of days. We know of that Good
Friday which Christianity holds to have been that of the Cross. But the
non-Christian, the atheist, knows of it as well. That is to say that he
knows of the injustice, of the interminable suffering, of the waste, of the
brute enigma of ending, which so largely make up not only the historical dimension of the human condition, but the everyday fabric of our
personal lives. We know, ineluctably, of the pain, of the failure of love,
of the solitude which are our history and private fate. We know also
about Sunday. To the Christian, that day signifies an intimation, both
assured and precarious, both evident and beyond comprehension, of
resurrection, of a justice and a love that have conquered death. If we are
non-Christians or non-believers, we know of that Sunday in precisely
analogous terms. We conceive of it as the day of liberation from in-
humanity and servitude. We look to resolutions, be they therapeutic or
political, be they social or messianic. The lineaments of that Sunday
carry the name of hope (there is no word less deconstructible).

But ours is the long day's journey of the Saturday. Between suffering,
aloneness, unutterable waste on the one hand and the dream of liberation, of rebirth on the other. In the face of the torture of a child, of the
death of love which is Friday, even the greatest art and poetry are almost
helpless. In the Utopia of the Sunday, the aesthetic will, presumably, no
longer have logic or necessity. The apprehensions and figurations in the
play of metaphysical imagining, in the poem and the music, which tell
of pain and of hope, of the flesh which is said to taste of ash and of the
spirit which is said to have the savour of fire, are always Sabbatarian.
They have risen out of an immensity of waiting which is that of man.
Without them, how could we be patient?

[GEORGE STEINER from *Real Presences*]

*This brings to our consciousness the 'geist' of our particular time. And what do
we do on this Saturday? Is there a harrowing of hell as well as the silence after a
burial? Steiner wrote that having abolished hell we have established it on earth.
Are we to endure the full force of evil?*

14th May

And the goblins – they had not really been there at all? They were only the phantoms of cowardice and unbelief? One healthy human impulse would dispel them? Men like the Wilcoxes, or President Roosevelt, would say yes. Beethoven knew better. The goblins really had been there. They might return – and they did. It was as if the splendour of life might boil over and waste to steam and froth. In its dissolution one heard the terrible, ominous note, and a goblin, with increased malignity, walked quietly over the universe from end to end. Panic and emptiness! Panic and emptiness! Even the flaming ramparts of the world might fall.

Beethoven chose to make all right in the end. He built the ramparts up. He blew with his mouth for the second time, and again the goblins were scattered. He brought back the gusts of splendour, the heroism, the youth, the magnificence of life and of death, and, amid vast roarings of a superhuman joy, he led his Fifth Symphony to its conclusion. But the goblins were there. They could return. He had said so bravely, and that is why one can trust Beethoven when he says other things.

[E. M. Forster, from *Howard's End*]

We almost forget that evil can be quiet, an insistent silent menace, so serpentine. And Forster knew that you could be effective quietly. He was a listener who made an occasional comment. Here he leaves you in no doubt that it is vitally important to be aware and alert. The goblins do return! Elsewhere his great line was 'Only connect': it is the ones who do not connect who cast the first stone.

15th May

I asked for health
that I might do great things:
I was given infirmity,
that I might do better things . . .

I asked for riches that I might be happy:
I was given poverty that I might be wise,

I asked for power
that I might have the praise of men:
I was given weakness
that I might feel the need of God.

I asked for all things
that I might enjoy life:
I was given life
that I might enjoy all things . . .

I got nothing that I asked for,
but everything that I hoped for,
almost despite myself:

My unspoken prayers were answered,
I am among all men most richly blessed.

[ANON.]

This makes its own point simply – as does much that we remember without being able to recall its source. It really does become part of the common stock.

16th May

And thinking over the long pilgrimage of his past, he accepted it joy-fully. He accepted the deformity which had made life so hard for him; he knew that it had warped his character, but now he saw also that by reason of it he had acquired that power of introspection which had given him so much delight. Without it he would never have had his keen appreciation of beauty, his passion for art and literature, and his interest in the varied spectacle of life. The ridicule and contempt which had so often been heaped upon him had turned his mind inward and called forth those flowers which he felt would never lose their fragrance. Then he saw that the normal was the rarest thing in the world. Everyone had some defect, of body or of mind; he thought of all the people he had known, (the whole world was like a sick-house, and there was no rhyme or reason in it) he saw a long procession, deformed in body and warped in mind, some with illness of the flesh, weak hearts or weak lungs, and some with illness of the spirit, languor of will or a craving for liquor. At this moment he could feel a holy compassion for them all . . . They could not help themselves. The only reasonable thing was to accept the good of men and be patient with their faults. The words of the dying God crossed his memory: "Forgive them, for they know not what they do."

[W. SOMERSET MAUGHAM, from *Of Human Bondage*]

A sad yet generous contemplation of human relationships (Dickens does it with a lighter touch.) Surely compassion is vital. So many of us are damaged but we go on being human in an extraordinary way, heroically trying to make sense of life.

17th May

> Heart of the heartless world,
> Dear heart, the thought of you
> Is the pain at my side,
> The shadow that chills my view.
>
> The wind rises in the evening,
> Reminds that autumn is near.
> I am afraid to lose you,
> I am afraid of my fear.
>
> On the last mile to Huesca,
> The last fence for our pride,
> Think so kindly, dear, that I
> Sense you at my side.
>
> And if bad luck should lay my strength
> Into the shallow grave,
> Remember all the good you can;
> Don't forget my love.
>
> [JOHN CORNFORD, *Huesca*]

John Cornford was a talented young poet who was killed in Spain fighting against Fascism. I am still moved by the self-sacrifice of young men and women who went to Spain from this country and were promptly killed. It was all so horrible – on both sides – but can we stand on the sidelines? Most of us do not want to be present to the history of our own day. And of course Guernica was but the prelude to something much worse. "If they do this when the wood is green, what will they do when it is dry?"

18th May

. . . He became aware that a blackbird, in the dark twilight of hazel-stems, was uttering notes of extraordinary purity and poignance.

He listened, fascinated. That particular intonation of the blackbird's note, more full of the spirits of air and of water than any sound upon earth, had always possessed a mysterious attraction for him. It seemed to hold, in the sphere of sound, what amber-paved pools surrounded by hart's tongue ferns contain in the sphere of substance. It seemed to embrace in it all the sadness that it is possible to experience without crossing the subtle line into the region where sadness becomes misery . . .

. . . Wolf sat entranced, just giving himself up to listen; forgetting all else. He was utterly unmusical; and it may have been for that very reason that the quality of certain sounds in the world melted the very core of his soul. Certain sounds could do it; not very many. But the blackbird's note was one of them. And then it was that without rising from the ground he straightened his back against the sycamore-tree and got furiously red under his rugged cheeks. Even his tow-coloured hair, protruding from the front of his cap, seemed conscious of his humiliation. Waves of electricity shivered through it; while beads of perspiration ran down his forehead into his scowling eye-brows.

For he realised, in one rush of shame, that Gerda was the blackbird!

He realised this before she made a sound other than that long-sustained tremulous whistle. He realised it instantaneously by a kind of sudden absolute knowledge, like a slap in the face. And then, immediately afterwards, she came forward, quite calmly and coolly, pushing aside the hazels and the elder-bushes.

[JOHN COWPER POWYS, from *Wolf Solent*]

Any moment in life, quite ordinary, may carry with it more than you expect. Powys could write evocatively like this (even if he wrote at great length and with an intensity that is too much for the story being told.)

19th May

Imagination is always the fabric of social life and the dynamic of history. The influence of real needs and compulsions, of real interests and materials, is indirect because the crowd is never conscious of it. To become conscious of even the simplest realities one needs to pay attention. Nor, from this point of view, do culture, education, or social position make much difference. A couple of hundred leaders of industry assembled in a hall are no less of an unconscious herd than a meeting of workers or tradesmen. Anyone who invented a method of assembly which could avoid the extinction of thought in each of the participants would make a revolution in human history comparable to the dis-

covery of fire, or of the wheel, or of the use of implements. In the meanwhile, imagination remains and will remain a factor in human affairs
whose real importance it is almost impossible to exaggerate. But its
effects are very different according to how it is manipulated, or not
manipulated. The state of men's imagination at a given moment dictates
the limits to which power can be effectively used at that moment, so as to
produce real results. Once the moment has passed, different limits come
into operation. It may happen that the state of imagination would
allow a government to make a certain measure three months before it
becomes necessary, while at the moment when it is necessary the
imagination cannot be persuaded to accept it. Therefore it should have
been taken three months earlier. The art of government consists in
being continually sensitive and aware in these matters.

[SIMONE WEIL, from *Note on Social Democracy*]

*Simone Weil was insistent that we face the political, yet with the imagination
that senses the mood, the 'geist' of the particular time.*

20th May

What was he doing, the great god Pan,
  Down in the reeds by the river?
Spreading ruin and scattering ban,
Splashing and paddling with hoofs of a goat,
And breaking the golden lilies afloat
  With the dragon-fly on the river.

He tore out a reed, the great god Pan,
  From the deep cool bed of the river;
The limpid water turbidly ran,
And the broken lilies a-dying lay,
And the dragon-fly had fled away,
  Ere he brought it out of the river.

High on the shore sat the great god Pan,
  While turbidly flow'd the river;
And hack'd and hew'd as a great god can
With his hard bleak steel at the patient reed,
Till there was not a sign of the leaf indeed
  To prove it fresh from the river.

He cut it short, did the great god Pan
  (How tall it stood in the river!),
Then drew the pith, like the heart of a man,
Steadily from the outside ring,
And notch'd the poor dry empty thing
  In holes, as he sat by the river.

"This is the way," laugh'd the great god Pan
  (Laugh'd while he sat by the river),
"The only way, since gods began
To make sweet music, they could succeed."
Then dropping his mouth to a hole in the reed,
  He blew in power by the river.

Sweet, sweet, sweet, O Pan!
  Piercing sweet by the river!
Blinding sweet, O great god Pan!
The sun on the hill forgot to die,
And the lilies revived, and the dragon-fly
  Came back to dream on the river.

Yet half a beast is the great god Pan,
  To laugh as he sits by the river,
Making a poet out of a man:
The true gods sigh for the cost and pain –
For the reed which grows never more again
  As a reed with the reeds of the river.

[ELIZABETH BARRETT BROWNING, *A Musical Instrument*]

*This poem, like that of Swinburne, goes back to my boyhood. The penultimate
verse haunts me.*

21st May

For when thy folding star arising shews
His paly circlet, at his warning lamp
  Thy fragrant Hours, and Elves
  Who slept in buds the day,

And many a Nymph who wreaths her brows with sedge,
And sheds the fresh'ning dew, and lovelier still,
  The Pensive Pleasure sweet,
  Prepare thy shadowy ear.

Then lead, calm Votaress, where some sheety lake
Cheers the lone heath, or some time-hallow'd pile,
   Or upland fellows grey
   Reflect its last cool gleam.

Or if chill blust'ring winds or driving rain,
Prevent my willing feet, be mine the hut,
   That from the mountain's side,
   Views wilds, and swelling floods,

And hamlets brown, and dim-discover'd spires,
And hears their simple bell, and marks o'er all
   Thy dewy fingers draw
   The gradual dusky veil.

While Spring shall pour his show'rs as oft he wont,
And bathe thy breathing tresses, meekest Eve!
   While Summer loves to sport
   Beneath thy ling'ring light:

While sallow Autumn fills thy lap with leaves;
Or Winter yelling thro' the troublous air,
   Affrights thy shrinking train,
   And rudely rends thy robes.

So long, sure-found beneath the Sylvan shed,
Shall Fancy, Friendship, Science, rose-lipp'd Health,
   Thy gentlest influence own,
   And hymn thy fav'rite name!

[WILLIAM COLLINS, from *Ode to Evening*]

Eighteenth century poetry is formal, often squeezed dry. There is neither the
exuberance of a Herrick nor a Romantic rush. But some of the poems have a
quiet dignity which is not to be written off.

22nd May

I admit that my first night home I woke up in a sudden sweat of fear.
I was no longer in the favoured position of an observer in a foreign
country. I was back in a very uncertain battle. Ever since the first atom
bomb was dropped I have seldom been free of the sense that we are all
living on the margin of disaster. But these six months of detachment
from America have served to strengthen what I already believe in.

I have renewed a sense of the responsibility of the intellectual – a word honoured by William James and scorned by Fascists – of the necessity for him to be as true as possible to what his experience has taught him, and to speak for those truths as fully and as fearlessly as he can. So far as American politics are concerned, progressives can no longer allow themselves to be deflected into delaying actions, into supporting the lesser of two evils. If you believe in a democratic socialism, you must act accordingly, and work for it. Many of the positions you take will of course be vilified for that. But however bad the odds, the final stakes are international co-operation or a war that will at the very least complete the destruction of Europe: the heart of our civilisation.

[F. O. MATTHIESSEN, from *From the Heart of Europe*]

Have we learned this lesson?

23rd May

Nothing, it seemed, between them and the grave.
No, as I looked, there was nothing anywhere.
You'd think no ground could be so flat and bare:
No little ridge or hump or bush to brave
The horizon. Yet they called that land their land,
Without a single thought drank in that air
As simple and equivocal as despair.
This, this was what I could not understand.

The reason was, there was nothing there but faith.
Faith made the whole, yes, all they could see or hear
Or touch or think, and arched its break of day
Within them and around them every way
They looked: all was transfigured far and near,
And the great world rolled between them and death.

[EDWIN MUIR, *Nothing there but faith*]

Muir had a sense of being beholden to previous generations. He could recognize the disaster but he could also see further in faith – which is the power to contemplate and respond. So many of us live on the surface of events. Few look at the depths and ask what is their significance. 'News' beats us about the head into inertia.

24th May

Perfect little body, without fault or stain on thee,
With promise of strength and manhood full and fair!
   Though cold and stark and bare,
The bloom and the charm of life doth awhile remain on thee.

Thy mother's treasure wert thou; – alas! no longer
To visit her heart with wondrous joy; to be
   Thy father's pride; – ah, he
Must gather his faith together, and his strength made stronger.

To me, as I move thee now in their last duty,
Dost thou with a turn or gesture anon respond;
   Startling my fancy fond
With a chance attitude of the head, a freak of beauty.

Thy hands clasps, as 'twas wont, my finger, and holds it:
And the grasp is the clasp of Death, heartbreaking and stiff;
   Yet feels to my hand as if
'Twas still thy will, thy pleasure and trust that enfolds it.

So I lay thee there, thy sunken eyelids closing, –
Go, lie thou there in thy coffin, thy last little bed! –
   Propping thy wise, sad head,
Thy firm, pale hands across thy chest disposing.

So quiet! – doth the change content thee? – Death, wither hath he
                   taken thee?
To a world do I think, that rights the disaster of this?
    The vision of which I miss,
 who weep for the body, and wish but to warm thee and
                   awaken thee?

Ah, little at best can all our hopes avail us
To lift this sorrow, or cheer us, when in the dark,
   Unwilling, alone we embark,
And the things we have seen and have known and have heard of,
                   fail us.

[ROBERT BRIDGES, *On a dead child!*]

*I remember I. A. Richards telling this in my undergraduate days. We want
things to be all right in another world, but there is no simple comfort.*

25th May

Never be happy until the golden hour
Creates its living death upon the instant
Just beyond perception: be happy then,
That you shall never understand that radiant
Mastery. It is gone as soon as known,
Known only as a breath of incalculable spirit,
Wordless peak except verbs prick at it;
Perhaps never known, but in this mating time.

Never be broken by the things of evil
That pass upon the years to true forgetfulness,
Giving themselves back to nature; man's evil
Forget, for in time forget you must,
Whether man wrought them from his crooked heart,
Or life imposed them in a cruel majesty
Impersonal and blind. Do not shake the fist
Or cry the brutal rage: time heals the time.

Baffled by instances of malice, keep
The calm of solitary imaginings,
That harmony inhere although the flesh be maimed,
Keep struggle pure with a white intent,
Revising possibility. Pare the naked nature
And in dark hours accept what fate is.
What toys we are to crippling chance
When victim, not the callers, of a savage dance.

Look upon the passing scene with tenderness.
All suffers change. The blight is in the air,
Within the lungs, within the light, within
The eye. Great nature is our master.
All our will and our flushed, enticed brains
Cannot unmake the world. Talk to the night
When the woods are deep, the stars alight,
Talk out the long instancy of mankind.

[RICHARD EBERHART, *Formative Mastership*]

Words always hint at what has been seen but they can never adequately express it. 'The long instancy' – the present, the presence, the eternal moment, that which is much more than we know – is glimpsed but never captured. Blake talked of time as the 'mercy of eternity'.

26th May

It is when men and women who are sinned against become our concern that God can put in our mouths the word that witnesses to Christ, the saver of sinners. In China we have come to realize how lacking we really were in true love for our people. It is not enough to smile and be nice to them. It is to put ourselves in their position, to understand the justice of their cause, to be fellow-fighters with them. It is to see how all their revolutionary strivings – industrial, agricultural, educational and artistic – could achieve a deeper grounding and bear better fruit if consciously related to the purposes of God and to the spiritual resources at the base of the whole universe. Love does mean all this.

The sinned against of the world are so helpless and loveless that they must form themselves into groups, collectives, fellowships. The evils of fascist and semi-fascist groups should not lead theologians to condemn all human collectives. Even those which are not Christian can often be the vehicles of the grace of God. To me, an incompletely Christianized intellectual with a sprinkling of Confucianist elitism, it was quite a pilgrimage to come to realize the spiritual potential of human social organisation. There is an inspiration in human fellowship enabling comrades to rise to levels unattainable by mere individuals. Common purpose and common enthusiasm transforms and uplifts. More and more Christians realize now that the transcendent is encountered not so much 'out there' as within the interpersonal relationships of finite beings. We open ourselves to the sacred and to encountering God as we dive into the depths of human relations, no matter how secular they seem.

[TING KUANG-HSUN, from *No Longer Strangers*]

Under house arrest during the Cultural Revolution, his work smashed, Ting came to Darnall in 1949 as Mao was poised to take Beijing. He became a bishop when he went back to China, and he has since become the 'president' of the undenominational Church of China. I remember his saying that he and his people wanted our prayers but asked us to keep out of his country.

27th May

In this epoch of full-grown history men have not acquiesced in the given conditions of their lives. Taking little for granted they have sought to know the ground they stand on, and the road they travel, and the reason why. Over them, therefore, the historian has obtained an increasing ascendancy. The law of stability was overcome by the power of ideas, constantly varied and rapidly renewed; ideas that give life and motion, that take wing and traverse seas and frontiers, making it futile to pursue the consecutive order of events in the seclusion of a separate nationality. They compel us to share the existence of societies wider than our own, to be familiar with distant and exotic types, to hold our march upon the loftier summits, along the central range, to live in the company of heroes, and saints, and men of genius, that no single country could produce. We cannot afford wantonly to lose sight of great men and memorable lives, and are bound to store up objects for admiration as far as may be; for the effect of implacable research is constantly to reduce their number. No intellectual exercise, for instance, can be more invigorating than to watch the working of the mind of Napoleon, the most entirely known as well as the ablest of historical men. In another sphere, it is the vision of a higher world to be intimate with the character of Fenelon, the cherished model of politicians, ecclesiastics, and men of letters, the witness against one century and precursor of another, the advocate of the poor against oppression, of liberty in an age of arbitary power, of tolerance in an age of persecution, of the humane virtues among men accustomed to sacrifice them to authority, the man of whom one enemy says that his cleverness was enough to strike terror, and another, that genius poured in torrents from his eyes. For the minds that are greatest and best alone furnish the instructive examples. A man of ordinary proportions or inferior metal knows not how to think out the rounded circle of his thought, how to divest his will of its surroundings and to rise above the pressure of time and race and circumstances, to choose the star that guides his course, to correct, and test, and assay his convictions by the light within, and, with a resolute conscience and ideal courage, to remodel and reconstitute the character which birth and education gave him . . .

[LORD ACTON, from *A Lecture on the Study of History*]

Acton was horrified by historians who regarded human beings as mere puppets in an impersonal process. He insists on the morally responsible human soul.

28th May

Yet God chooses to enter into relationship with man, he chooses to disclose himself to man. This is the meaning of the closing couplet of the poem,

Behold, the fear of the Lord, that is wisdom;
and to depart from evil is understanding. [Job 28.28]
It is through man's religion, his relationship with God – for that is what
'fear of the Lord' means – that man will find that order, peace, and
harmony which he seeks and which he cannot experience otherwise
from this disordered world. But how that disorder arose, the book of
Job does nothing to explain.

Of all the Wisdom literature Job, then, is the most profound, for the
author brings home to man what must be the nature of his belief. For
although Job ends up in the same position as the three friends, unable to
place God in the dock, he knows, as the friends do not know, that the
believer is an agnostic too. He is freed from the necessity of having to
give an explanation to everything. And more than that, he can stand
with the unbeliever in the horror of the uncertainties, unjustness, and
meaninglessness of life and can share with him the full lot of being
human. If only the Church would meet man where he is in his natural
loneliness and despair, and show him that we all stand together and
God stands with us, instead of talking about atonement and salvation in
language and ideas that are as meaningless as Chinese to a Brazilian
peasant! . . . It is always the temptation of the faithful to think that they
must know all the answers. Job affirms that knowledge of God and
knowledge of all the answers about God are two different things. Man
can in fact have only the former – he can only be an agnostic believer.

[ANTHONY PHILLIPS, from *God B.C.*]

Most people think of religion as something you know. *Here it is not knowing,
but trusting.*

29th May

There lived a singer in France of old
    By the tideless dolorous midland sea.
In a land of sand and ruin and gold
    There shone the woman, and none but she.
And finding life for her love's sake fail,
Being fain to see her, he bade set sail,
Touched land, and saw her as life grew cold,
    And praised God, seeing; and so died he.

Died, praising God for his gift and grace:
    For she bowed down to him weeping and said

"Live", and her tears were shed on his face
   Or ever the life in his face was shed.
The sharp tears fell through her hair and stung
Once, and her close lips touched him and clung
Once, and grew one with his lips for a space;
   And so drew back, and the man was dead.

O brother, the gods were good to you.
   Sleep, and be glad while the world endures.
Be well content as the years wear through;
   Give thanks for life, and the loves and lures;
Give thanks for life, O brother, and death,
For the sweet last sound of her feet, her breath,
For gifts she gave you, gracious and few
   Tears and kisses, that lady of yours.

Rest, and be glad of the gods; but I
   How shall I praise them, or how take rest?
There is not room under all the sky
   For me that know not of worst or best,
Dream or desire of the days before,
Sweet things or bitterness, any more.
Love will not come to me now though I die,
   As love came close to you, breast to breast.

[A. C. SWINBURNE, from *The Triumph of Time*]

As a youth I was fascinated by Swinburne's musical dancing verse. It was a schoolboy enthusiasm, but what a sense he gives of the haunting quality of words. You realize what can be done with them and what they can do with you.

30th May

Poets in all ages have contemplated the medium of their art with an ambivalent set of emotions. They love it, because only in words can their poems attain palpable form, yet they hate it because they see in language an intractable Protean element which they must ceaselessly strive to redeem and to transfigure.

There have even been poets who have been haunted by a lingering fear that the effort to write poetry is foredoomed to failure because they can never express in words that Truth which it is the object of poetry to reveal. Roy Fuller has told us of these gnawing doubts:

Perhaps the object of art
Is this: the communication
Of that which cannot be told.
Worse: the rich explanation
That there is nothing to tell;
Only the artificial
Plot and ambiguous word,
The forged but sacred missal.

His doubts have been echoed by David Gascoyne . . .

Before I fall
Down silent finally, I want to make
One last attempt at utterance, and tell
How absurd desire was to compose
A single poem with my mental eyes
Wide open, and without even one lapse
From that most scrupulous Truth which I pursue
When not pursuing Poetry. – Perhaps
Only the poem I can never write is true.

If we are inclined to blame poets for yielding to such pessimistic reflections, we should remember that, in this present age of anxiety and introspection, all human activities are subjected to a minute and subtle scrutiny by minds whose knowledge of psycho-analysis leads them to question all established values. It is only to be expected that poets will be tainted by the prevailing malady, and that they will become increasingly self-conscious and self-critical. Indeed we may suspect that a poet who has never been assailed by these doubts is either too stupid to understand the agony that torments the finest spirits among his contemporaries, or too cowardly to contemplate a truth that may wreck his fondest illusions.

[JOHN PRESS, from *The Fire and the Fountain*]

A rare admission that poetry is doomed to failure. Yet you keep on trying. In Hamlet *Shakespeare is aware that he is using words that betray him as a person. Yet he carried on and wrote* The Tempest. *The problem is that the good will always be assailed. Words are corrupted almost as soon as they are uttered.*

31st May

Beneath a growing lethargy and a constant sense of shaky foundations, which might at any moment finally collapse, he kept a gaiety in his inmost heart and fed it with gratitude for what life had given him and still gave. "When I think of the friends I have had," he characteristically remarked one day, "I forget the enemies I have made." And he gave "thanks in old age – thanks ere I go";

> For health, the midday sun, the impalpable air – for life, mere life,
> For precious ever-lingering memories (of you my mother dear – you
>   father – you, brothers, sisters, friends),
> For all my days – not those of peace alone – the days of war the same.
> For gentle words, caresses, gifts from foreign lands,
> For shelter, wine and meat – for sweet appreciation,
> (You distant, dim, unknown – or young or old – countless,
>   unspecified, readers, belov'd,
> We never met, and ne'er shall meet – and yet our souls embrace,
>   long, close, and long;)
> For beings, groups, love, deeds, words, books – for colours, forms,
> For all the brave strong men – devoted, hardy men – who've forward
>   sprung in freedom's help, all years, all lands.
> As soldier from an ended war return'd – As traveller out of myriads,
>   to the long procession retrospective,
> Thanks – joyful thanks! – a soldier's traveller's thanks.

[HUGH L'ANSON FAUSSET, from *Walt Whitman*]

Few poets were so footloose to human culture as Whitman. He was born on this day in 1819. Most people in America (unlike the Jews in exile) were slung out of a tradition. Whitman is saying that he has a whole new continent to sing about. And sing he does – even if at times it feels like compulsive raving.

JUNE

1st June

What is there in my heart that you should sue
so fiercely for its love? What kind of care
brings you as though a stranger to my door
through the long night and in the icy dew

seeking the heart that will not harbour you,
that keeps itself religiously secure?
At this dark solstice filled with frost and fire
your passion's ancient wounds must bleed anew.

So many nights the angel of my house
has fed such urgent comfort through a dream,
whispered. "Your lord is coming, he is close."

that I have drowsed half-faithful for a time
bathed in pure tones of promise and remorse;
"tomorrow I shall wake to welcome him."

[GEOFFREY HILL, *Lachrimae Amantis*]

*The questions are important. And astringent too. It is hard to admit that we
come only reluctantly and half-way out of our religious security.*

2nd June

My body's self deserts me now,
  The half of me that was her own,
Since all I knew of brightness died
  Half of me lingers, half is gone.

The face that was like hawthorn bloom
  Was my right foot and my right side;
And my right hand and my right eye
  Were no more mine than hers who died.

117

Poor is the share of me that's left
   Since half of me died with my wife;
I shudder at the words I speak;
   Dear God, that girl was half my life.

And our first look was her first love;
   No man had fondled ere I came
The little breasts so small and firm
And the long body like a flame.

For twenty years we shared a home,
   Our converse milder with each year;
Eleven children in its time
   Did that tall stately body bear.

It was the King of hosts and roads
   Who snatched her from me in her prime:
Little she wished to leave alone
   The man she loved before her time.

Now King of churches and of bells,
   Though never raised to pledge a lie,
That woman's hand – can it be true? –
   No more beneath my head will lie.

[FRANK O'CONNOR, from *The Irish of Murrough O'Daly*]

A common experience told uncommonly well.

3rd June

The liquid call of a curlew made him raise his head and regard the sky through his tears. Stars were aflicker in the deep spaces between luminous clouds. A dim light filled the lane, and revealed the haystack in the field over the hedge. He stood up, and looked towards the eastern horizon, where the beeches on the ridge showed massy and black against the tawny glow spreading up the sky. Slowly an umbered moon lifted above the forest, like a shield forged in fire and slowly cooling, a red-smoking dross about its face. The grasshoppers began to risp in the hedges.

   He walked down the lane. Time had no significance, his home was of no account. Nothing mattered any more. Better if the flames had consumed his heart that night years ago when they had resolved the body of Jim into irreclaimable ash, freeing his spirit for the sun and the corn. Was that stir of wind in the hedge nothing more than wandering air? Why was his back so icy and strange? He glanced over his shoulder, seeing strange things in the light of the moon. An owl hooted suddenly near him . . .

Alone at the edge of the corn, Willie was standing. "I shall return one day," he whispered, his eyes on the fiery red star above the beechwood. "Jim, are you there? I shall not forget you. Goodbye, Big Wheatfield. Goodbye, spinney – Jim, Dolly, Bill Nye, and now Willie, – goodbye. Brooks, and meadows where the plovers nested, goodbye. And downs, goodbye. Longpond, – Heron Island –"

He leant against a tree, while an aerymouse passed round his head as it flew along the edge of the spinney, returning with a dark erratic flutter of its skin wings. "Goodbye, aerymouse, too."

When the ruddy star was clear again, he went back to his waiting friend. Silently, and with arms linked they passed down the right-of-way, leaving behind the wind sighing in the silver-swaying wheat.

[HENRY WILLIAMSON, from *Dandelion Days*]

My birthday. And a quotation from one of a sequence of novels about boyhood. Here is a farewell to those days which have awkward likes and extraordinary accumulations of knowledge. (I memorised all three thousand locomotive numbers of the London and North-Western Railway!)

4th June

So beautiful – God himself quailed
at her approach: the long body curved
like the horizon. Why had he made
her so? How would it be, she said
Leaning towards him, if, instead of
Quarrelling over it, we divided it
between us? You can have all the credit
for its invention, if you will leave the ordering
of it to me. He looked into her
eyes and saw far down the bones
of the generations that would navigate
by those great stars, but the pull of it
was too much. Yes, he thought, give me their minds'
tribute, and what they do with their bodies

is not my concern. He put his hand in his side
and drew out the thorn for the letting
of the ordained blood and touched her with
it. Go, he said. They shall come to you for ever
with their desire, and you shall bleed for them in return.

[R. S. THOMAS, *The Woman*]

*Most of Thomas's poetry is what you would expect of a sensitive Christian
living amidst dereliction – the irony, the bitterness, the occasional glimpse of
God. Here he comes into the field of human relationships and the daunting
aspect of feminine beauty. The background is the Eve who captures Adam
away from the divine command. Few religious poets tackle the relationship
between men and women today, and any attempt is important – however
bungling women may judge such as this. But here is an assertion that the
feminine is at the basis of it all, and God would have it so. And even God
quails!]*

5th June

But what after all is one night? A short space, especially when the
darkness dims so soon, and so soon a bird sings, a cock crows, or a faint
green quickens, like a turning leaf, in the hollow of the wave. Night,
however, succeeds to night. The winter holds a pack of them in store
and deals them equally, evenly, with indefatigable fingers. They
lengthen, they darken. Some of them hold aloft clear planets, plates of
brightness. The autumn trees, ravaged as they are, take on the flash of
tattered flags kindling in the gloom of cool cathedral caves where gold
letters on marble pages describe death in battle and how bones bleach
and burn far away in Indian sands. The autumn trees gleam in the
yellow moonlight, in the light of the harvest moons, the light which
mellows the energy of labour, and smooths the stubble, and brings the
wave lapping blue to the shore. It seemed now as if, touched by human
penitence and all its toil, divine goodness had parted the curtain and
displayed behind it, single, distinct, the hare erect; the wave falling; the
boat rocking, which, did we deserve them, should be ours always. But,
alas, divine goodness, twitching the cord, draws the curtain; it does not
please him; he covers his treasures in a drench of hail, and so breaks
them, so confuses them that it seems impossible that their calm should
ever return or that we should ever compose from their fragments a

perfect whole or read in the littered pieces the clear words of truth. For our penitence deserves a glimpse only, our toil respite only.

[VIRGINIA WOOLF, from *To the Lighthouse*]

I first read this novel in Durham, staying up all night to do so! It is the kind of book that from time to time makes me gulp. This passage comes from an interlude in the narrative.

6th June

                                              . . . My mariners,
Souls that have toil'd and wrought, and thought with me –
That ever with a frolic welcome took
The thunder and the sunshine, and opposed
Free hearts, free foreheads – you and I are old;
Old age hath yet his honour and his toil;
Death closes all: but something ere the end,
Some work of noble note, may yet be done,
Not unbecoming men that strove with gods.
The lights begin to twinkle from the rocks;
The long day wanes: the slow moon climbs; the deep
Moans round with many voices. Come, my friends,
'Tis not too late to seek a newer world.
Push off, and sitting well in order smite
The sounding furrows; for my purpose holds
To sail beyond the sunset, and the baths
Of all the western stars, until I die.
It may be that the gulfs will wash us down:
It may be we shall touch the Happy Isles,
And see the great Achilles whom we knew.
Tho' much is taken, much abides; and tho'
We are not now the strength which in old days
Moved earth and heaven; that which we are, we are;
One equal temper of heroic hearts,
Made weak by time and fate, yet strong in will
To strive, to seek, to find, and not to yield.

[ALFRED TENNYSON, from *Ulysses*]

I had to learn this poem as a ten-year-old at school. It is Tennyson at his most authentic, using his gift of a sense of the music of words.

7th June

What needest thou? – a few brief hours of rest
Wherein to seek thyself in thine own breast;
A transient silence wherein truth could say
Such was thy constant hope, and this thy way?
  O burden of life that is
  A lifelong tangle of perplexities!

What seekest thou? – a truce from that thou art;
Some steadfast refuge from a fickle heart;
Still to be thou, and yet no thing of scorn,
To find no stay here, and yet not forlorn –
  A riddle of life that is
  An endless war 'twixt contrarieties.

Leave this vain questioning. Is not sweet the rose?
Sings not the wild bird ere to rest he goes?
Hath not in miracle brave June returned?
Burns not her beauty as of old it burned?
  O foolish one to roam
  So far in thine own mind away from home.

Where blooms the flower when her petals fade.
Where sleepeth echo by earth's music made,
Where all things transient to the changeless win,
There waits the peace thy spirit dwelleth in.

[WALTER DE LA MARE, *Vain Questioning*]

I once heard Walter de la Mare lecture in Cambridge. He was genuine in what he had to say and did not slip into sentimentality. He was the most acutely sensitive of the Georgian poets and the most accurate in his wording. He was gently aware of fragile beauty that we apprehend amidst the 'tangle of perplexities', a beauty that is enough to justify this life.

8th June

I'll come to thee at eventide
When the west is streaked wi' grey
I'll wish the night thy charms to hide
And daylight all away.

I'll come to thee at set o'sun
Where white thorns i' the May
I'll come to thee when work is done
And love thee till the day.

When Daisey stars are all turned green
And all is meadow grass
I'll wander down the bank at e'en
And court the bonny lass.

The green banks and the rustleing sedge
I'll wander down at e'en
All slopeing to the water's edge
And in the water green.

And theres the luscious meadow sweet
Beside the meadow drain
My lassie there I once did meet
Who I wish to meet again.

The water lilies were in flower
The yellow and the white
I met her there at even's hour
And stood for half the night.

We stood and loved in that green place
When Sundays sun got low
Its beams reflected in her face
The fairest thing below.

My sweet Ann Foot my bonny Ann
The meadow banks are green
Meet me at even when you can
Be mine as you have been.

[JOHN CLARE, *Song*]

As good a simple love poem as you can find.

9th June

There could be no development of the personality of individuals, no
fulfilment of those gifts in which one man differs from another without
the freedom for each man to grow in his own direction.

... Sometimes men have tried to find freedom along quiet paths of change, as the humanists did on the eve of the Reformation, and as the dissenting manufacturers of the 18th century did. At other times, the drive for freedom has been explosive, intellectually explosive in the Elizabethan age and the Scientific Revolution, economically explosive in the Industrial Revolution, and politically explosive in the other great revolutions of our period, from Puritan times to the age of Napoleon.

Yet our study shows that freedom is a supple and elusive idea, whose advocates can at times delude themselves that obedience to tyranny is a form of freedom. Such a delusion ensnared men as diverse as Luther and Rousseau, and Hegel and Marx. Philosophically, there is indeed no unlimited freedom. But we have seen that there is one freedom which can be defined without contradiction, and which can therefore be an end in itself. This is freedom of thought and speech: the right to dissent.

The evidence of history is strong, that those societies are most creative and progressive which safeguard the expression of new ideas. Societies appear to remain vigorous only so long as they are organized to receive novel and unexpected – and sometimes unpleasant – thoughts. It may seem odd that the government of some countries gives a special status to the opposition; Canada, like Great Britain, actually pays a salary to the leader of the opposition. Yet this legalization of opposition, this balance between power and dissent, is the heart of the Western tradition ...

The conflict of minds is still an abstract phrase – as abstract as the history of ideas. Behind the minds are men: ideas are made, are held, and are fought for, by men. To read the history of ideas out of its context of men and events is to violate it. Ideas are as human as emotions, as powerful, as conflicting, and as indestructible. The aim of this book has been to show ideas in their full setting: of men, of groups of men, and of events ...

[J. BRONOWSKI & B. MAZLISH, from *The Western Intellectual Tradition*]

Few books have the breadth of Bronowski's mind. We need to see the broad sweep, the contexts, in order to locate ourselves and feel part of something greater than ourselves.

10th June

Darkling I listen; and, for many a time
  I have been half in love with easeful Death,
Call'd him soft names in many a mused rhyme,

To take into the air my quiet breath;
Now more than ever seems it rich to die,
   To cease upon the midnight with no pain,
      While thou art pouring forth thy soul abroad
         In such an ecstasy!
      Still wouldst thou sing, and I have ears in vain –
         To thy high requiem become a sod.

Thou wast not born for death, immortal Bird!
   No hungry generations tread thee down;
The voice I knew this passing night was heard
   In ancient days by emperor and clown:
Perhaps the self-same song that found a path
      Through the sad heart of Ruth, when, sick for home,
         She stood in tears amid the alien corn;
         The same that oft-times hath
      Charm'd magic casements, opening on the foam
         Of perilous seas, in faery lands forlorn.

Forlorn! the very word is like a bell
   To toll me back from thee to my sole self!
Adieu! the fancy cannot cheat so well
   As she is famed to do, deceiving elf.
Adieu, adieu, thy plaintive anthem fades
      Past the near meadows, over the still stream
         Up the hill-side; and now 'tis buried deep
         In the next valley-glades:
      Was it a vision, or a waking dream?
         Fled is that music; Do I wake or sleep?

[JOHN KEATS, from *Ode to a Nightingale*]

*Keats was conscious of impending death and this saved him from being merely a
nature poet. There is a clear sense of the transitory and the fragile, and of the
pathos of the bird singing in the darkness, image of our humanity.*

11th June

We shall not come again. We shall never come back again. Over the
dawn a lark (that shall not come again). And wind and music far. O lost!
(It shall not come again.) And over your mouth the earth. O ghost!
But over the darkness, what? Wind pressed the boughs; the withered

leaves were quaking. We shall not come again. We shall never come back again. It was October, but we shall never come back again.

When will they come again? When will they come again?

The laurel, the lizard, and the stone will come no more. The women weeping at the gate have gone and will not come again. And pain and pride and death will pass, and will not come again. And light and dawn will pass, and the star and the cry of a lark will pass, and will not come again. And we shall pass, and shall not come again.

What things will come again? O Spring, the cruellest and fairest of the seasons, will come again. And the strange and buried men will come again, and death and dust will never come again, for death and the dust will die. And Ben will come again, he will not die again, in flower and leaf, in wind and music far, he will come back again.

O lost, and by the wind grieved, ghost, come back again!

It had grown dark. The frosty night blazed with great brilliant stars. The lights in the town shone with sharp radiance. Presently, when he had lain upon the cold earth for some time, Eugene got up and went away towards the town. Wind pressed the boughs; the withered leaves were shaking.

[THOMAS WOLFE, from *Look Homeward, Angel*]

Wolfe is haunted by the sense of not being able to go back to childhood's first awareness of the joy and pain of relationships. Some things will never come again. And yet it seems, some do. Are we caught into wondering again and again whether we are possessed of anything that is lasting?

12th June

> So, some tempestuous morn in early June,
>   When the year's primal burst of bloom is o'er,
> Before the roses and the longest day –
>   When garden-walks, and all the grassy floor,
> With blossoms, red and white, of fallen May,
>   And chestnut-flowers are strewn –
> So have I heard the cuckoo's parting cry,
>   From the wet field, through the vext garden-trees,
>   Come with the volleying rain and tossing breeze:
> The bloom is gone, and with the bloom go I.
>
> Too quick despairer, wherefore wilt thou go?
>   Soon will the high Midsummer pomps come on,

Soon will the musk carnations break and swell,
  Soon shall we have gold-dusted snapdragon,
Sweet-William with its homely cottage smell,
  And stocks in fragrant blow;
Roses that down the alleys shine afar,
  And open, Jasmine-muffled lattices,
  And groups under the dreaming garden-trees,
And the full moon and the white evening-star.

He hearkens not! Light-comer, he is flown!
  What matters it? Next year he will return,
And we shall have him in the sweet spring-days,
  With whitening hedges, and uncrumpling fern,
And blue-bells trembling by the forest-ways,
  And scent of hay new-mown.
But Thyrsis never more we swains shall see!
  See him come back, and cut a smoother reed,
  And blow a strain the world at last shall heed –
For Time, not Corydon, hath conquered thee.

[MATTHEW ARNOLD, from *Thyrsis*]

This is Arnold at his elegaic best. In both Thyrsis *and* The Scholar Gypsy *he sees particular bits of the countryside and of gardens that have gone for ever and are yet still present to his heart. And he finds words that are an evocation of that landscape. It still works for me – but what of those who live in the Upper Thames Valley now? Perhaps the memory lingers in counties such as Shropshire. And certainly even city dwellers have formed their resistance movement against concrete and swoop on garden centres to buy plants and flowers.*

13th June

And once more he was completely puzzled and baffled by the enigma of his father.

He did not hold the key and even had he held it he was too young, too inexperienced, to have used it. As with gathering passion the eyes of Darius assaulted the window pane, Darius had a painful intense vision of that miracle, his own career. Edwin's grand misfortune was that he was blind to the miracle. Edwin had never seen the little boy in the Bastille. But Darius saw him always, the infant who had begun life at a ropes-end. Every hour of Darius's present existence was really an astounding marvel to Darius. He could not read the newspaper without thinking how wonderful it was that he should be able to read the newspaper. And it was wonderful! It was wonderful that he had three different suits of clothes, none of them with a single hole. It was wonderful that he had three children, all with complete outfits of good clothes. It was wonderful that he had never to think twice about buying coal, and that he could have more food than he needed! It was wonderful that he was not living in a two-roomed cottage. He never came into his house by the side-entrance without feeling proud that the door gave on to a preliminary passage and not direct into a living-room; he would never lose the idea that a lobby, however narrow, was the great distinguishing mark of wealth. It was wonderful that he had a piano, and that his girls could play it and sing.

[ARNOLD BENNETT, from *Clayhanger*]

My father was born in the same year as Bennett, and in Edwin Clayhanger I see my father in an uncanny way. He too had this sense of miracle. And it is this recognition of 'miracle' that makes Arnold Bennett a man of genuine imagination – a man who salutes the wonder that is being disclosed to us in the often grim pageant of human life. To be aware of that miracle, in however small a degree – and all our awareness falls short of it as did that of Peter and his companions on the Mount of Transfiguration – is to meet the Glory of God, to acknowledge the 'wonder' that a lover like Ferdinand salutes in the person of Miranda. It is more rare for a man bruised from his earliest years and then possessed of some success in the enterprises of the world, to retain the capacity to perceive that wonder. It is a gift – that goes without saying – but it is also a testimony to something else – to an ability to receive it as a gift and to treasure it accordingly. It does not lose itself in the contemplation of the treasure as a miser might do. It does not grow careless and unseeing because it now has an abundance of good things to savour – but it retains an essential purity of heart that does not cease to exclaim, to cry out, its reverence for the wonder.

14th June

The story of Europe and the West has been richer than that of any other civilisation, as is fitting since it is a phase not of a local cycle but of the general development of man. In Europe we see the spirit of man living in this world and yet aspiring; striving to escape the sordid and restricted into the open, free and generous life; opening its eyes to facts and yet saying yes to life; refusing imprisonment either in the world as it is or in dreams of another world; living and dying for illusions, but achieving greatness; separating the ideal and the real and so impelled to perpetual creation in its desire to re-combine them; and finally frustrated because its pride blinded it to the changes proceeding within itself...

The only true European today is one who recognizes that the old values are no longer valid and is occupied in transmuting them within himself so that Europe may find herself again within a new and universal community. Whoever weeps for the old world justifies the gangster who asserts that the spirit of man is effete and the game open to revenge and hate.

When a great ideal has ceased to illuminate the human understanding and has therefore lost its power, man has no choice but to search afresh for some element in the process of the real world with which he can identify himself. At such a moment men may believe that they have lost something beyond price, for a grand vision has faded into despair and self-assurance given place to the humiliation of man's inability to understand himself... The change may have been long prepared, but dominance is single and until the old has gone the new cannot take its place. The change cannot come until neither loyalty to the old nor fear of the new can no longer delay it. Such a transformation is all the more difficult because it seems to require the greater to be exchanged for the less. Each real advance is paid for by aiming at less in order to achieve more. The crucial step cannot be taken until men are ready to choose the less which can be realised in place of the more which had remained a dream...

[LANCELOT L. WHYTE, from *The Next Development in Man*]

One of the seminal books of this century, published during the Second World War and therefore not given the attention it ought to have had. Whyte asked the fundamental question, What do we do when we can turn anything to destruction? A passage that is so pertinent to the nineties!

15th June

Lorenzo   The moon shines bright. In such a night as this,
When the sweet wind did gently kiss the trees,
And they did make no noise, in such a night
Troilus methinks mounted the Trojan walls,
And sigh'd his soul toward the Grecian tents
Where Cressid lay that night.

Jessica	In such a night
	Did Thisbe fearfully o'ertrip the dew,
	And saw the lion's shadow ere himself,
	And ran dismayed away.
Lorenzo	In such a night
	Stood Dido with a willow in her hand
	Upon the wild sea banks, and waft her love
	To come again to Carthage.
Jessica	In such a night
	Medea gathered the enchanged herbs
	That did renew Old Aeson.
Lorenzo	In such a night
	Did Jessica steal from the wealthy Jew
	And with an unthrift love did run from Venice
	As far as Belmont.
Jessica	In such a night
	Did young Lorenzo swear he loved her well,
	Stealing her soul with many vows of faith
	And ne'er a true one.
Lorenzo	In such a night
	Did pretty Jessica (like a little shrew)
	Slander her love, and he forgave it her. . .

How sweet the moonlight sits upon this bank!
Here will we sit, and let the sounds of music
Creep in our ears – soft stillness and the night
Become the touches of sweet harmony;
Sit Jessica – look how the floor of heaven
Is thick inlaid with patens of bright gold,
There's not the smallest orb which thou behold'st
But in his motion like an angel sings,
Still quiring to the young-ey'd cherubims;
Such harmony is in immortal souls,
But whilst this muddy vesture of decay
Doth grossly close it in, we cannot hear it.

[WILLIAM SHAKESPEARE, from *The Merchant of Venice*]

This is the third quotation this month which concerns the night. It is at its most enjoyable in June, with the half light, the scents, and the glittering stars. There is all the beauty of summer, even if the elegaic is not far away. Shakespeare is conscious of a divinely created order whereas Arnold had become more doubtful.

16th June

> Slow sarabande of pain in all the air;
> Everywhere cadence, decay of a tune, of time,
> Death of the gold days and the feathered joy
> And across the purple hills and the purple sky
> The long undying rosary of despair.
>
> It has come too soon, this sorrow's psalm,
> The dog-faced cloud-rack scowling in the West,
> Where brethren moving like uprooted trees
> In a Birnam of blood drop aching twigs of hands,
> And from leaves in an ancient way stare round about
>
> At callous undulating plains of salt,
> Where nightjar leers through a broken note,
> And the scarecrow dog at the end of his rope
> Gnaws at the door, howls as he feels as we,
> The wide immeasurable knowledge of an end.

[HENRY TREECE, from *Invitation and Warning*]

This has a strange link with Mrs Gradgrind's words about a pain in the room though she could not exactly say that she'd got it. The poet is aware of pain as a kind of dance that involves the whole human situation in this post-war world. It recalls the best of all that Macbeth had counted on until Birnam Wood disclosed its real menace. Now the frightened watchdogs only give warning of the approaching end . . . Yet apocalyptic literature had, by contrast, a more than doom-laden message: within it there is always at least a hint of hope.

17th June

Never before did language possess such freedom. Shakespeare's art appeared to have shaken off all the orthodoxies and limitations of the flat Ptolemaic cosmos. But this was also why he opposed the threat of relativism, the loss of degree, the incipient confusions of belief, with an emphasis on order and the moral verities of tradition, a conservatism that wholly and fascinatingly contrasts with the liberties he took with words. And then, in the midst of it, Hamlet's scruples about language, worries that would not be Hamlet's if his author had not known them himself . . .

With the great monologue of self-indictment and self-humiliation in the second scene of the second act, Hamlet, at the same time, is denigrating language itself and thereby brings into question the tradition of humanistic certainties insofar as they are founded upon language. Moreover, he slanders the very genre of poetic drama – one of which, a very famous one, is being performed at that moment:

> This is most brave
> That I, the son of a dear father murdered,
> Prompted to my revenge by heaven and hell,
> Must, like a whore, unpack my heart with words.

Although it is doubtful whether whores have ever been in the habit of doing this, the 'must' is extraordinary. For it is the 'must' of every hero of every tragedy even if his resolution to act is less inhibited than Hamlet's. Could there be poetic drama at all if their leading actors simply 'acted' and not, before the act, unpacked their hearts with words put together in long and moving speeches? And indeed, Hamlet's very hesitancy to act is inseparable from his misgivings, intense and oppressive, that his inner condition is inexpressible, be it in words or deeds, in love or murder . . .

[ERICH HELLER, from *In the Age of Prose*]

Heller is asking this question about the way in which words betray. In Hamlet Polonius and Rosencrantz and Guildenstern contaminate words because of their hidden motives. And Hamlet cannot speak the truth – and if he does it doesn't register with those he speaks it to. So at least let us be aware of such betrayals and ask how speech can be purified. I am a man of unclean lips. Do I let God purge them? (And what of the words of the Gospels?)

18th June

. . . The cart was halted before the enclosure; and rejecting the offers of assistance with the same air of simple self-reliance he had displayed throughout, Tennessee's Partner lifted the rough coffin on his back, and deposited it, unaided, within the shallow grave. He then nailed down the board which served as a lid; and mounting the little mound of earth beside it, took off his hat, and slowly mopped his face with his handkerchief. This the crowd felt was a preliminary to speech; and they disposed themselves variously on stumps and boulders, and sat expectant.

"When a man," began Tennessee's Partner, slowly, "has been running free all day, what's the natural thing for him to do? Why, to come home. And if he ain't in a condition to go home, what can his best friend do? Why, bring him home! And here's Tennessee has been running free, and we brings him home from his wandering." He paused, and picked up a fragment of quartz, rubbed it thoughtfully on his sleeve, and went on: "It ain't the first time that I've packed him on my back, as you'd see'd me now. It ain't the first time that I brought him to this yer cabin when he couldn't help himself; it ain't the first time that I and 'Jinny' have waited for him on yon hill, and picked him up and so fetched him home, when he couldn't speak and didn't know me. And now that it's the last time, why" – he paused, and rubbed the quartz gently on his sleeve, – "you see it's sort of rough on his partner. And now, gentlemen," he added, abruptly, picking up his long-handled shovel, "the fun'l's over; and my thanks and Tennessee's thanks to you for your trouble."

. . . one night, when the pines beside the cabin were swaying in the storm, and trailing their slender fingers over the roof, and the roar and rush of the swollen river were heard below, Tennessee's Partner lifted his head from the pillow, saying, "It is time to go for Tennessee; I must put 'Jinny' in the cart," and would have risen from his bed but for the restraint of his attendant. Struggling, he still pursued his singular fancy: "There, now, steady, 'Jinny' – steady, old girl. How dark it is! Look out for the ruts, – and look out for him too, old gal. Sometimes, you know, when he's blind drunk, he drops down right in the trail. Keep straight up to the pine on the top of the hill. Thar – I told you so! – thar he is, – coming this way, too, – all by himself, sober, and his face a-shining. Tennessee! Pardner!"

And so they met.

[BRET HARTE, from *Tennessee's Partner*]

I can never read this without crying. Why?

19th June

> For when it dawned – they dropped their arms,
> And clustered round the mast;
> Sweet sounds rose slowly through their mouths,
> And from their bodies passed.

Around, around, flew each sweet sound,
Then darted to the Sun;
Slowly the sounds came back again,
Now mixed, now one by one.

Sometimes a-dropping from the sky
I heard the sky-lark sing;
Sometimes all little birds that are,
How they seemed to fill the sea and air
With their sweet jargoning!

And now 'twas like all instruments,
Now like a lonely flute;
And now it is an angel's song,
That makes the heavens be mute.

It ceased; yet still the sails made on
A pleasant noise till noon,
A noise like of a hidden brook
In the leafy month of June,
That to the sleeping woods all night
Singeth a quiet tune.

[S. T. COLERIDGE, from *The Rime of the Ancient Mariner*]

Editor's note: *Alan chose this passage a few weeks before he died and I was unable to ask him why he chose it. But see his comments on Coleridge and* Kubla Khan (10*th May*).

20th June

Just when we are safest, there's a sunset-touch,
A fancy from a flower-bell, someone's death,
A chorus-ending from Euripides, –
And that's enough for fifty hopes and fears
As old and new at once as Nature's self,
To rap and knock and enter in our soul,
Take hands and dance there, a fantastic ring,
Round the ancient idol, on his base again, –
The grand Perhaps! We look on helplessly, –
There the old misgivings, crooked questions are –
This good God, – what he could do, if he would,
Would, if he could – then must have done long since;

If so, when, where, and how? some way must be, –
Once feel about, and soon or late you hit
Some sense, in which it might be, after all.
Why not, "The Way, the Truth, the Life?" . . .
                              I say faith is my waking life.
One sleeps, indeed, and dreams at intervals,
We know, but waking's the main point with us,
And my provision's for life's waking part.
Accordingly, I use heart, head and hands
All day, I build, scheme, study and make friends;
And when night overtakes me, down I lie,
Sleep, dream a little, and get done with it,
The sooner the better, to begin afresh.
What's midnight's doubt before the dayspring's faith? . . .
With me, faith means perpetual unbelief
Kept quiet like the snake 'neath Michael's foot
Who stands calm just because he feels it writhe . . .

[ROBERT BROWNING, from *Bishop Blougram's Apology*]

Does the doubting bishop go on because he is doing very nicely, thank you? This is too cynical. For the bishop is aware of the questions: he can't get away from them. There is always 'the grand perhaps'. So there is always something to be said in defence of the Blougrams of this world. He does not pretend to know all the answers, only enough to keep the writhing serpent under control. And it is enough to get by with. In the face of Victorian doubt, Arnold gave in, Tennyson turned away, Browning kept steady and held the question.

21st June

Girl of the musing mouth,
The mild archaic air,
For whom do you subtly smile?
Yield to what power or prayer
Breasts vernally bare?

I seem to be peering at you
Through the wrong end of time
That shrinks to a bright, far image –
Great Mother of earth's prime –
A stature sublime.

So many golden ages
Of sunshine steeped your clay,
So dear did the maker cherish
In you life's fostering ray,
That you warm us today.

Goddess or girl, you are earth.
The smile, the offered breast –
They were the dream of one
Thirsting as I for rest,
As I, unblest.

[CECIL DAY LEWIS, *Statuette: Late Minoan*]

Art transcends material stuff to 'warm us today'. So there is a grace about the faces of some sculptures of a vanished age. They give me a sense that their perception is linked to my own, and that if I stand and look they will give me something – a miracle again.

22nd June

See you the ferny ride that steals
Into the oak-woods far?
O that was whence they hewed the keels
That rolled to Trafalgar . . .

See you the dimpled track that runs
All hollow through the wheat?
O that was where they hauled the guns
That smote King Philip's fleet. . .

See you our little mill that clacks,
So busy by the brook?
She has ground her corn and paid her tax
Ever since Domesday Book . . .

See you the windy levels spread
About the gates of Rye?
O that was where the Northmen fled
When Alfred's ships came by . . .

And see you, after rain, the trace
of mound and ditch and wall?
O that was a Legion's camping-place,
When Caesar sailed from Gaul.

And see you marks that show and fade,
Like shadows on the Downs?
O they are the lines the Flint Men made,
To guard their wondrous towns.

Trackway and Camp and City lost,
Salt Marsh where now is corn –
Old Wars, old Peace, old Arts that cease,
And so was England born!

She is not any common Earth,
Water or wood or air,
But Merlin's Isle of Gramarye,
Where you and I will fare!

[RUDYARD KIPLING, from *Puck's Song*]

This kind of writing gives me a shiver of pleasure because it touches so closely on a historical relationship which I feel very deeply. The earth in all the details which Kipling mentions presents a living record of human effort and is 'present' to us in so far as we become sensitive to it – as a Presence – *a disclosure of divine Reality.*

23rd June

It happens to nearly everyone occasionally to find himself appreciating a situation not solely according as it gratifies instincts of self-respect or sex or domination, and not solely because it offers escape from fear of insecurity or want. The recollection and anticipation of these experiences is cherished profoundly and intimately to a degree not adequately expressed by the label of Good, True, or Beautiful, and devotion to them is as reckless of gain and as unquestioning as a parent's devotion to an invalid child. In fact, response to such moments of illumination has an intensity not accountable for by arguable judgment and not publicly justifiable, and it constitutes an attitude which it can only describe as 'worship'. Any kind of experience which evokes this attitude we can suitably call 'holy' or 'sacred'. In terms of this fact of experience we invert any definition implied by tradition, and we say that The Holy is 'that which someone worships'. Obviously these words must not be limited to the belongings of any religious institution, for some of the most memorable of such occasions are encountered in contemplating works of art or natural beauty or personalities of a historical past or

contemporaries to whom we have given affection, honour, and devotion
. . . To worship, and to treat some portions of our experience as holy,
belongs inevitably and undeniably to all of us, whether we choose to
call ourselves Christians or atheists or anything else whatever, and in
this sense none of us escapes being religious: differences between us
arise, however, as soon as we enter that age-long competition to give a
name to the 'object' of our worship. Some avoid this competition and
call themselves agnostic; it would be a mistake to imagine that these
are necessarily irreligious merely because they refuse to become
theological.

[MARTIN JOHNSON, from *Modern Art and Scientific Thought*]

*We need to extend the range of our sense of what is holy – so much wider than
what happens in church.*

24th June

June 29th, 1919: I am leaving Paris, after eight fateful months, with
conflicting emotions. Looking at the Conference in retrospect there is
much to approve and much to regret. It is easy to say what should have
been done, but more difficult to have found a way for doing it...

While I should have preferred a different peace, I doubt whether it
could have been made, for the ingredients for such a peace as I would
have had were lacking at Paris. And even if those of us like Smuts,
Botha, and Cecil could have had our will, as much trouble might have
followed a peace of our making as seems certain to follow this.

The same forces that have been at work in the making of this peace
would be at work to hinder the enforcement of a different kind of
peace, and no one can say with certitude that anything better than has
been done could be done at this time. We have had to deal with a
situation pregnant with difficulties and one which could not be met only
by an unselfish and idealistic spirit, which was almost wholly absent and
which was too much to expect of men come together at such a time and
for such a purpose.

And yet I wish we had taken the other road, even if it were less
smooth, both now and afterward, than the one we took. We would at
least have gone in the right direction, and if those who follow us had
made it impossible to go the full length of the journey planned, the
responsibility would have rested with them and not with us.

[EDWARD HOUSE, from *The Intimate Papers of Colonel House*]

Edward House was the man behind Woodrow Wilson and so was near the heart of the negotiations. During the Second World War I used to read this to WEA classes on twentieth century history.

25th June

> What is our innocence,
> what is our guilt? All are
> naked, none is safe. And whence
> is courage: the unanswered question,
> the resolute doubt, –
> dumbly calling, deafly listening – that
> in misfortune, even death,
> > encourages others
> > and in its defeat stirs
>
> > the soul to be strong? He
> sees deep and is glad, who
> accedes to mortality
> and in his imprisonment, rises
> upon himself as
> the sea in a chasm, struggling to be
> free and unable to be,
> > in its surrendering
> > finds its continuing.
>
> > So he who strongly feels,
> behaves. The very bird,
> grown taller as he sings, steels
> his form straight up. Though he is captive,
> his mighty singing
> says, satisfaction is a lowly
> thing, how pure a thing is joy.
> > This is mortality,
> > this is eternity.

[MARIANNE MOORE, *What are Years?*]

There are no concessions here to human sentiment. Defeat is real, but in response we test the spirit. (The picture of the sea reminds me of a cleft in the coast of Anglesey where the waves roar in.)

26th June

The greatest mistake that we make with our own lives is to snatch at the particular objects we desire . . . If we realized the riches that lie within every one of us we should know that we can afford to be spendthrift of nine-tenths of the possessions which we treasure; success, praise, and good opinion among men, achievements and still more material well-being . . . Never be afraid of throwing away what you have. If you *can* throw it away it is not really yours. If it is really yours you cannot throw it away. And you may be certain that if you throw it away, whatever in you is greater than you will produce something in its place. Never be afraid of pruning your branches. Trust the future and take risks. In moral, as in economic affairs, the rash man is he who does not speculate.

[R. H. TAWNEY, from *Diary*, 30th June 1912]

We do miss people like Tawney and the other founders of the WEA. He repre-sented a generous spirit which reached out from universities to share with others who knew the tumults of the time something of what was being explored and understood. So I was drawn to tutor WEA classes in Durham in the twenties. Face to face dialogue in a class was so important. And Tawney knew his stuff and could carry people with him.

27th June

Is it birthday weather for you, dear soul?
Is it fine your way,
With tall moon-daisies alight, and the mole
Busy, and elegant hares at play
By meadow paths where once you would stroll
In the flush of day?

I fancy the beasts and flowers there beguiled
By a visitation
That casts no shadow, a friend whose mild
Inquisitive glance lights with compassion,
Beyond the tomb, on all of this wild
And humbled creation.

It's hard to believe a spirit could die
Of such generous glow,
Or to doubt that somewhere a bird-sharp eye

Still broods on the capers of men below,
A stern voice asks the Immortals why
They should plague us so.

Dear poet, wherever you are, I greet you.
Much irony, wrong,
Innocence you'd find here to tease or entreat you,
And many the fate-fires have tempered strong,
But none that in ripeness of soul could meet you
Or magic of song.

Great brow, frail frame – gone. Yet you abide
In the shadow and sheen,
All the mellowing traits of a countryside
That nursed your tragi-comical scene;
And in us, warmer hearted and brisker-eyed
Since you have been.

[C. DAY LEWIS, *Birthday Poem for Thomas Hardy*]

A lovely poem that gets the sense of Hardy more than most have done – the brooding, the grim stories and tragedies, and yet a gentle sensitivity to people in their relationships which is personal rather than literary.

28th June

Suddenly, released by a couple of shots somewhere, the war, the catastrophe, was upon us. What had been universally felt for two years in its sultriness, what diplomatic shuffling and footling had partly provoked and partly caged as a dangerous monster, suddenly burst upon the stage. The dream was shattered overnight. The whole spiritual and intellectual world, so detached from reality, crumbled. It collapsed not only in Germany; over the entire earth it was smashed to smithereens as with a mighty hammer-blow.

Never has anything more unwanted and more unintended by those in the know descended on mankind. Never have the dark and subterranean forces let loose as though from the dungeons of Nature broken out more terribly. We do not yet know, we who stand today in the midst of their fury and in the thick of the second phase of that unleashing, whether they can really ever be locked up again.

. . . The question as to what we are to do in the midst of this most monstrous cataclysm known to human history is addressed to us – and,

speaking as a German – particularly to us Germans who, surrounded by
hate today, were the immediate authors – we cannot shake this off – of
this gigantic holocaust – even though we also, when it began, found
ourselves ensnared in a terrorism that had been cast over us, not that we
were to blame of course. It would be pitiable cowardice not to face this
question as deeply, as ruthlessly and as comprehensively as possible, an
act of spiritual desertion to put the blame on to one man – for whom,
indeed, no allowances need to be made – and his clique . . .

We must start with a new spiritual will if we are to come to terms
with the inner and outer conditions of our life, now reduced to almost
nothing; and we must modify them if we want to try to regain, spiritually – and only spiritually is it possible – a place, a dignity and a significance among the peoples of the world.

[ALFRED WEBER, from *Farewell to European History*]

*This day is the anniversary of Sarajevo in 1914. And here is a German historian
asking the pertinent questions. I read it at the beginning of the Second World
War. Do we ever learn?*

29th June

Friend that I never knew,
Ringed with a hedge of yew
  You lie:
Calm in that stately bed
Rests your life-wearied head,
  Your saddened eye . . .

For though in Time's stern list
You as protagonist
  Were forced to try
Your steel against the blind
Zeal that would shut the mind
  And close the eye.

Not thus you now appear,
Not thus I hold you dear
  And neighbourly;
But as a questing soul
That knew no finite goal,
  Whose constant sigh

Was for the life we dream
No necromancer's dream –
    Conjured to fly –
That life wherein the clod
Is sentient of God
    And lives thereby;

Where beyond mortal gains
Pure deity constrains
    To harmony,
And our discords become
In joy the perfect sum
    Of minstrelsy.

Thus, friend, your resting place
Is made a means of grace,
    And I
Know fair things yet more fair
Because your presence rare
    Is nigh.

[MAX PLOWMAN, from *On Living Near the Grave of Father Tyrrell*]

A Quaker writing about an obstreperous Jesuit!

30th June

Pile the bodies high at Austerlitz and Waterloo.
Shovel them under and let me work –
    I am the grass; I cover all.

And pile them high at Gettysburg
And pile them high at Ypres and Verdun.
Shovel them under and let me work.
Two years, ten years, and passengers ask the conductor:
    What place is this?
    Where are we now?

    I am the grass
    Let me work.

[CARL SANDBURG, *Grass*]

It is good to have this confrontation with something as humble as grass. There is the same quietness after struggle that comes with the wind on the moor at the end of Wuthering Heights. *It is an unpretentious healing of the agony, putting it to sleep.*

JULY

1st July

O lyric Love, half-angel and half-bird
And all a wonder and a wild desire, –
Boldest of hearts that ever braved the sun,
Took sanctuary within the holier blue.
And sang a kindred soul out to his face, –
Yet human at the red-ripe of the heart –
When the first summons from the darkling earth
Reached thee amid thy chambers, blanched their blue,
And bared them of the glory – to drop down,
To toil for man, to suffer or to die, –
This is the same voice: can thy soul know change?
Hail then, and hearken from the realms of help!
Never may I commence my song, my due
To God who best taught song by gift of thee,
Except with bent head and beseeching hand –
That still, despite the distance and the dark,
What was, again may be; some interchange
Of grace, some splendour once thy very thought,
Some benediction anciently thy smile:
– Never conclude, but raising hand and head
Thither where eyes, that cannot reach, yet yearn
For all hope, all sustainment, all reward,
Their utmost up and on, – so blessing back
In those thy realms of help, that heaven thy home,
Some whiteness which, I judge, thy face makes proud,
Some wanness where, I think, thy foot may fall!

[ROBERT BROWNING, from *The Ring and the Book*]

Browning's long-winded yet inspired poem. This extract is the invocation at the beginning. He is trying to express the heart of the romantic. Into the squalor and violence of human relationships there come courageous acts which illuminate the

145

redemption of the world, step by step. The poem expresses this lyrically. It can only be sung.

2nd July

O to break loose, like the chinook
salmon jumping and falling back,
nosing up to the impossible
stone and bone-crushing waterfall –
raw-jawed, weak-fleshed there, stopped by ten
steps of the roaring ladder, and then
to clear the top on the last try,
alive enough to spawn and die . . .

When will we see Him face to face?
Each day, He shines through darker glass –
In this small town where everything
is known, I see His vanishing
emblems, His white spire and flag-
pole sticking out above the fog,
like old white china doorknobs, sad,
slight, useless things to calm the mad. . . .

O to break loose. All life's grandeur
is something with a girl in summer . . .
elated as the President
girdled by his establishment
this Sunday morning, free to chaff
his own thoughts with his bear-cuffed staff,
swimming nude, unbuttoned, sick
of his ghost-written rhetoric.

No weekends for the gods now. Wars
flicker, earth licks its open sores,
fresh breakages, fresh promotions, chance
assassinations, no advance.
Only man thinning out his kind
Sounds through the Sabbath noon, the blind
Swipe of the pruner and his knife
busy about the tree of life. . . .

Pity the planet, all joy gone
from the sweet volcanic cones;

peace to our children when they fall
in small war on the heels of small
war – until the end of time
to police the earth, a ghost
orbiting for ever lost
in our monotonous sublime.

[ROBERT LOWELL, from *Waking Early Sunday Morning*]

This is America at its most vigorously impulsive, this hungering shout for emancipation. How do we break loose? (We have to want to.)

3rd July

The unpurged images of day recede;
The Emperor's drunken soldiery are abed;
Night resonance recedes, night-walkers' song
After the great cathedral gong;
A starlit or a moonlit dome disdains
All that man is,
All mere complexities,
The fury and the mire of human veins.

Before me floats an image, man or shade,
Shade more than man, more image than a shade;
For Hades' bobbin bound in mummy-cloth
May unwind the winding path;
A mouth that has no moisture and no breath
Breathless mouths may summon;
I hail the superhuman;
I call it death-in-life and life-in-death.

Miracle, bird or golden handiwork,
More miracle than bird or handiwork,
Planted on the star-lit golden bough,
Can like the cocks of Hades crow,
Or, by the moon embittered, scorn aloud
In glory of changeless metal
Common bird or petal
And all complexities of mire and blood.

At midnight on the Emperor's pavement flit
Flames that no faggot feeds, nor steel has lit,

Nor storm disturbs, flames begotten of flame,
Where blood-begotten spirits come
And all complexities of fury leave,
Dying into a dance.
An agony of trance,
An agony of flame that cannot singe a sleeve.

Astraddle on the dolphin's mire and blood.
Spirit after spirit! The smithies break the flood.
The golden smithies of the Emperor!
Marbles of the dancing floor
Break bitter furies of complexity,
Those images that yet
Fresh images beget,
That dolphin-torn, that gong-tormented sea.

[W. B. YEATS, *Byzantium*]

A jump back from yesterday's twentieth-century America! Yeats is a great but mystifying poet. He had a curious glimpse of our humanity, that we are but one step short of the majestic and glorious. He knew that craftsmen in wood and stone and metal also give hints of this glory. But it feels too timeless for me. Granted that you cannot push this side of life aside, does it really get involved in history and time and the material?

4th July

She was a little startled by seeing the Cheshire Cat sitting on a bough of a tree a few yards off. The Cat only grinned when it saw Alice. It looked good-natured, she thought; still it had very long claws and a great many teeth, so she felt that it ought to be treated with respect.

"Cheshire-Puss," she began, rather timidly, as she did not know whether it would like the name: however, it only grinned a little wider. "Come, it's pleased so far," thought Alice, and she went on. "Would you tell me, please, which way I ought to go from here?"

"That depends a good deal on where you want to get to," said the Cat.

"I don't much care where –" said Alice.

"Then it doesn't matter which way you go," said the Cat.

"– so long as I get *somewhere*," Alice added as an explanation.

"Oh, you're sure to do that," said the Cat, "If you only walk long enough."

Alice felt that this could not be denied, so she tried another question. "What sort of people live about here?"

"In that direction," the Cat said, waving its right paw round, "lives a Hatter: and in that direction," waving the other paw, "lives a March Hare. Visit either you like; they're both mad."

[LEWIS CARROLL, from *Alice in Wonderland*]

Lewis Carroll is one of the greatest commentators on nineteenth-century England. He was one of the Surrealists fifty years before their time. We are like this! And I was brought up on Lewis Carroll. I remember reciting him to my great-aunts at the age of seven.

5th July

Look, stranger, at this island now
The leap light for your delight discovers,
Stand stable here
And silent be,
That through the channels of the ear
May wander like a river
The swaying sound of the sea.

Here at the small field's ending pause
Where the chalk wall falls to the foam, and its tall ledges
Oppose the pluck
And knock of the tide,
And the shingle scrambles after the suck-
ing surf, and the gull lodges
A moment on its sheer side.

Far off like floating seeds the ships
Diverge on urgent voluntary errands;
And the full view
Indeed may enter
And move in memory as now these clouds do,
That pass the harbour mirror
And all the summer through the water saunter.

[W. H. AUDEN, *Look Stranger*]

One of Auden's early poems. He asks us to look at what has happened to us, and to listen to the sound of the sea. There is something to be heard. We have moved on from Arnold's Dover Beach, *and are bidden not to be oppressed by what has gone. We are simply to listen and look, that 'the full view indeed may enter and move . . .' (A few were trying to do this in the twenties and thirties, disturbed by the breaking down of European culture through the First World War and wanting to create a new order. So did Fascism want to restore an imperium. There were enough around who believed it could be done.)*

6th July

Come down from heaven to meet me when my breath
Chokes, and through drumming shafts of stifling death
I stumble toward escape, to find the door
Opening on morn, where I may breathe once more
Clear cock-crow airs across some valley dim
With whispering trees. While dawn along the rim
Of night's horizon flows in lakes of fire,
Come down from heaven's bright hill, my song's desire.

Belov'd and faithful, teach my soul to wake
In glades deep-ranked with flowers that gleam and shake
And flock your paths with wonder. In your gaze
Show me the vanquished vigil of my days.
Mute in that golden silence hung with green,
Come down from heaven and bring me in your eyes
Remembrance of all beauty that has been,
And stillness from the pools of Paradise.

[SIEGFRIED SASSOON, *Invocation*]

A sheer good lyric, and so much stronger than the Georgian poets – presumably because of the First World War. Binyon and Bridges are prissy by comparison.

7th July

. . . art is in the last resort a social activity, and no great work of art was ever produced in a social vacuum . . . and the crucial moment in the development of any artist, great or small, is the moment at which the private world of the studio must be adjusted to the world outside . . . No artist who is any good can stand aside from the attitudes of his time, any more than by an effort of will he can reject the vocabulary of form which is current at that time . . .

. . . 'Alerted' was his adjective for the state of mind of the Time-Life figure, and a generalized vigilance, an anxiety just held in check, is the note of many of the pre-war Reclining Figures.

The birth of the feminine archetype in modern man signifies (Neumann) at the same time the development of human relatedness, of his social capacity, and the growing consciousness of the unity of mankind on earth.

What they stand for, fundamentally, is the ability of the human body to survive and dominate, no matter how catastrophic its surroundings . . . Never are they merely inert – they must be toured, not quizzed, lived in, not visited, read from end to end and not encapsulated. They suggest that there is, after all, an alternative to pettiness and self-destruction . . . it is by his readiness to let the demons loose that we recognize this Moore: less metaphorically, we realize that in the mid 1930s, long before the imagery of the 'divided self' was formulated by R. D. Laing, Moore was probing the extent to which an individual personality could be divided, and split off, and set against itself, and yet retain its identity.

[JOHN RUSSELL, from *Henry Moore*]

John Russell is a perceptive critic of art. He says what you are not expecting. And Moore brings the feminine into the centre of attention, resisting the force of death – in contrast to Epstein who is vigorous but much more aligned with the Jewish tradition. With Moore there is so much movement, yet none of the prettiness of the Renaissance. Here is the feminine that can outlast the madness of the masculine-dominated world.

8th July

"You see, Nancy," he said, "I reverse your whole process. I believe that Duck Caldwell – like you or me or any of us – is wholly responsible for his acts. Wholly, and for eternity, for everlasting. That is what gives him value in my eyes – his eternal everlasting responsibility. His very act to me involves the whole universe. And when it breaks the moral law of the whole universe, I consider that his punishment might be infinite, everlasting. And yet in my system there is one thing that yours lacks. In my system, although there is never-ending responsibility, there is such a thing as mercy."

Maxim was not finished with what he had to say, but he paused here for a moment to let the word have its full weight. He went on. "Duck

can be forgiven. I can personally forgive him because I believe God can
forgive him. You see, I think his will is a bad one, but not much worse,
not different in kind, from other wills. And you and I stand opposed.
For you – no responsibility for the individual, but no forgiveness. For
me – ultimate, absolute responsibility for the individual, but mercy.
Absolute responsibility: it is the only way that men can keep their value,
can be thought of as other than mere things. Those matters that Arthur
speaks of – social causes, environment, education – do you think they
really make a difference between one human soul and another? In the
eyes of God are such differences of any meaning at all? Can you suppose
that they condition His mercy? Does He hold a Doctor of Philosophy
more responsible than a Master of Arts, or a high-school graduate more
responsible than a man who has not finished the eighth grade? Or is His
mercy less to one than another?"

   None of them had ever heard language like this, although they may
have read it, and they did not know how to respond . . .

[LIONEL TRILLING, from *The Middle of the Journey*]

In the story Maxim had left the Communist Party in America and feared for his
life. Here he is talking to American liberals who are unable to understand him.

9th July

. . . in the Fens, on a pumping-station between Pymore and Suspension-
Bridge the following remarkable inscription is to be found, written in
black letters on a white board in a style suggesting a date such as 1812:

> These Fens have oft-times been by Water drown'd;
>   Science a Remedy in Water found;
> The Power of Steam, she said, shall be employ'd
>   And the destroyer be itself destroy'd.

Pondering the reason for the strange charm of these rustic lines, far in
the wilderness, with nothing in view but flat fields of black earth and a
geometrically straight canal, it occurred to me that it echoes one of the
favourite paradoxes of the great Latin hymns. The 'Vexilla Regis' for
example –

> On whose dear arms, so widely flung
> The Price of this world's ransom hung.
> The Price which He alone could pay,
> And spoil the Spoiler of his prey . . .

However sophisticated we become, the resurrection remains the symbol of the triumphant rise of humanity from the dark night of animality into the bright day of the heavenly city. And the cost of it is that voluntary sacrifice of that innumerable company of beings at all stages of social evolution who have given themselves for others in the assurance of a hope that they only dimly understand. Of this sacrifice the Cross is the ever-enduring symbol. And the compassionate Kwen-Lin also turns back on the very threshold of Paradise, unable to leave the world of suffering while her ears are still assailed by so many little cries. Long may it be before we cease to appreciate the beauty of old words recording these things, such as the runes on the Ruthwell Cross, where the tree itself is speaking:

> Then the young hero, who was mightiest God,
>   Strong and with steadfast mind,
> Up to the Cross with steps unfaltering trod
>   There to redeem mankind.
> I trembled but I durst not fail.
>   I on my shoulders bore the glorious King.
> They pierce my sides with many a darksome nail
>   And on us both their cruel curses fling.

[JOSEPH NEEDHAM, from *Cambridge Summer*]

Needham is a biologist who went on to study China and the history of science and civilisation there. He is also steeped in Cambridge and the Fens and English Catholicism. He came to Darnall once and talked to the parish meeting. During his visit he was reading the proofs of the first volume of his history. Not long ago six Chinese journalists came to Gosforth and on the mention of Needham's name, they rose and bowed, and one of them said, "He is the greatest Englishman."

10th July

> One by one they appear in
> the darkness: a few friends, and
> a few with historical
> names. How late they start to shine!
> but before they fade they stand
> perfectly embodied, all

the past lapping them like a
cloak of chaos. They were men
who, I thought, lived only to
renew the wasteful force they
spent with each hot convulsion.
They remind me, distant now.

True, they are not at rest yet,
but now that they are indeed
apart, winnowed from failures,
they withdraw to an orbit
and turn with disinterested
hard energy, like the stars.

[THOM GUNN, *My Sad Captains*]

What we want from historical writing is something it rarely gives: a revelation of what humanity at any one time can become sensitive to and capable of expressing. Thom Gunn uses a phrase from Antony and Cleopatra *for the title of this poem. Antony's captains are bound up with him in the tragedy, even if they withdraw. But our failures do not matter if, in our recall of one another from a distance, we sense how mutually indebted we are across time and space.*

11th July

They told me I had three months to live,
So I crept to Bernadotee,
And sat by the mill for hours and hours
Where the gathered waters deeply moving
Seemed not to move:
O world, that's you!
You are but a widened place in the river
Where Life looks down and we rejoice for her
Mirrored in us, and so we dream
And turn away, but when again
We look for the face, behold the low-lands
And blasted cotton-wood trees where we empty
Into a larger stream!
But here by the mill the castled clouds
Mocked themselves in the dizzy water:
And over its agate floor at night

The flame of the moon ran under my eyes
Amid a forest stillness broken
By a flute in a hut on the hill.
At last when I came to lie in bed
Weak and in pain, with the dreams about me,
The soul of the river had entered my soul.
And the gathered power of my soul was moving
So swiftly it seemed to be at rest
Under the cities of cloud and under
Spheres of silver and changing worlds –
Until I saw a flash of trumpets
Above the battlements over Time!

[EDGAR LEE MASTERS, *Isaiah Beethoven*]

A prickly Southerner who loathed Abraham Lincoln and claimed that even in defeat there was something in the South that should not be lost as it was part of the American inheritance. This is one of a sequence of poems in each of which he speaks as a particular character. Unusual in American poetry he strikes this lyrical note – though the image of the river is common enough.

12th July

"But you can tell him, Leo, tell him everything, just as it was. Tell him it was nothing to be ashamed of, and that I'm nothing to be ashamed of, his old grandmother whom people came miles to see. There was nothing mean and sordid in it, was there? and nothing that could possibly hurt anyone. We did have sorrows, bitter sorrows, Hugh dying, Marcus and Denys killed, my son Hugh killed, and his wife – though she was no great loss. But they weren't our fault – they were the fault of this hideous century we live in, which has denatured humanity and planted death and hate where love and living were. Tell him this, Leo, make him see and feel it, it will be the best day's work you ever did. Remember how you loved taking our messages, bringing us together and making us happy – well, this is another errand of love, and the last time I shall ever ask you to be our postman. Why does he think I stay on here, except to be near him? And yet he has this grudge against me, he won't come near me if he can help it, though shoals of people come that I don't want to see. Sometimes I think he would rather I didn't live here, but I won't believe it. And make him get out of his head this ridiculous idea that he can't marry: it's that that wounds me most . . . but every man should get married – you ought to have married, Leo, you're all dried up inside, I can tell that. It isn't too late; you might marry still: why don't you? Don't you feel any need of love? But Edward – (only don't call him that) he must; he's young – he's the same age Ted was when you came to Brandham. He has all his life before him. Tell him he must get rid of these silly scruples – his grandfather would have had them, if I'd let him. Poor Ted, if he'd had more brains, he wouldn't have blown them out. You owe it to us, Leo, you owe it to us; and it'll be good for you too. Tell him there's no spell or curse except an unloving heart. You know that, don't you? Tell him to think kindly of his old grandmother, who only lives to love him."

[L. P. HARTLEY, from *The Go-Between*]

The speaker, Marion, had used Leo as a small boy to carry messages to the lover she could not marry. At this, the novel's close, she asks him again to be a go-between, to explain to her grandson Edward the events of the affair – he had known of it and begrudged her it.

13th July

Do you remember that hour
In a nook of the flowering uplands
When you found for me, at the cornfield's edge,
A golden and purple flower?
Heartsease, you said. I thought it might be
A token that love meant well by you and me.

I shall not find it again
With you no more to guide me.
I could not bear to find it now
With anyone else beside me.
And the heartsease is far less rare
Than what it is named for, what I can feel nowhere.

Once again it is summer;
Wildflowers beflag the lane
That takes me away from our golden uplands,
Heart-wrung and alone.
The best I can look for, by vale of hill,
A herb they tell me is common enough – self-heal.

[CECIL DAY-LEWIS, *The Heartsease*]

Cecil Day-Lewis's father was a grim parson in Derbyshire. His mother died when he was young. An aunt came from Ireland to be housekeeper but was forced to return when his father married again. He looked turbulently in his later life for the kind of loving he had only glimpsed. He was conscious of making a mess of adult relationships, losing as much as he ever found. In his poetry he has a delicate and sensitive touch, and is more vulnerable than Auden and others of his generation.

14th July

The English Bible, again, with its archaic homeliness and majesty, sets the mind brooding, not less than the old ballad most redolent of the native past and the native imagination; it fills the memory with solemn and pungent phrases; and this incidental spirit of poetry in which it comes to be clothed is a self-revelation perhaps more pertinent and welcome to the people than the alien revelations it professes to transmit. English law and parliaments, too, would be very unjustly judged if judged as practical contrivances only; they satisfy at the same time the moral interest people have in uttering and enforcing their feelings. These institutions are ceremonious, almost sacramental; they are instinct with a dramatic spirit deeper and more vital than their utility. Englishmen and Americans love debate; they love sitting round a table as if in consultation, even when the chairman has pulled the wires and settled everything beforehand, and when each of the participants listens only to his own remarks and votes according to his party . . . Without the English spirit, without the faculty of making themselves believe in public what they never feel in private, without the habit of clubbing together and facing facts, and feeling duty in a cautious, consultative, experimental way, English liberties forfeit their practical value; as we see when they are extended to a volatile histrionic people like the Irish, or when a jury in France, instead of pronouncing simply on matters of fact and the credibility of witnesses, rushes in the heat of its patriotism to carry out, by its verdict, some political policy.

The practice of English liberty presupposes two things: that all concerned are fundamentally unanimous, and that each has a plastic nature, which he is willing to modify.

[GEORGE SANTAYANA, from *English Liberty in America*]

The Authorised Version of the Bible still moves me more than any other. Why did the translators use what was somewhat archaic English? Did the commit-

tee act in the way Santayana describes? This readiness to be old-fashioned but
not hostile to those who are not is actually richer than compromise. The true
meaning of tradition is not to be locked in to what we have inherited and to be
unable to see outside it. Nor is it to repel the new. But it is to evaluate what is
new from the richness of the past. Adjustments and re-fashioning (as in
English architecture) do not destroy our sense of continuity – though it needs
great imagination to know what to conserve.

15th July

A fool there was and he made his prayer
  (Even as you and I!)
To a rag and a bone and a hank of hair
(We called her the woman who did not care)
But the fool called her his lady fair –
  (Even as you and I!)

Oh, the years we waste and the tears we waste
And the work of our head and hand
Belong to the woman who did not know
(And now we know she could never know)
  And did not understand!

A fool there was and his goods he spent
  (Even as you and I!)
Honour and faith and a sure intent
(And it wasn't the least what the lady meant)
But a fool must follow his natural bent
  (Even as you and I!)

Oh, the toil we lost and the spoil we lost
And the excellent things we planned
Belong to the woman who didn't know why
(And now we know that she never knew why)
  And did not understand!

The fool was stripped to his foolish hide
  (Even as you and I!)
Which she might have seen when she threw him aside –
(But it isn't on record the lady tried)
So some of him lived but most of him died –
  (Even as you and I!)

And it isn't the shame and it isn't the blame
That stings like a white hot brand –
It's coming to know that she never knew why
(Seeing, at last, she could never know why)
    And never could understand!

[RUDYARD KIPLING, *The Vampire*]

This is Kipling at his most impish! A failure to understand produces the
tragedy. And it isn't either men or women who are to blame – each has a share.

16th July

Meanwhile the mind from pleasure less
Withdraws into its happiness;
The mind, that ocean where each kind
Does straight its own resemblance find;
Yet it creates, transcending these,
Far other worlds, and other seas;
Annihilating all that's made
To a green thought in a green shade.

Here at the fountain's sliding foot,
Or at some fruit-tree's mossy root,
Casting the body's vest aside,
My soul into the boughs does glide;
There like a bird, it sits and sings,
Then whets and combs its silver wings,
And, till prepared for longer flight,
Waves in its plumes the various light.

Such was that happy Garden-state
While man there walked without a mate:
After a place so pure and sweet,
What other help could yet be meet!
But 'twas beyond a mortal's share
To wander solitary there:
Two Paradises 'twere in one,
To live in Paradise alone.

How well the skilful gardener drew
Of flowers and herbs this dial new!
Where from above, the milder sun

Does through a fragrant zodiac run:
And, as it works, th'industrious bee
Computes its time as well as we.
How could such sweet and wholesome hours
Be reckon'd, but with herbs and flowers!

[ANDREW MARVELL, from *The Garden*]

Marvell has some lines one always wants to remember. Sometimes the poetry is artificial, typically late seventeenth-century, but it is dignified and it has a graciousness that Dryden and Pope lacked.

17th July

I will be quiet and talk with you,
    And reason why you are wrong,
You wanted my love – is that much true?
And so I did love, so I do:
    What has come of it all along?

I took you – how could I otherwise?
    For a world to me, and more;
For all, love greatens and glorifies
Till God's a-glow, to the loving eyes
    In what was mere earth before.

Yes, earth – yes, mere ignoble earth!
    Now do I mis-state, mistake?
Do I wrong your weakness and call it worth?
Expect all harvest, dread no dearth,
    Seal my sense up for your sake?

Oh, Love, Love, no, Love, not so, indeed!
    You were just weak earth, I knew:
With much in you waste, with many a weed,
And plenty of passions, run to seed,
    But a little good grain too.

And such as you were, I took you for mine:
    Did you not find me yours,
To watch the olive and wait the vine,
And wonder when rivers of oil and wine
    Would flow, as the Book assures?

> Well, and if none of these good things came,
>   What did the failure prove?
> The man was my whole world, all the same,
> With his flowers to praise or his weeds to blame,
>   And, either or both, to love . . .

[ROBERT BROWNING, from *James Lee's Wife: IV. Along the Beach*]

Our wedding day. And this is the best expression I know of what a husband and wife can say to each other.

18th July

If it had not been for these things, I might have lived out my life, talking at street corners to scorning men. I might have died, unmarked, unknown, a failure. Now we are not a failure. This is our career and our triumph. Never in our full life can we hope to do such work for tolerance, for justice, for man's understanding of man, as now we do by an accident. Our words – our lives – our pains – nothing. The taking of our lives – lives of a good shoemaker and a poor fish peddler – all! That last moment belongs to us – that agony is our triumph.

[VANZETTI, *Speech before Execution*]

Two Italian Americans, Vanzetti and Sacco were members of the Communist Party who were executed for being traitors, though they did little more than express their opinions. The incident belongs to my younger days when I was involved in sending a telegram to Roosevelt in an attempt to stop the executions. This speech is an example of how the least educated can become truly lyrical.

19th July

He was wide awake and was seized by the word. It is a biblical happening in a modern setting: "The prophet that hath a dream, let him tell a dream; and he that hath my word, let him speak my word faithfully . . . For ye have perverted the words of the living God." (Jeremiah 23.28,36) The word for Karl Kraus was an event, as concrete as the word that "the Lord sent unto Jacob, and it hath lighted upon Israel." (Isaiah 9.8)

(His work) is rich in words. And every single word is of the greatest possible precision. It is precise through its infinite ambiguity . . . All thoughts are in the world before they are thought. They are dispersed

among the elements of language. The artist gathers them together and
welds them into his thought. He once said, "Language is the divining-rod
which discovers the wells of thought." Thus language, for him, is a
means not so much of communicating what he knows, but of finding out
what he does not yet know. Words are living organisms, not labels
stuck on objects. They are at home in a cosmos of the spirit, not in a
chance assembly of 'atoms of perception' . . . The greater the number of
associations into which the word enters, the greater its value in a piece
of writing.

(His polemical talent) Behind every dwarf that Karl Kraus attacked
there loomed the shadow of a giant . . . Into his language he had gathered
the storm at a time when his age was busy with sowing the wind . . . It
was Austrian in its idiom – "a people, in whom faith had always had
preponderance over the intellect, enthusiastically embraced political
ideologies which offered a substitute for evaporating convictions of
religion." We have not yet grasped the demonic possibilities of mediocrity . . . It was Karl Kraus who discovered to what satanic heights in-
feriority may rise. He anticipated Hitler long before anyone knew his
name.

[ERIC HELLER, from Karl Kraus: The Disinherited Mind]

*Heller regards Kraus as having the most sensitive mind in Vienna in the
twenties. He was saying these things when the then unknown Hitler was
wandering the streets of that city.*

20th July

A Book of Verse underneath the Bough,
A Jug of Wine, a Loaf of Bread, and thou
   Beside me singing in the Wilderness –
Oh, Wilderness were Paradise enow!

Some for the Glories of this World, and some
Sigh for the Prophet's Paradise to come –
   Ah take the Cash and let the Credit go
Nor heed the rumble of a distant Drum!

Look to the blowing Rose about us. "Lo,
Laughing," she says, "into the world I blow,
   At once the silken tassel of my Purse
Tear, and its Treasure on the Garden throw."

The Worldly Hope men set their Hearts upon
Turns Ashes, or it prospers; and anon,
  Like Snow upon the Desert's dusty face
Lighting a little hour or two is gone.

Think, in this batter'd Caravanserai
Whose Portals are alternate Night and Day,
  How Sultan after Sultan with his Pomp
Abode his destined Hour, and went his way . . .

Ah, my Beloved, fill the Cup that clears
Today of past Regrets and future fears:
  Tomorrow? – Why, Tomorrow I may be
Myself with Yesterday's Sev'n thousand Years.

For some we loved, the loveliest and the best
That from his Vintage rolling Time hath prest,
  Have drunk their Cup a Round or two before,
And one by one crept silently to rest . . .

[EDWARD FITZGERALD, from *The Rubdiydt of Omar Khayam*]

*It is extraordinary the effect this poem had on the English in the grime of the
industrial cities. Like Islamic art, it is beautiful decoration. It reverberates in
your mind, but you don't absorb it. It has been abstracted from life. Nevertheless there is something about it that is moving. There is a great history, there is
sadness, there is the fleeting now to notice. And there is an evasiveness that
appeals when reality is too harsh. The mood may be one of wistful regret, but
there is no point in asking for more.*

21st July

. . . I think I can truly say that I do believe and have always believed,
even in my most anti-Catholic moments, in the possibility of a spiritual
life and that a spiritual life must involve a certain method and discipline.
Reading St. Francis de Sales, I feel what I'm afraid I don't feel about all
the saints: "Here is a truly spiritual man, towards whom I feel humble
and loving and who has not only vision but a kind of divine common
sense and I will take more from him on faith than I can take from
the brilliant dialecticians and theologians who browbeat my feeble
reasoning faculties."
    Because I am interested in 'metaphysics' it does not follow that I have
a head for them or can move easily or confidently amongst abstractions.

All that I feel I can grope after and occasionally grasp is something which appears to me true and revealing and which I find now here, now there, in my own experience, in works of art, in things said by spiritual teachers and sometimes by philosophers. I have never stopped loving the Gospels, even when I have doubted the Catholic interpretation of them and even if I don't stay in the Church, I don't think I can ever lose my reverence for them . . .

"Let me not be afraid of going in to myself or going out of myself. Let me be content to be anonymous, despised, intermittent. Let me not be puffed up by my suffering or ashamed to be happy. Give me grace to wait, always to wait, to expect nothing and to be ready at any moment to part with all I have. Take away from me the desire to be loved and admired and give me instead the power to love without desiring to possess. Give me eyes to see with, remembering always that the eye sees nothing but what the light that falls on it permits it to see."

Well, I can't live up to that, as you know. But it is still what I want. And when I want it enough, it will be answered . . .

[Antonia White, from *The Hound and the Falcon*]

Her father was a convert to Rome and sent her to a convent school where she was mercilessly treated. Her novel about her childhood is called Frost in May. *She resisted the attempt to impose a framework on her. She was rebellious and refused to be crushed.*

22nd July

When in the chronicle of wasted time
I see descriptions of the fairest wights,
And beauty making beautiful old rime,
In praise of ladies dead and lovely knights,
Then, in the blazon of sweet beauty's best,
Of hand, of foot, of lip, of eye, of brow,
I see their antique pen would have express'd
Even such beauty as you master now,
So all their praises are but prophecies
Of this our time, all you prefiguring;
And, for they look'd but with divining eyes,
They had not skill enough your worth to sing:
　　For we, which now behold these present days,
　　Have eyes to wonder, but lack tongues to praise.

[William Shakespeare, *Sonnet CVI*]

From the group of sonnets in which Shakespeare uses his memories as the back-
ground to his straightforward awareness and appreciation of the worth of this
man he contemplated. In summoning my memories I enhance the way in which I
see a person now.

23rd July

Kafka knew Kierkegaard's warning: "An individual cannot assist or save
a time, he can only express that it is lost." He saw the coming of the age
of the inhuman and drew its intolerable visage. But temptation of
silence, the belief that in the presence of certain realities art is trivial or
impertinent, was near at hand. The world of Auschwitz lies outside
speech as it lies outside reason. To speak of the unspeakable is to risk the
survivance of language as creator and bearer of humane, rational truth.
Words that are saturated with lies or atrocity do not easily resume life.
The apprehension was not Kafka's alone. The fear of the erosion of the
Logos, of the gain of letter on spirit, is strong in Hofmannsthal's *Letter of
Lord Chandos* and the polemics of Karl Kraus. Wittgenstein's *Tractatus*
and Broch's *The Death of Virgil* (which may, in part, be read as a gloss on
Kafka's dilemma) are pervaded by the authority of silence.

In Kafka the question of silence is posed most radically. It is this which
gives him his exemplary place in modern literature. Should the poet
cease? In a time when men are made to pipe and squeak their sufferings
like beetles and mice, is literate speech, of all things the most human,
still possible? Kafka knew that in the beginning was the Word; he asks
us: What of the end?

[GEORGE STEINER, from *Language and Silence*]

Kafka is so baffling, yet he saw clearly what lies outside our capacity to explain.
The Castle *portrays a man who believes he has a job but never makes contact
with it; in* The Trial *a man is accused, but he never knows of what; in* The
Metamorphosis *a man wakes up changed into a beetle.*

24th July

i thank you God for most this amazing
day: for the leaping greenly spirits of trees
and a blue dream of sky; and for everything
which is natural which is infinite which is yes.

(i who have died am alive again today,
and this is the sun's birthday; this is the birth
day of life and of love and wings: and of the gay
great happenings illimitably earth)

how should tasting touching hearing seeing
breathing any – lifted from the no
of all nothing – human merely being
doubt unimaginable You?

(now the ears of my ears awake and
now the eyes of my eyes are opened)

[e. e. cumming, *Poems*]

Such an enjoyable prayer to use!

25th July

"Where is the life that late I led?"
[2 HENRY IV, 5.3]

They come not now that came before –
    Evening of spring and blossom white,
The footstep hushed, the whispering door,
    The thin form glimmering into sight,
The moon half-seen in clouded night,
    One star, and wind, and passing rain,
The smell of lilac in the lane;
    Where is the foot, the lovely head,
My moon that never was to wane?
    Where is the life that late I led?

Tossed by the sea from shore to shore,
    Wheeled to the battle's left and right;
In wreck of storm, in wreck of war,
    In tides that clashed, and clashing fight,
When the deep guns out-boomed the might
    Of the deep-booming hurricane,
And like the shriek of ropes astrain,
    The wind wailed with the death that sped
Sheer through the battery's galloping train –
    Where is the life that late I led?

They come not now, they come no more
   The thoughts that sprang with daily light,
As gems upon an enchanted floor,
   Matching the sun in promise bright;
Even sorrow, too, has taken flight –
   Sorrow and consecrating pain –
And rage comes never here again,
   Pleasure and grief alike are dead;
What fear can more? What hopes remain?
   Where is the life that late I led?

                    Envoi

So should a man recall in vain
   The dreams of a scarce-wakened brain
Forgotten e'er the sleep is fled
   And buried down in Time's inane,
Where is the life that late I led?

            [H. W. NEVINSON, *A Ballade of Time*]

This leaves you to answer the question which Henry IV *poses, What does it all add up to?*

26th July

Thackeray's sense of well-being depended, however, not so much on his ability to work, his health, or his faith, as on his sense of loving and being loved. "People say that I have no heart," he remarked to Langley. "Now I think myself a very soft person." And he liked to quote Lord Ashburton's judgment that he was "as tender as a woman but as cruel as Robespierre." Indeed, his anger, as the shrewd French critic saw, was at bottom, simply "La réaction d'une nature tendre, furieux d'avoir été désappointé." The tale of disappointments was a long one. Thackeray never let the fourteenth of March pass without remembering the death of little Jane Thackeray a few months after her birth. "I have had a child in (the world beyond) for twenty years now," he wrote in 1891, "and love her still." Though he kept away from Isabella, "because I think it is best not to see her," and though he once said to a friend, heartbroken at the death of his wife, "Dear fellow . . . a dead sorrow is better than a living one," he made sure that she was excellently looked after, and the memory of their happy years together remained green in his mind. He wrote not long before he died: "Yesterday, in the street, I saw a pair of eyes so like two which used to brighten at my coming once, that the whole past came back as I walked lonely, in the rush of the Strand, and I was young again in the midst of joys and sorrows, alike sweet and sad, alike sacred and fondly remembered." . . .

All these memories contributed to the "bankruptcy of his heart" which was so fundamental a feature of Thackeray's character in later life and intensified "the deep steady melancholy of his nature". He was constantly "snarling away in the old 'poco curante' theme", "To stay is well enough," he felt, but he would not "be very sorry to go". His carriage was headed downhill, he told his old schoolfellow Boyes, "after having had some pleasant travelling, after being well-nigh upset, after being patched up again, after being robbed by footpads etc, etc. I couldn't care to travel over the ground again: though I have had some pleasant days and dear companions." Yet, though he continued to feel that "a man without a woman is a lonely wretch," and computed that he was not happy "above four days in a month", he had many consolations . . .

[GORDON N. RAY, from *Thackeray: The Age of Wisdom*]

Though most people would have regarded him as the diner-out of the century, Thackeray was a person greatly hurt by life yet undefeated. He retained something of the kindness he had been shown, especially by women.

27th July

I understand you well enough, John Donne.
First, that you were a man of ability
Eaten by lust and by the love of God,
Then, that you crossed the Sevenoaks High Street
As rector of Saint Nicholas:
I am of that parish.

To be a man of ability is not much.
You may see them on the Sevenoaks platform any day,
Eager men with despatch cases
Whom ambition drives as they drive the machine,
Whom the certainty of meticulous operation
Pleasures as a morbid sex a heart of stone . . .

You brought body and soul to this church
Walking there through the park alive with deer,
But now what animal has climbed into your pulpit?
One whose pretension is that the fear
Of God has heated him into a spirit,
An evaporated man no physical ill can hurt.

Well might you hesitate at the Latin gate
Seeing such apes denying the church of God:
I am grateful particularly that you were not a saint
But extravagant whether in bed or in your shroud.
You would understand that in the presence of folly
I am not sanctified but angry.

Come down and speak to the men of ability
On the Sevenoaks platform and tell them
That at your Saint Nicholas the faith
Is not exclusive in the fools it chooses,
That the vain, the ambitious and the highly sexed
Are the natural prey of the incarnate Christ.

[C. H. SISSON, from *A letter to John Donne*]

What is a poet who is also a Christian to say at the present time about the flesh? Certainly no other Anglican poet has got anywhere near the fleshliness of Donne – and in English poetry Lawrence is the next! Though Eliot went back to the seventeenth century, that was to Andrewes. Among the occasional attempts today, this is one – odd but more printable than most. There isn't much here, except that Donne is needed, that sex is significant, and that there is compassion in the verse. Since the sound barrier was breached by Lady Chatterley's Lover, *Christianity has to take Donne and Lawrence on board, and go further into what we have avoided. (On 27 July 1617 Donne preached at the parish church at Sevenoaks, of which he was Rector, and was entertained at Knole, then the country residence of Richard Sackville, Third Earl of Dorset.)*

28th July

The cliff was sheer, rising at an angle, I would say, of more than eighty degrees: I have a distinct impression that in some places in Wind-Box Gorge parts of the mighty precipice actually overhang the river. Where it began, the path was about thirty feet above the surface of the water, so that from the deck of the junk we looked up at it, more than half the

height of our mast. Su-ling told me that in winter, at low water, at what
the river men call 'zero', the path would be more than sixty feet above
the surface, while late in the spring, perhaps a month after we were
there, it would be nearly as much, or more, under the surface . . .

What giddied me then, and still does now, about this awful path was
not just its hazardous appearance. I was most intensely disturbed by the
sense it gave me of the gap between the Chinese on the junk and myself
. . . To begin with the path was more than a thousand years old, so
Su-ling said: T'ang dynasty, she said, and perhaps earlier. Chinese river-
men had been satisfied for a millenium – for more than five times the
whole of my native country – to use this awful way of getting through
Wind-Box Gorge. How could I, in the momentary years of my youth,
have a part in persuading these people to tolerate the building of a great
modern dam that would take the waters of Tibet and inner China, with
their age-old furies on its back, there to grow lax and benign? How
could I span a gap of a thousand years . . . in a day?

There was something else about the path: I could not help feeling the
incredible patience that had gone into its making. Surely only one man
at a time could have worked there, hammering and chiselling out fragments of stone and dropping the pieces into the river below. How many
years did these miles of jeopardous corridor take to cut? What patience!
What all-enduring patience! And what a chasm between such patience
and my hasty world!

[JOHN HERSEY, from *A Single Pebble*]

*A glimpse of a world on a larger (and smaller!) scale than anything in Western
Europe. And I recall that at one stage in the Long March the army climbed a
cliff like the one described here, peg by peg, in the process losing many who
slipped.*

29th July

> Since there's no help, come let us kiss and part,
> Nay I have done, you get no more of me;
> And I am glad, yea glad with all my heart,
> That thus so cleanly I myself can free;
> Shake hands for ever, cancel all our vows,
> And when we meet at any time again
> Be it not seen in either of our brows
> That we one jot of former love retain.
> Now at the least gasp of Love's latest breath,

When, his pulse failing, Passion speechless lies,
When Faith is kneeling by his bed of death,
And Innocence is closing up his eyes:
Now if thou wouldst, when all have given him over,
From death to life thou mightest him yet recover!

[MICHAEL DRAYTON, *Sonnets to Idea: IV*]

The poem that most truly expresses what happens when you love, get across each other, are wrenched apart, and go your separate ways – and then, at the last breath, turn again.

30th July

She testifies to that first truth
The hour-glass cannot hold.
Her voice recalls the voice of Ruth
When she to Naomi told
A pledge too dear for time to break
Or Earth to render vain:
Dark is the radiance doomed to wake
This Danae to the rain.

Delicate as the foal whose hooves
Seem moving to the sky,
Clear as the questioning moon that moves
And feels the waves' reply,
Fragrant as when spring rains renew
The lilac and the lime,
Rich as the Earth which Adam knew
Before the birth of time:

In every form I see the stamp
And image of the fair,
And yet Copernicus' lamp
Was always burning there.
How could interpreters divine
The depth of eye and hand
If the lost myth that made them shine
They could not understand? . . .

[VERNON WATKINS, from *Testimony*]

I like the sound of this poem, a testimony to the bond of affection that stands the strain of whatever pressure is put upon it. 'She' is not identified, but represents those who have made the same choice and act of faith that the present 'She' is making.

31st July

Across the gap made by our English hinds,
Amid the Roman's handiwork, behold
Far off the long-roofed church; the shepherd binds
The withy round the hurdles of his fold;
Down in the foss the river fed of old,
That through long lapse of time has grown to be
The little grassy valley that you see.

Rest here awhile, not yet the eve is still,
The bees are wandering yet, and you may hear
The barley mowers on the trenched hill,
The sheep-bells, and the restless changing weir.
All little sounds made musical and clear
Beneath the sky that burning August gives,
While yet the thought of glorious Summer lives.

Ah, Love! such happy days, such days as these,
Must we still waste them, craving for the best,
Like lovers o'er the painted images
Of those who once their yearning hearts have blessed?
Have we been happy on our day of rest?
Thine eyes say 'Yes' – but if it came again,
Perchance its ending would not seem so vain.

[WILLIAM MORRIS, *The Earthly Paradise: August*]

Morris did indeed know the English countryside. It mattered to him, but he also knew that human relationships matter more. And he was also aware that his marriage was flawed. Could the craftsman in human relationships be happy with less than the best? But you make the best of it, knowing that you never have the control that you would like over the material in front of you. Do you endure? Or do you cut?

AUGUST

1st August

"One mustn't worry too much. All human solutions are temporary.
Pass your glass will you, dear boy? One has to live in one's own little
local world of religion, mostly. For nearly everyone religion is something primitive. We hardly ever get beyond the beginning any more
than we do in philosophy. If it's natural to you to cry out 'Christ help
me!', cry it and then be quiet. You may be helped."

"But how do I know what it means, how do I know what's true?"

"That sort of truth is local too. I don't mean any relativism nonsense.
Of course there's science and history and so on. I mean that one's
ordinary tasks are usually immediate and simple and one's own truth
lives in these tasks. Not to deceive oneself, not to protect one's pride
with false ideas, never to be pretentious or bogus, always to try to be
lucid and quiet. There's a kind of pure speech of the mind which one
must try to attain. To attain it is to be in the truth, one's own truth,
which needn't mean any big apparatus of belief. And when one is *there*
one will be truthful and kind and able to see other people and what they
need!"

[IRIS MURDOCH, from *The Sacred and Profane Love Machine*]

*Here is an indication of the attempt to get religion out of its bony structures of
belief and devotions and into these personal relationships, especially seeing who
people are and what they need. So many people have slipped quietly and
thoughtfully away from organized religion. But if there is no sense of religion at
all, what remains but pleasure, leisure, and power?*

2nd August

The death that we shall die
Is here, we know, coiled like a spring inside us,
Waiting its time.
When what is now becomes the past, we can see its future implied.
As seed in the fruit, child in the womb.

The gardener, stooping down to tie
His bootlace, died so,
And acts through a lifetime multiplied
Foreshadowed this: when as a boy
He learnt to tie a bow,
Or when he stooped each day to dibble his plants,
Something was meant, he could not know.

So men seem walking histories
Of their own futures: we look to see the design
Forward or backward, plain,
As rings in a tree-trunk tell the sequence of years.
The jilted boy in pain
Trudging the pavement under the heartless stars
Now with his darling joyfully walks the same street.
Old words, old phrases, fly homing into the future
Where the poem is complete.

Parting a week ago,
The baby waved, through tears. I waved back lightly
With no foreboding fears;
But I remember it now,
And scan and search the memory, as though it should explain
All that came after, the anguish of last night,
The ambulance dash, the kind indifferent nurses,
And now the cot, where she lies in a hospital gown
And waves to me, through tears.

Suppose, when we are dead,
The soul moves back, over the gulf of nescience,
To relive a lifetime, all that was done and said . . .
Some say remorse impels it, the pitiless conscience
That drives toward expiation;
But it might be a different need:
To live each now in the illumination
Of what's to come; wholly to understand
Those tears, that waving hand.

[ANNE RIDLER, *A Waving Hand*]

I think of this now when I bend down to tie my bootlaces. Anne Ridler illuminates the ordinary which we usually do not notice. Once it is recognized, the dimensions of life expand.

3rd August

Mr Gaul and Perdita were both walking quite slowly now – the one
three or four feet higher than, and a little in advance of, the other, as if,
in spite of an occasional car or truck driving into Weymouth, they were
so solitary there that the place had begun to take notice of them. This is
a frequent experience with wayfarers. Leaving a town or hamlet they
chat to one another for a while, and are accosted by others; but let them
walk long enough along the same beach, and the time arrives when that
inanimate pathway subdues them to itself, hypnotises them into silence,
into a curious passivity. It is then that under the spell of the simplest
forms of matter, a mudbank, a flint track, a stone wall, they are allowed
to listen to a speech too deep for sound; and they become eaves-
droppers of the ancient litany of aboriginal matter and grow confederate
with the long piety of the cosmos, whose religion is to wait. The whitish-
grey sea-wall under the girl's feet and at the man's side, had the air – as
the sunlight fell upon it – of being something that had moved forward
just a fraction of an inch towards their conscious souls. It had the air of
posing a question to these self-absorbed intelligences. The shelving
pebbles – whose surface was like a sound that might set a dinosaur's
teeth on edge – seemed to join with the wall in asking them this
question.

[JOHN COWPER POWYS, from *Weymouth Sands*]

*Here is a familiar experience – an ordinary walk – where you come face to face
with larger questions.*

4th August

> Come down, O maid, from yonder mountain height:
> What pleasure lives in height (the shepherd sang),
> In height and cold, the splendour of the hills?
> But cease to move so near the Heavens, and cease
> To glide a sunbeam by the blasted Pine
> To sit a star upon the sparkling spire;
> And come, for Love is of the valley, come,
> For Love is of the valley, come thou down
> And find him; by the happy threshold, he,
> Or hand in hand with Plenty in the maize,
> Or red with spirited purple of the vats,
> Or foxlike in the vine; nor cares to walk

With Death and Morning on the Silver Horns,
Nor wilt thou share him in the white ravine,
Nor find him dropt upon the firths of ice,
That huddling slant in furrow-cloven falls
To roll the torrent out of dusky doors:
But follow; let the torrent dance thee down
To find him in the valley; let the wild
Lean-headed Eagles yelp alone, and leave
The monstrous ledges there to slope, and spill
Their thousand wreaths of dangling water-smoke,
That like a broken purpose waste in air:
So waste thou not; but come; for all the vales
Await thee; azure pillars of the hearth
Arise to thee; the children call, and I
Thy shepherd pipe, and sweet is every sound,
Sweeter thy voice, but every sound is sweet;
Myriads of rivulets hurrying thro' the lawn,
The moan of doves in immemorial elms,
And murmuring of innumerable bees.

[ALFRED TENNYSON, from *The Princess*]

Those last two lines are quintessentially Tennyson: words that mooch along,
enveloped by waves of sound! He was the most bodily sensuous of the Victorian
poets and wasn't afraid of it. He broke through the prudishness, knowing that
flesh and blood humans want more. And here he touches something of the
passion and beauty of sexuality – and its rapture.

&

5th August

"Take an old man's word: there's nothing worse than a muddle in all
the world. It is easy to face Death and Fate, and the things that sound so
dreadful. It is on my muddles that I look back with horror – on the
things that I might have avoided. We can help one another but little.
I used to think I could teach young people the whole of life, but I know
better now, and all my teaching of George has come down to this:
beware of muddle. Do you remember in that church, when you pretended to be annoyed with me, but weren't? Do you remember before,
when you refused the room with the view? Those were muddles – little
but ominous – and I am fearing that you are in one now." She was
silent. "Do trust me, Miss Honeychurch. Though life is very glorious, it

is difficult." She was still silent. "Life, wrote a friend of mine, 'is a public performance on the violin in which you must learn the instrument as you go along'. I think he puts it well. Man has to pick up the use of his functions as he goes along – especially the function of Love." Then he burst out excitedly, "That's what I mean. You love George!" And after his long preamble, the three words burst against Lucy like waves from the open sea. "But you do," he went on, not waiting for contradiction. "You love the boy body and soul, plainly, directly, as he loves you, and no other word expresses it . . .

". . . You can transmute love, ignore it, muddle it, but you can never pull it out of you. I know by experience that the poets are right: Love is eternal . . .

". . . I only wish poets would say this too: that love is of the body; not the body, but of the body. Ah! the misery that would be saved if we confessed that! Ah, for a little directness to liberate the soul! Your soul, dear Lucy! I hate the word now, because of all the cant with which superstition has wrapped it round. But we have souls! I cannot say how they came nor whither they go, but we have them, and I see you ruining yours. I cannot bear it. It is again the darkness creeping in; it is hell."

[E. M. FORSTER, from *A Room with a View*]

Forster is gently saying that we are not really evil, but we are muddled about what we feel and so get ourselves into a mess and prevent one another from being straightforward. And yet there are moments too when we clear a path . . .

6th August

Neither on horseback nor seated,
But like himself, squarely on two feet,
The poet of death and lilacs
Loafs by the footpath. Even the bronze looks alive
Where it is folded like cloth. And he seems friendly.

"Where is the Mississippi panorama
And the girl who played the piano?
Where are you, Walt?
The Open Road goes to the used-car lot.

"Where is the nation you promised?
Those houses of wood built to sustain
Colossal snows,
And the light above the street is sick to death . . ."

"I am here," he answered.
"It seems you have found me out.
Yet, did I not warn you that it was Myself
I advertised? Were my words not sufficiently plain?

"I gave no prescriptions,
And those who have taken my moods for prophecies
Mistake the matter."
Then, vastly amused – "Why do you reproach me?
I freely confess I am wholly disreputable.
Yet I am happy, because you have found me out."

A crocodile in wrinkled metal loafing . . .

Then all the realtors,
Pickpockets, salesmen, and the actors performing
Official scenarios,
Turned a deaf ear, for they had contracted
American dreams.

But the man who keeps a store on a lonely road,
And the housewife who knows she's dumb.
And the earth, are relieved.

All that grave weight of America
Cancelled! Like Greece and Rome.
The future in ruins!
The castles, the prison, the cathedrals
Unbuilding, and roses
Blossoming from stones that are not there . . .

[LOUIS SIMPSON, from *Walt Whitman at Bear Mountain*]

*A dialogue poem giving Whitman, as it were, an opportunity to reply to a
modern critic. Underneath his glorious shouts there was a sombre note, a
wondering what it was all leading to, an uncertainty.*

7th August

O meek anticipant of that sure pain
Whose sureness grey-hair'd scholars hardly learn!
What wonder shall time breed, to swell thy strain?
What heavens, what earth, what suns shalt thou discern?

Ere the long night, whose stillness brooks no star,
Match that funereal aspect with her pall,
I think thou wilt have fathom'd life too far
Have known too much – or else forgotten all.

The Guide of our dark steps a triple veil
Betwixt our senses and our sorrow keeps:
Hath sown with cloudless passages the tale
Of grief, and eas'd us with a thousand sleeps.

Ah! not the nectarous poppy lovers use,
Not daily labour's dull Lethaean spring,
Oblivion in lost angels can infuse
Of the soil'd glory, and the trailing wing;

And though thou glean, what strenuous gleaners may,
In the throng'd fields where winning comes by strife;
And though the just sun gild, as all men pray,
Some reaches of the storm-vext stream of life;

Though that blank sunshine blind thee; though the cloud
That sever'd the world's march and thine, is gone;
Though ease dulls grace, and Wisdom be too proud
To halve a lodging that was all her own:

Once, ere the day decline, thou shalt discern,
Oh, once, ere night, in thy success, thy chain.
Ere the long evening close, thou shalt return
And wear this majesty of grief again.

[MATTHEW ARNOLD, from *To a Gipsy Child by the Sea-Shore*]

The poet was sensitive enough to react to the fact that a child's glance had fallen on him. He is made aware of the sorrow and pain that has been inflicted. More generally, Dickens was one of the few who were able to look at children as they are and not as chattels or labour. Oh, it is so horrible what we have done to children.

8th August

Thus the English portrait also keeps long silences, and when it speaks, speaks in a low voice, just as the Englishman does to this day, and as indeed, the muffled sound of the English language seems to demand.

Or, to put it differently, the English portrait conceals more than it reveals, and what it reveals it reveals with studied understatement. These men and women illustrate what Jane Austen in *Emma* calls 'the true English style' by 'burying under a calmness that seems all but indifference, the real attachment'. 'Dr Livingstone, I presume?' is the locus classicus of this aspect of Englishness, and if that assertion is countered by a reminder of Shakespeare and the passions raging in his plays, one ... can equally refer to the words which he put into the mouth of Hamlet: "In the very torrent, tempest, and, as I may say, whirlwind of passion, you must acquire and beget a temperance that may give it smoothness." He also warns that what is "overdone ... cannot but make the judicious grieve."

There could be no better way of characterizing the portraits of Reynolds and Gainsborough: temperance, smoothness, judiciousness, moderation...

A decent home, a temperate climate, and a moderate nation. It has its disadvantages in art. There is no Bach, no Beethoven, no Brahms. There is no Michaelangelo, no Titian, no Rembrandt, no Dürer or Grünewald. There are no vast compositions in the churches, and only bad if vast compositions in the palaces, but there are exquisite water-colours and miniatures, things on a small scale, and there are in the Middle Ages exquisitely carved bosses and capitals rather than the superhuman dramatis personae of French church portals. England also produces a nice crop of amateur painters from maiden aunts to Prime Ministers, and what the amateur painter must be lacking in, in order to remain an amateur, is a violent compulsion towards a single-minded self-expression. The amateur is altogether characteristic of England, and not the specialist.

[N. Pevsner, from *The Englishness of English Art*]

Well, if you are English and recognize yourself ... To the Chinese Bishop Tings of this world, we must be a very small bird's nest!

9th August

To those who know a little of Christian history probably the most moving of all the reflections it (the command to 'do this in remembrance of me') brings is . . . the thought of those innumerable millions of entirely obscure faithful men and women, everyone with his or her own

individual hopes and fears and sorrows and loves – and sins and tempta-
tions and prayers – once every whit as vivid and alive as mine are now.
They have left no slightest trace in this world, not even a name but have
passed to God utterly forgotten by men. Yet each of them once believed
and prayed as I believe and pray, and found it hard and grew slack and
sinned and repented and fell again. Each of them worshipped at the
eucharist and found their thoughts wandering and tried again, and felt
heavy and unresponsive and yet knew – just as really and pathetically
as I do these things. There is a little ill-spelled, ill-carved rustic epitaph
of the fourth century from Asia Minor: "Here sleeps the blessed Chione
who has found Jerusalem for she prayed much." Not another word is
known of Chione, some peasant woman who lived in that vanished
Christian world of Anatolia. But how lovely if all that should survive
after sixteen centuries were that one had prayed much, so that the
neighbours who saw all one's life were sure one must have found
Jerusalem! What did the Sunday eucharist in her village church every
week for a lifetime mean to the blessed Chione – and to the millions
like her then, and every year since? The sheer stupendous quantity of
the love of God which this ever-repeated action has drawn from the
obscure Christian multitudes through the centuries is in itself an overwhelming thought . . . It is because it became embedded deep down in
the life of the Christian peoples, colouring all the 'via vitae' of the ordinary man and woman, marking its personal turning points, marriage,
sickness, death and the rest, running through it year by year with the
feasts and fasts and the rhythm of the Sundays, that the eucharistic
action became inextricably woven into the public history of the Western
world. The thought of it is inseparable from its great turning-points also:
Pope Leo doing this in the morning before he went out to daunt Attila,
on the day that saw the continuity of Europe saved; and another Leo
doing this three and a half centuries later when he crowned Charle-
magne Roman Emperor on the day that saw that continuity fulfilled.
Or again, Alfred wandering defeated by the Danes staying his soul on
this, while medieval England struggled to be born; and Charles I also,
on that morning of his execution when medieval England came to its
final end. Such things strike the mind with their suggestions of a certain
timelessness about the eucharistic action and an independence of its
setting, in keeping with the stability in an ever-changing world of the
forms of the liturgy themselves.

[GREGORY DIX, from *The Shape of the Liturgy*]

At Thaxted we celebrated the Eucharist with this sense of public history (not least the martyrs and saints of England, whom we mostly forget) interwoven with the intimate and personal and everyday. Much of the joyous life experienced there has gone.

10th August

> She walks in beauty, like the night
> Of cloudless climes and starry skies;
> And all that's best of dark and bright
> Meet in her aspect and her eyes:
> Thus mellowed to that tender light
> Which heaven to gaudy day denies.
>
> One shade the more, one ray the less,
> Had half-impair'd the nameless grace
> Which waves in every raven tress,
> Or softly lightens o'er her face;
> Where thoughts serenely sweet express
> How pure, how dear their dwelling place.
>
> And on that cheek, and o'er that brow,
> So soft, so calm, yet eloquent,
> The smiles that win, the tints that glow,
> But tell of days in goodness spent,
> A mind at peace with all below,
> A heart whose love is innocent.

[LORD BYRON, *She Walks in Beauty*]

It is hard to imagine a Europe in which the British Romantics were so dominant. Byron at one time personified the whole movement. He was no charlatan, though eaten up by his troubles. His talent was largely wasted because he was so damaged. But this poem, though slick, is restrained and moving.

11th August

"The world in which I am at present living is the world I have attempted to paint in these pictures. The resurrection is meant to indicate the passing of the state of non-realisation of the possibilities of heaven in this life to the sudden awakening to that fact. That is what is inspiring the people as they resurrect, namely, the new meaning they find in what they have seen before." This explanation accords with Spencer's ideas as they have been gradually unfolded in his total *œuvre*. It was his belief that the golden age was just round the corner for it is a state of mind, the apprehension of the sublime truth that this world is governed by love, pervaded by joy and transfigured by a sense of the oneness of all life, if only we would have it so. We could enter upon the millenium tomorrow if we put away hatred, fear, suspicion, cruelty, lust for power, pride and especially the feeling of otherness. That is the gospel of the erotic paintings, it is also the gospel of the resurrections. Though it is close to the spirit of the Evangelists, it is not quite the same, for at the root of it lies the doctrine of non-duality, the basic metaphysic of the orient. The doctrine runs right through the whole of his painting from first to last. It pervades all his outlook and is reflected in his conception of you-me, the non-dual relationship between a man and a woman. That he had this vision of oneness entitles him to be called a religious man in the highest sense of the word. His day-to-day life was marked, as we have seen, by behaviour very far from what is thought of as piety. Nevertheless . . . by his very impieties he became sacred. They gave him strength to wrestle all night and at last force the angel to bless him. The blessing is best seen in the resurrection pictures, the most elaborate compositions achieved in our time in England. With their total of something like seven hundred figures, in the intricacy of their arabesques, their inexhaustible variety, the ecstasy which pervades them in some parts, in others their simple joy, the fertility of their invention, their unity of mood and their absolute originality, they represent the most mature expression of his art.

[MAURICE COLLIS, from *Stanley Spencer*]

Spencer paints impossible creatures! He has glorious dustmen sorting out the fragments! (Dickens creates such creatures too.) But he saw something of which the rest of us barely have intimations. The artist walks in a countryside that the rest of us do not see. It all looks inconceivable and mad, and yet . . . What is 'vision', what is the artist's 'seeing'? And what is the writer's 'hearing'?

12th August

When William Morris describes a house of any kind, and makes his description poetical, it is always, I think, some house that he would have liked to live in, and I remember him saying about the time when he was writing of that great house of the Wolfings, "I decorate modern houses

for people, but the house that would please me would be some great
room where one talked to one's friends in one corner and ate in another
and slept in another and worked in another." Indeed all he writes
seems to me like the make-believe of a child who is re-making the
world, not always in the same way, but always after its own heart; and
so, unlike all other modern writers, he makes his poetry out of unending pictures of a happiness that is often what a child might imagine,
and always a happiness that sets mind and body at ease. Now it is a
picture of some great room full of merriment, now of the wine-press,
now of the golden threshing-floor, now of an old mill among apple trees,
now of cool water after the heat of the sun, now of some well-sheltered,
well-tilled place among woods or mountains, where men and women
live happily, knowing of nothing that is too far off or too great for the
affections . . . I often see him in my mind as I saw him once at Hammer-
smith holding up a glass of claret towards the light and saying, "Why do
people say it is prosaic to get inspiration out of wine? Is it not the sunlight and the sap in the leaves? Are not grapes made by the sunlight and
the sap?"

[W. B. YEATS, from *The Happiest of Poets*]

*Here is Morris the domestic and workaday person who is always doing things
and making things. (Have we done our worst by giving children too many toys?)*

13th August

When I consider every thing that grows
Holds in perfection but a little moment,
That this huge stage presenteth nought but shows
Whereon the stars in secret comment;
When I perceive that men as plants increase,
Cheered and check'd even by the self-same sky,
Vaunt in their youthful sap, at height decrease,
And wear their brave state out of memory:
Then the conceit of this inconstant stay
Sets you most rich in youth before my sight,
Where wasteful Time debateth with Decay,
To change your day of youth to sullied night;
    And, all in war with Time for love of you,
    As he takes from you, I engraft you new.

[WILLIAM SHAKESPEARE, *Sonnet XV*]

Shakespeare must have been conscious of the stage quite early in his life, and of the 'huge stage' with its few years between youth and death. It is hard for us to imagine that life was so much shorter then.

14th August

The mind is brushed by sparrow wings;
Numbers, rebuffed by asphalt, crowd
The margins of the day, accent the curbs,
Convoying divers dawns on every corner
To druggist, barber and tobacconist,
Until the graduate opacities of evening
Take them away as suddenly to somewhere
Virginal perhaps, less fragmentary, cool.
     There is the world dimensional for those untwisted
     by the love of things irreconcilable.
And yet, suppose some evening I forgot
The fare and transfer, yet got by that way
Without recall, – lost yet poised in traffic.
Then I might find your eyes across an aisle,
Still flickering with those prefigurations –
Prodigal, yet uncontested now,
Half-riant before the jerky window frame.

The earth may glide diaphanous to death;
But if I light my arms it is to bend
To you who turned away once, Helen, knowing
The press of troubled hands, too alternate
With steel and soil to hold you endlessly.
I meet you, therefore, in that eventual flame
You found in final chains, no captive then –
Beyond their million brittle, bloodshot eyes;
White, through white cities passed on to assume
That world which comes to each of us alone.

Accept a lone eye riveted to your plane,
Bent axle of devotion along companion ways
That beat, continuous, to hourless days –
One inconspicuous, glowing orb of praise.

[HART CRANE, from *For the Marriage of Faustus and Helen*]

A very literary poet of the city and of the crowd, but aware too of beauty. He knows the city but is confronted from time to time by that which he must honour and adore.

15th August

Busy old fool, unruly Sun,
Why dost thou thus,
Through windows, and through curtains call on us?
Must to thy motions lovers' seasons run?
Saucy, pedantic wretch, go chide
Late school-boys, and sour prentices,
Go tell Court-huntsmen, that the King will ride,
Call country ants to harvest offices;
Love, all alike, no season knows, nor clime,
Nor hours, days, months, which are the rags of time.

Thy beams so reverend, and strong
Why shouldst thou think?
I could eclipse and cloud them with a wink,
But that I would not lose her sight so long:
If her eyes have not blinded thine,
Look, and tomorrow late, tell me,
Whether both th'Indias of spice and mine
Be where thou left'st them, or lie here with me.
Ask for those Kings whom thou saw'st yesterday
And thou shalt hear, All here in one bed lay.

She's all States, and all Princes, I,
Nothing else is.
Princes do but play us; compar'd to this,
All honour's mine; all wealth alchemy.
Thou sun art half as happy as we,
In that the world's contracted thus;
Thine age asks ease, and since thy duties be
To warm the world, that's done in warming us.
Shine here to us, and thou art everywhere;
This bed thy centre is, these walls, thy sphere.

[JOHN DONNE, *The Sun Rising*]

To think he was Dean of St Paul's!

16th August

Like you I am ruminating the results of a year's grazing. I can do it best leaning over a gate and watching a cow similarly employed – the most tranquillising influence in Nature. The world is too much with us; Nature too little. I used to keep a Buddha under my crucifix – to the shock of my confrères. Henceforth I shall keep a cow – a sacred cow, emblem of the quiet weary East . . .

I feel more and more that as regards God and immortality man was made not to know but to hope. Hope, rather than faith; for faith is so hopelessly confounded with knowledge. There the Buddha is so right; for we do not, we cannot know. And there the Christian with his theology-faith is so wrong, so poor, so thin, so shallow, so provincial. For him the fringe of mystery that lends life its dignity, its pathos, its humility, is torn away, and replaced by a brick wall with nothing beyond. When I contrast the temper of Job xxxviii-ix with that of the ordinary cocksure Christian, I find it hard to believe in the steady development of the religious sense. Are our theologies more than an attempt to give shape and substance to our Hope? And are they not to be rated by a moral rather than an intellectual criterion – i.e., according to the quality, the elevation, and the 'truth' of the Hope? The gods we fashion are the measure of the Divine that is in us, whose face we dream of, but cannot see. I know we should not be frightened by the star-dust on these dark nights; that a particle of mind is more than a universe of matter, etc. But is there not probably some proportion, some relation of analogy? Or is it not merely that our spiritual conceit and self-importance have not yet been detected by a metaphysical Galileo? We are so young and cocksure that from man to God there is but one or at most two steps – mineral, vegetable, human, (angelic), divine. Is it not infinity to one that as the earth is, quantitatively, to the universe of star-dust so, qualitatively, is man's spirit to the divine? All I dare say is that the divine has a human aspect which alone concerns man; just as it has a canine aspect which alone concerns dogs; but that it is as little human as it is canine. It is that all-pervading indwelling Power which moves dogs and men towards their proper perfection; which, for them, is the Divine Will. It is man's privilege to think of it, to wonder; to hope; to figure it to himself in terms of his own spirit . . .

[GEORGE TYRRELL, from *The Life of George Tyrrell*]

Typically the ruminating Tyrrell, astonishingly ahead of his time – he died in 1919.

17th August

> The thought of our past years in me doth breed
> Perpetual benediction: not indeed
> For that which is most worthy to be blest –
> Delight and liberty, the simple creed
> Of childhood, whether busy or at rest,
> With new-fledged hope still fluttering in his breast –
>   Not for these I raise
>   The song of thanks and praise
>   But for those obstinate questionings
>   Of sense and outward things,
>   Fallings from us, vanishings;
>   Blank misgivings of a creature
> Moving about in worlds not realized,
> High instincts before which our mortal Nature
> Did tremble like a guilty thing surprized:
>   But for those first affections
>   Those shadowy recollections,
>   Which be they what they may,
> Are yet the fountain light of all our day,
> Are yet the master light of all our seeing,
>   Uphold us, cherish and have power to make
> Our noisy years seem moments in the being
> Of the eternal silence: truths that wake
>   To perish never.

[WILLIAM WORDSWORTH, from *Intimations of Immortality*]

The best that Wordsworth ever wrote. When he loses the sense of 'obstinate questionings', of mystery impinging on the social scene, he becomes an insufferable old Tory.

18th August

It is remarkable, in spite of his ardent simplicity and openness of heart, how insensible Dickens was to the greater themes of the human imagination – religion, science, politics, art. He was a waif himself, and utterly disinherited. For example, the terrible heritage of contentious religions which fills the world seems not to exist for him. In this matter he was like a sensitive child, with a most religious disposition, but no

religious ideas. Perhaps, properly speaking, he had no ideas on any subject; what he had was a vast sympathetic participation in the daily life of
mankind; and what he saw of ancient institutions made him hate them,
as needless sources of oppression, misery, selfishness, and rancour . . .
Common life as it is lived was varied and lovable for Dickens, if only the
pests and cruelties could be removed from it. Suffering wounded him,
but not vulgarity; whatever pleased his senses, and whatever shocked
them filled his mind alike with romantic wonder, with the endless
delight of observation. Vulgarity – and can we relish, if we recoil at
vulgarity? – was innocent and amusing; in fact, for the humorist, it was
the spice of life. There was more piety in being human than in being
pious. In reviving Christmas, Dickens transformed it from the celebration of a metaphysical mystery into a feast of overflowing simple kindness and good cheer; the church bells were still there – in the orchestra;
and the angels of Bethlehem were still there – painted on the back-
curtain. Churches, in his novels, are vague, desolate places where one
has ghastly experiences, and where only the pew-opener is human; and
such religious and political conflicts as he depicts in *Barnaby Rudge* and
A Tale of Two Cities are street brawls and prison scenes and conspiracies
in taverns without any indication of the contrasts in mind or interests
between the opposed parties . . .

[GEORGE SANTAYANA, from *Dickens*]

*Dickens was constantly saying, Look at how we damage one another and look at
other possibilities – Florence Dombey, Little Dorrit. One drop of compassion is
worth all the institutions.*

19th August

Many people . . . are so accustomed to regarding 'recognized facts' as the
natural basis of attitudes that they cannot conceive how anyone can be
otherwise organized. The hard-headed positivist and the convinced
adherent of a religion from opposite sides encounter the same difficulty.
The first at best suffers from an insufficient material for the development of his attitudes; the second from intellectual bondage and unconscious insincerity. The one starves himself; the other is like the little
pig in the fable who chose to have his house built of cabbages and ate it
and so the grim wolf with privy paw devoured him. For clear and
impartial awareness of the nature of the world in which we live and the
development of attitudes which will enable us to live in it finely are
both necessities, and neither can be subordinated to the other. They are

almost independent, such connections as exist in well-organized individuals being adventitious. Those who find this a hard saying may be
invited to consider the effect upon them of those works of art which
most unmistakeably attune them to existence. The central experience
of Tragedy and its chief value is an attitude indispensable for a fully
developed life.

[I. A. RICHARDS, from *Principles of Literary Criticism*]

*I bought this book in Cambridge the day it came out, and my room-mate and I
read it to each other, chapter by chapter until we had finished it. It gave us a
new way of looking at literature. A poem is not a set of words but an experience
made available to you through the words, and your response depends on your
availability to sharing that experience. Most people don't even read a poem you
might give them. It does not register, especially if you omit the name of the poet.
Imagery, thought, sentiment, feeling, knowledge, – all are there beneath your
response, whether stock or free. And Richards knew that what had been
unconscious was becoming conscious and that we had to face it. Genuine criticism
shapes your attitude to life.*

20th August

August for the people and their favourite island.
Daily the steamers sidle up to meet
The effusive welcome of the pier, and soon
The luxuriant life of the steep stone valleys,
The sallow oval faces of the city
Begot in passion or good-natured habit
Are caught by waiting coaches, or laid bare
Beside the undiscriminating sea . . .

For now the moulding images of growth
That made our interest and us, are gone.
Louder today the wireless roars
Its warning and its lies, and it's impossible
Among the well-shaped cosily to flit,
Or longer to desire about our lives
The beautiful loneliness of the banks, or find
The stoves and resignations of the frozen plains . . .

Greed showing shamelessly her naked money
And all Love's wondering eloquence debased
To a collector's slang, smartness in furs,

And Beauty scratching miserably for food.
Honour self-sacrificed for Calculation,
And Reason stoned by Mediocrity,
Freedom by Power shockingly maltreated,
And Justice exiled till Saint Geoffrey's Day.

So in this hour of crisis and dismay,
What better than your strict and adult pen
Can warn us from the colours and the consolations,
The showy arid works, reveal
The squalid shadow of academy and garden,
Make action urgent and its nature clear?
Who give us nearer insight to resist
The expanding fear, the savaging disaster?

[W. H. AUDEN, from *August for the People*]

Written in the thirties, within ten years of the outbreak of the Second World War, Auden expresses his outrage at what was happening, not least at the aridity of the spirit.

21st August

The conspicuous and remarkable failure of the churches to provide the basis for a new society is obviously not due to the 'godless spirit' of our age which is so often deplored from the pulpits. On the contrary, an age in which an elite can turn to the churches must have a very strong urge towards religion. In spite of this need and search, Christianity and the churches are unable to provide a religious social solution. All they can do today is to give the individual a private haven and refuge in an individual religion. They cannot give a new society and a new community. Personal religious experience may be invaluable to the individual; it may restore his peace, may give him a personal God and a rational understanding of his own function and nature. But it cannot recreate society and cannot make social and community life sensible. Even the most devout Catholic today is in the religious position of an extreme Protestant like Kierkegaard, for whom God was a purely personal, untranslatable and incommunicable experience, which only emphasized his own isolation and loneliness, and the utter irrationality of society ...

This is a worse failure for the Christian church than even a complete loss of all believers. A church that is only a tiny, persecuted minority in a vast sea of atheists might still be strong and successful if it gave its adherents a real community. It would emerge triumphantly as soon as materialism had revealed itself as hollow. That happened in the French Revolution. It might well happen again in Soviet Russia in a generation or two, since the tiny minorities who preserve and reform their church form a real community. But a Christian church which, though strong in number and quality of believers, cannot give them more than private religion and private satisfaction, ceases to be a church altogether – at least in the sense in which Europe understands the word. It loses its essential quality as the basis of a rational order of the cosmos and admits that Christianity, which has banished or rationalized so many earlier demons, cannot banish or rationalize the demons that beset our society and our times. It fails completely to understand their real nature as irrational forces outside the accepted European system of beliefs, in the same way in which bourgeois liberalism and socialism fail to under-stand these forces and try to conceive them as part of their own routine pattern – what I have called above 'the anti-fascist illusion'.

[PETER DRUCKER, from *The End of Economic Man*]

A blast of revelation again, a warning that Europe could break down, with the doom of 'economic man'. 'Finance' has become a machine which you judge by its efficiency rather than by its morality. But this cannot be a basis for human relationships. At least a quarter of the population have no access to it anyway – and that is without even thinking of the poorer parts of the world.

22nd August

There sang a fountain in a Syrian courtyard leaping
Near to the place where Lazarus, the loved of Jesus, lay,
Lazarus, four days dead, alone in the shadow sleeping . . .

Then, as the people passed, the fountain ceased from leaping,
While yet unwakened by the Son of God he slept.
By this were many gathered near the tomb mouth with much weeping,
Then did the fountain stop. That moment, Jesus wept.

Then sang those little birds upon the very stone
Where the dead spoke for that first time and all the folk drew near;
So great a marvel had not yet on Earth been known,
For the young man came forth, and it was he they knew;
And they drew back amazed; it shook their hearts with fear

To see the young man walk. Then that white retinue
Knew that their own last resurrection had come near.
Come, O Redeemer, come; come down, and make Earth new.

Love, newly-born, come down: for yon the fountain playing
Leaps into light, then spills, and fills the basin's brim.
Water gives life to stone, and light renews our saying:
For you the sages wait, and listening cherubim
Support the fountain's weight around its marble base.
For you the ages wait, old prophets are not still
Around this font of birth; they strain to see your face.
For you his winding horn a Triton's lips are playing;
His crooked eyes in water watch the fountains fill.
For you the doves of light return from their far straying,
Too long away, too long, in that Italian town
Open my eyes at last, my eyes shut long with praying,
And let me see your eyes: Love, newly born, come down.

[VERNON WATKINS, from *Cantata for the Waking of Lazarus*]

There is nothing quite like the Lazarus story anywhere else in the Gospels, not least because he had been dead four days! What did John mean by it? What experience is he interpreting? If the Gospel of John is a poem here at least is another poem which also uses an image of new life.

23rd August

If the present social situation is to be controlled by Christian principles, thoughts will be necessary which have not yet been thought, and which will correspond to this new situation as the older forms met the needs of the social situation in earlier ages. These ideas will have to be evolved out of the inner impulse of Christian thought, and not out of its vital expression at the present time, and not exclusively out of the New Testament, in precisely the same way as both those great main types of Christian-social philosophy were evolved out of the Christian thought of their own day, and not solely from the New Testament. And when they have been created and expressed, they will meet the fate which always awaits every fresh creation of religious and ethical thought: they will render indispensable services and they will develop profound energies, but they will never fully realize their actual ideal intention within the sphere of our earthly struggle and conflict.

As little as any other power in this world will they create the Kingdom of God upon earth as a completed social ethical organism. One of the most serious and important truths which emerge as a result of this enquiry is this: every idea is still faced by brutal facts, and all upward movement is checked and hindered by interior and exterior difficulties. Nowhere does there exist an absolute Christian ethic, which only awaits discovery; all that we can do is to learn to control the world-situation in its successive phases just as the earlier Christian ethic did in its own way. There is also no absolute ethical transformation of material nature or of human nature: all that does exist is a constant wrestling with the problems which they raise . . . Only doctrinaire idealists or religious fanatics can fail to recognize these facts. Faith is the source of energy in the struggle of life, but life still remains a battle which is continually renewed upon ever new fronts . . .

[ERNST TROELTSCH, from *The Social Teaching of the Christian Churches*]

This passage comes near the end of Troeltsch's immense work. The Church, either as dominating the political scene or as separate citadel over against the world, cannot meet the needs of the present time. A new relationship between the two is called for.

24th August

If mere fanaticism had been their motive, the men who were most active in the massacre would not have spared so many lives. While Guise was galloping after Fernères and Montgomery, who had taken horse betimes, and made for the coast, his house at Paris was crowded with families belonging to the proscribed faith, and strangers to him. A young girl who was amongst them has described his return, when he sent for the children, spoke to them kindly, and gave orders that they should be well treated as long as his roof sheltered them. Protestants even spoke of him as a humane and chivalrous enemy. Nevers was considered to have disgraced himself by the number of those whom he enabled to escape. The Nuncio was shocked at their ill-timed generosity. He reported to Rome that the only one who had acted in the spirit of a Christian and had refrained from mercy, was the King; while the other princes, who pretended to be good Catholics, and to deserve the favour of the Pope, had striven, one and all, to save as many Huguenots as they could.

The worst criminals were not the men who did the deed. The crime of mobs and courtiers, infuriated by the lust of vengeance and of power, is not so strange a portent as the exultation of peaceful men, influenced by no present injury or momentary rage, but by the permanent and incurable perversion of moral sense wrought by distorted piety.

[LORD ACTON, from *History of Freedom and Other Essays*]

This is the anniversary of the St Bartholomew's Day Massacre of the Huguenots in France.

25th August

It was in the mid-1960s that Bacon was given a little book by Michael Leiris . . . in which there appears a passage which he at once ringed with a thick flat nib. Leiris traces back to its origins in Baudelaire the notion of an ideal beauty that is quintessentially modern in that it refuses to fall back on "the emptiness of a beauty that is absolute and cannot be defined". . . "beauty cannot come into being without the intervention of something accidental (a misfortune, or the contingence of modernity) which drags the beautiful clear from its glacial stagnation; it is at the price of degradation that the mummified One turns into the living Many . . . "

. . . "Beauty must have in it an element that plays the motor-role of the first sin. What constitutes beauty is not the confrontation of opposites but the mutual antagonism of the opposites, and the active and vigorous manner in which they invade one another and emerge from the conflict marked as if by a wound or a depredation." . . .

And what if the act of painting, of committing a human figure to canvas, is also an act at once of love and of murder? Love is the instinct which creates that figure and nurtures it to fulfilment; murder, the instinct which pins it down and finishes it off. An interpretation of this kind would accord very well with the nervous reaction which communicates itself even to those who do not really care for Bacon's painting. Very few people can stand before one of his pictures and not feel that it stands for a human activity pushed to its limit. . . .

[JOHN RUSSELL, from *Francis Bacon*]

I first came to Bacon when I saw his Figures in a Landscape *in Birmingham Art Gallery. There is a figure bent over as if being flung into a pit. Systematized and impersonal violence has been so characteristic of our century. The figures are broken and the wounds are prominent. This is what we have done and we must look at what we have done if we are to be honest. Crucifixes no longer get under our skin. But the artist can ask, What then of this human being that faces you?*

26th August

And death shall have no dominion.
Dead men naked they shall be one
With the man in the wind and the west moon;
When their bones are picked clean and the clean bones gone,
They shall have stars at elbow and foot;
Though they go mad they shall be sane,
Though they sink through the sea they shall rise again;
Though lovers are lost love shall not;
And death shall have no dominion.

And death shall have no dominion.
Under the windings of the sea
They lying long shall not die windily;
Twisting on racks when sinews give way,
Strapped to a wheel, yet they shall not break;
Faith in their hands shall snap in two,
And the unicorn evils run them through;
Split all ends up they shan't crack;
And death shall have no dominion.

And death shall have no dominion.
No more may gulls cry at their ears
Or waves break loud on the foreshores;
Where blew a flower may a flower no more
Lift its head to the blows of the rain;
Though they be mad and dead as nails,
Heads of the characters hammer through daisies;
Break in the sun till the sun breaks down,
And death shall have no dominion.

[DYLAN THOMAS, *And death shall have no dominion*]

Thomas was a man who physically responded the whole time – here it is to the ebb and pluck of the tide. Keats described the poet as the one who has no personality but who fills in for others, an instrument to be played upon.

27th August

... the understanding of how others have reacted to situations unlike his own reveals to (the historian) possibilities in his own nature of which his own circumstances had never made him aware. Dilthey instances the effect of his own study of Luther and the Reformation in enabling him at least to understand a religious experience of a depth and intensity such as in his own person he was not capable of sharing. "Man, bound and determined by the reality of life, is set free not only through art – as has often been set forth – but also through the understanding of history."

This widening of consciousness through historical knowledge has disconcerting results. Every age expresses its attitude to life and the world in certain principles of thought and conduct, which are regarded in that age as absolute and unconditionally valid, as constituting a 'law of nature' which only frivolity or ill-will can question. The historian discovers these principles in every age which he studies, but he also discovers that they vary from age to age, and that, in spite of the claim to absoluteness which is always made, changed circumstances always result in changed principles, which are therefore historically relative...

... If our grandfathers reacted to their situation in one way and we react to ours in another, the conclusion which Dilthey draws is not that no one can ever know how to act or think, but that in every situation man can find a way. Even our illusions reflect something in experience, and are therefore not wholly illusions. Dropping the claim of absoluteness does not mean surrendering every claim to truth, but merely admitting many truths where before we had only a few.

[H. A. HODGES, from *Wilhelm Dilthey*]

Dilthey, writing at the turn of the century, was a good thinker on the writing of history. Elsewhere Hodges comments that it is impossible to make syntheses – we are forced to make choices!

28th August

Why is our age so sick?

Every creative art has the task of creating its own approach to the world – its own key to the universe. Its task lies within the realm of irrationality: to give expression to the emotional feeling of a period. When this is not done it is a sign that that period has lost contact with its own inner self.

Everyone knows the reason why our period cannot find its equilibrium. It can neither control nor organize the possibilities that it has
itself produced ...

We have not been able to cope with the new reality. We have not
mastered the social consequences any better than the human ones, for
we have created a civilization which lacks any desire for tranquillity. We
do not know how to adapt ourselves to this civilization, for our culture
lacks an adequate balance between physical and mental tension.

In short, we have not found the key to reality, which lies hidden in our
emotion. This is the matter which we must discuss here. The rift
between the newly created reality and emotional feeling started with
the industrial revolution:
        ungoverned machines – outcast feeling:
        production as an end in itself – escape into romanticism.
This dichotomy explains the rise of the public art of the last century,
which is still the standard of taste of the general public ... (The art) that
came to govern the emotional world of the general public proved to be
merely a drug, a narcotic ...

Today, a safe distance away, the public art of the nineteenth century
quite often has the charm of a mask – half banal, half demoniac. It can
be likened to some pleasant-tasting medicinal powder that gives the
organism a momentary lift before the poison begins its fell work.

The consequence of this situation was that the greatest painters of
this period, the only ones whose work continues to survive today, were
forced to capitulate ... and become doomed to unimportance.

[S. GIEDION, from *Architecture, you and me*]

*He is so piercing about the false romanticism of the late nineteenth century. And a
generation that has witnessed the tower blocks and the heartless estates would
concur. Architecture both reflects and contributes to the character of an age.
It is the most significant of the arts because it produces the buildings in which
we live!*

29th August

It is in the modern revival of ancient methods of agriculture and in the
science of ecology that hitherto there has been the fullest appreciation of
the mutuality of function in the organism, with its essential shuttle-like
throw from environment to organism and from organism to environment, each throw changing the design, each change affording a stimulus

to the next change that is to follow. Yet plant, animal and man live by the same biological law. The laws that govern growth and development apply equally to the organism as a whole as to its parts.

. . . The mutual action of organism and environment, associated as we rise in the biological scale with an increasing degree of autonomy of the organism, recalls forcibly to mind the circumstances of a single cell, such for instance, as the liver cell, set in the body of which it is an infinitesimal part. The cell acts as liver cell carrying on the specific function of 'liverness', yet changes, in health, 'aware' of, and subject to, the wider needs of the body of which it is part and from which it derives sustenance. It is this relationship to the body which alone gives significance to its individuality as liver cell as well as to its unique function of liverness.

. . . Thus the body as an organisation is, in fact, the ultimate significance of the cell. Can it be that Man himself is but a cell in the body of the Cosmos; and that Cosmos is organismal as he is?

Without being able to define the factual basis for their intuition – for that can only come through science – wise men in all ages have acted with a deep intuitive apprehension of this as a truth. Upon it they have built their hopes, their conduct and their religions. Only now, as intuitive apprehension seems to be wearing thin and threadbare, are men of science being led, through the study of function, to suspect that there may even be a physical basis for these primitive intuitive actions; that in fact the significance of human living lies in the degree of mutuality established with an all pervading order – Nature – whether we deify her or not.

[INNES PEARSE and LUCY CROCKER, from *The Peckham Experiment*]

The Peckham Experiment was one of the revelatory points of my life. It started as a study of the nature of health. A health centre was formed in Peckham which could be joined only by complete families. Health checks were carried out every six months. The emphasis was on education and living rather than on pathology. It was observed that health did indeed improve. And this was sixty years ago.

30th August

Season of mists and mellow fruitfulness!
   Close bosom friend of the maturing sun;
Conspiring with him how to load and bless
   With fruit the vines that round the thatch-eaves run;

To bend with apples the mossed cottage-trees,
   And fill all fruit with ripeness to the core;
     To swell the gourd, and plump the hazel shells
With a sweet kernel; to set budding more,
   And still more, later flowers for the bees,
   Until they think warm days will never cease,
     For Summer has o'er-brimmed their clammy cells.

Who hath not seen thee oft amid thy store?
   Sometimes whoever seeks abroad may find
Thee sitting careless on a granary floor,
   Thy hair soft-lifted by the winnowing wind;
Or on a half-reaped furrow sound asleep,
   Drowsed with the fume of poppies, while thy hook
     Spares the next swath and all its twined flowers;
And sometimes like a gleaner thou dost keep
   Steady thy laden head across a brook;
   Or by a cider-press, with patient look,
     Thou watchest the last oozings hours by hours.

Where are the songs of Spring? Ay, where are they?
   Think not of them, thou hast thy music too, –
While barred clouds bloom the soft-dying day,
   And touch the stubble plains with rosy hue;
Then in a wailful choir the small gnats mourn
   Among the river sallows, borne aloft
     Or sinking as the light wind lives or dies;
And full-grown lambs loud bleat from hilly bourn;
   Hedge-crickets sing; and now with treble soft
   The redbreast whistles from a garden-croft;
     And gathering swallows twitter in the skies.

[JOHN KEATS, *Ode to Autumn*]

Autumn can begin early in Cumbria! Keats is so good at choosing the appro-
priate word. You couldn't substitute 'cats' or 'bats' for gnats!

31st August

I think we shall come soon
Beyond the sleep of meadows,
Out of these small green
Valleys of history,

Quit the reiteration
Of lintel and corbel,
Eaves secretive and laden,
Viola and apple,

And go back to the beginning,
Back beyond reaping and sowing,
Further than the Plantagenets,
Further than Boadicea dying,

To the thin air and the old rock,
The long bones unstirred by larksong
Cold under the blue of summer,
And the darkened hearthstone.

We climb now to the hills
That rise silent shoulder to shoulder
To the skies of summer hills
Azure and fainter than harebells.

I think that when we come
To the hills' roof we shall find
That perhaps for which
We have been searching always.

We hear the tongues of oaks:
We mount to the wind
Flowing from the rock. And still,
Always we climb.

[DIANA McLOGHLEN, *Hutton Roof*]

*Hutton Roof is a village near Penrith, and Diana McLoghlen is a local Gosforth
poet.*

SEPTEMBER

1st September

. . . Flora de Barral was not exceptionally intelligent but she was thoroughly feminine. She would be passive (and that does not mean inanimate) in the circumstances, where the mere fact of being a woman was enough to give her an occult and supreme significance. And she would be enduring, which is the essence of woman's visible, tangible power. Of that I was certain. Had she not endured already? Yet it is so true that the germ of destruction lies in wait for us mortals, even at the very source of our strength, that one may die of too much endurance as well as of too little of it . . .

A woman may be a fool, a sleepy fool, an agitated fool, a too-awfully noxious fool, and she may even be simply stupid. But she is never dense. She's never made of wood through and through as some men are. There is in woman always, somewhere, a spring. Whatever men don't know about women (and it may be a lot or it may be very little) men and even fathers do know that much. And that is why so many men are afraid of them . . .

Of all the forms offered to us by life it is the one demanding a couple to realize fully which is the most imperative. Pairing-off is the fate of mankind. And if two beings who are thrown together, mutually attracted, resist the necessity, fail in understanding, and voluntarily stop short of the embrace, in the noblest meaning of the word, then they are committing a sin against life, the call of which is simple. Perhaps sacred. And the punishment of it is an invasion of complexity, a tormenting, forcibly tortuous involution of feelings, the deepest form of suffering, from which indeed something significant may come at last, which may be criminal or heroic, may be madness or wisdom – or even a straight if despairing decision . . .

[JOSEPH CONRAD, from *Chance*]

An even better passage than the one from Almayer's Folly *(8th May), with a sting or two as you go along. Is there a resource between men and women to enable us to counteract our lurch towards self-destruction?*

2nd September

We use our imagination not to escape the world but to join it, and this exhilarates us because of the distance between our ordinary dulled consciousness and an apprehension of the real. The value-concepts are here patently tied on to the world, they are stretched as it were between the truth-seeking mind and the world, they are not moving about on their own as adjuncts of the personal will. The authority of morals is the authority of truth, that is of reality. We can see the length, the extension of these concepts as patient attention transforms accuracy without interval into just discernment. Here too we can see it as natural to the particular kind of creatures that we are that love should be inseparable from justice, and clear vision from respect for the real ...

The difficulty is to keep the attention fixed upon the real situation and to prevent it from returning surreptitiously to the self with consolations of self-pity, resentment, fantasy, and despair. The refusal to attend may even induce a fictitious sense of freedom – I may as well toss a coin. Of course, virtue is good habit and dutiful action. But the background condition of such habit and such action, in human beings, is a just mode of vision and a good quality of consciousness. It is a task to come to see the world as it is.

[IRIS MURDOCH, from *The Sovereignty of Good*]

For someone with at times fantasy in her novels, it is good to have this clear statement about imagination and reality. But how to do this when the wells are poisoned? There is so much now that is superficial and merely attention-holding for a moment or two.

3rd September

... (Cromwell's) failure to establish a permanent Government was not due merely to his deficiency in constructive imagination. It was due rather to two causes: the umbrage taken at his position as head of an army whose interference in political affairs gave even more offence than the financial burdens it imposed on a people unaccustomed to regular taxation; and the reaction which set in against the spiritual claims of that Puritanism of which he had become the mouthpiece. The first cause of offence requires no further comment. As for the second, it is necessary to lay aside all sectarian preoccupations, if ever a true historic judgment is to be formed. It was no reaction against the religious doctrines or ecclesiastical institutions upheld by the Protector that brought about the destruction of his system of government. It is in the highest degree unlikely that a revolution would ever have taken place merely to restore episcopacy or the Book of Common Prayer. So far as the reaction was not directed against militarism, it was directed against the introduction into the political world of what appeared to be too high a standard of morality, a reaction which struck specially upon Puritanism, but which would have struck with as much force upon any other form of religion which, like that upheld by Laud, called in the power of the State to enforce its claims.

Nor is this all that can be said. Even though Oliver was in his own person no sour fanatic, as Royalist pamphleteers after the Restoration falsely asserted, it is impossible to deny that he strove by acts of government to lead men into the paths of morality and religion beyond the limit which average human nature had fixed for itself ...

[S. R. GARDINER, from *Oliver Cromwell*]

When revolution happens, you see the turmoil of a society but also a reality that has not been seen before. Cromwell acted all of a piece – genuinely so, as far as he was made; but events revealed his own turmoil and limitations as well as his dependence on others. To be great-souled gives room for terrible inner conflict.

4th September

To make it new is to make it recur. In fulfilment is recurrence, re-capitulation. Fulfilment gathers up the past into the present in the form of a recapitulation: that in the dispensation of times there might be a recapitulation of all things in Christ. Recapitulate – with the metaphor of the head in both the Latin and the Greek words. It is a gathering up of time into eternity; a transfiguration of time; the transfiguration in which Moses and Elijah, who are the past, appeared unto them as present, talking with Jesus. Symbolic consciousness makes figural interpretations in order to accomplish the transfiguration.

. . . Redemptive history (anthropology) is anamnesis; to remember again what we have repressed; to recapitulate the phylogeny, a re-collection of previous incarnations. "In recollection all former births passed before His eyes. Born in such a place, of such a name, and down-wards to His present birth, so through hundreds, thousands, myriads, all His births and deaths He knew." Not an objective and distant study of strangers, but discovering and embracing ourselves, collecting the

previous incarnations into a unity with oneself; to constitute the collective self, the Son of Man. To recapitulate the phylogeny is to reconstitute
the phylum, the unity of the human race, the atonement. The atonement of mankind, not the forensic justification of the individual
believer. Dismembered, remembered. Symbolic consciousness is to
remember the unity; history as the history of one man. The unity is the
invisible reality; the unconscious is the collective. Literalism singles out
a separate holy church or nation, but "Christ Jesus, at His long typed-
out coming, abolished those national shadows and erected His spiritual
kingdom . . . Literalism is to take *pars pro toto*; symbolism reconstitutes
the lost (hidden) unity."

[NORMAN BROWN, from *Love's Body*]

*The book is a stream of quotation and insight. But there is so much – and it is
white hot. It needs another generation to cool it. Here is an insight that needs
more examination. As to the insight itself, if you bring something 'to a head',
have you created an idol? As to anamnesis, how much do we now remember and
connect with?*

5th September

Sometime during eternity
some guys show up
and one of them
who shows up real late
is a kind of carpenter
from some square-type place
like Galilee
and he starts wailing
and claiming he is hip
to who made heaven
and earth
and that the cat
who really laid it on us
is his Dad.

. . .
You're hot
they tell him
And they cool him
They stretch him on a Tree to cool
And everybody after that

                                              is always making models
                          of this Tree
                                    with Him hung up
              and always crooning His name
                                          calling Him to come down
                          and sit in
                                          on their combo
                    as if he is *the* king cat
                                                    who's got to blow
                          or they can't quite make it
                    Only he don't come down
                                                    from His Tree
                    Him just hang there
                                    on His Tree
                                          looking real Petered out
                          and real cool
                                          and also
                          according to a roundup
                                          of late world news
                    from the usual unreliable sources
                                                    real dead.

                [L. FERLINGHETTI, from *Sometime during Eternity*]

There is something that intrigues me here and it remains in the mind. How to be able to listen to new voices and distinguish the ephemeral from new metaphor? Difficult! Why, for example, 'cat'? [Slang for 'sure of himself'–ed.]

6th September

If I say that God is passionate, and that this gives us the key to the whole nature of reality, I am making a theological statement which is strictly poetic. The poetry of passionate love is the accurate language of theology . . .

But Jesus is 'the passionate God' supremely at that moment which turned all of living and loving inside out, which was his death and resurrection. But if he is that then, he is that always, and we have to see the passionate character of incarnation working out in his life as it moves towards that end. At the end, also, we shall see the ultimate encounter with evil . . .

The images of poetry are not confined to the categories of meaning which are consciously in the mind of the poet. He indeed receives them from conscious and also from deeply unconscious sources, and so he gives them, and from him they are received by others, and again given, changing and growing as they are thrown from one to another through many themes and ages, as the underlying reality is rediscovered and recreated. And ambiguity is of the essence of poetry, since it must speak at many levels and stir the depths of the mind in ways that words of single value – prose words – cannot do . . .

The right kind of language must have two characteristics. It must image the nature of the exchanges which are the life of God, and of God in humankind. But it must do so in a poetry which reflects for those who hear it the known truth of their particular cultural and personal experience. In other words, the poetry of good theology must grow from deep within the actual and concrete experience of people, so deep that when they hear that poetry they recognize in it both the accurate expression of their problems and hopes and loves and the evocation of deeper layers which they cannot touch but of which they are mutely aware, afraid and desirous. The need for such a language has been a problem weighing on the minds of many Christians.

[ROSEMARY HAUGHTON, from *The Passionate God*]

Very different from the God of the Thirty-Nine Articles, "without body, parts, or passions"! So many women writing about God are doing what men have not managed to do – with a more personal style, a new range of metaphor, and new suppositions. My wife used to ask men who were talking, "Are you speaking out of experience?"

7th September

> I am the great sun, but you do not see me,
>   I am your husband, but you turn away.
> I am the captive, but you do not free me,
>   I am the captain you will not obey.
>
> I am the truth, but you will not believe me,
>   I am the city where you will not stay,
> I am your wife, your child, you will leave me,
>   I am that God to whom you will not pray.
>
> I am your counsel, but you do not hear me,
>   I am the lover whom you will betray,
> I am the victor, but you do not cheer me,
>   I am the holy dove whom you will slay.

I am your life, but if you will not name me,
Seal up your soul with tears, and never blame me.

[CHARLES CAUSLEY, *I am the great sun*]

Sometimes a poet crystallises a set of contradictions which you can use as a basis
for reflection.

8th September

If love should count you worthy, and should deign
One day to seek your door and be your guest,
Pause! ere you draw the bolt and bid him rest,
If in your old content you would remain.
For not alone he enters; in his train
Are angels of the mist, the lonely guest
Dreams of the unfulfilled and unpossessed,
And sorrow, and life's immemorial pain.

He wakes desires you never may forget,
He shows you stars you never saw before,
He makes you share with him, for evermore,
The burden of the world's divine regret.
How wise you were to open not! and yet
How poor if you should turn him from the door.

[SIDNEY ROYSE LYSAGHT, *The Penalty of Love*]

How much easier life would be if we were not involved in these tensions, this
muted version of the Cross. And yes, we can evade it, but we shall never be
satisfied because we are not made to live without the demand!

9th September

In existentialist terminology man is 'thrown' into the world, con-
fronting alien and hostile powers which he seeks to understand and
master. The first confrontation was with nature, and for most of the
thousands of years of man's existence, life has been a game against
nature: to find shelter from the elements, to ride the waters and the
wind, to wrest food and sustenance from the soil, the waters, and other
creatures. The coding of much of man's behaviour has been shaped by

his adaptability to the vicissitudes of nature. In the nature of societal design, most of the world's societies still live in this game against nature.

Man as *homo faber* sought to make things, and in making things he dreamt of remaking nature. To be dependent on nature was to bend to its caprices and acknowledge its tyrannies and diminishing returns. To re-work nature, to make fabricated things, was to enhance man's powers. The industrial revolution was, at bottom, an effort to substitute a technical order, an engineering conception of function and rationality for the haphazard ecological distributions of resources and climates. In the industrial society, the cosmological vision was the game against fabricated nature.

The post-industrial society turns its back on both. In the salient experience of work, men live more and more outside nature, and less and less with machinery and things; they live with and encounter one another. The problem of group life is, of course, one of the oldest difficulties of human civilization, going back to the cave and the clan. But of necessity the context has changed. The oldest forms of group life were within the context of nature, and the overcoming of nature gave an external purpose to the lives of men. The group life that was hitched to things gave men a huge sense of power as they created mechanical artefacts to transform the world. But now these older contexts have been routinized, indeed have almost disappeared from men's view. In the daily round of work, men no longer confront nature, either as alien or beneficent, and fewer now handle artefacts and things. The post-industrial society is essentially a game between persons.

[DANIEL BELL, from *The Coming of Post-Industrial Society*]

I try once in a while to catch up with what others think has been happening in our world during the twenty years or so since I last thought about it!

10th September

The stranger tried the handle of the door, quietly, cautiously. But I had locked it on coming out. So he tried the handle of the kitchen door. Then he hesitated for a moment, turned towards me, and I saw him full face in the pale morning light. Only then did I recognize Le Grand Meaulnes.

For some time I stood still – frightened, despairing, helpless against the deep pain his return had suddenly reawakened. He had gone to the back of the house and now reappeared, still looking uncertain.

Then I went towards him, and embraced him, sobbing, unable to utter a word.

He understood at once:

"Then she is dead."

He stood motionless, insensible, forbidding, I took him by the arm and gently urged him towards the house. It was growing light. To get the worst over, I took him straight up to the room in which she had died. He went over to the bed, fell on his knees, and for a long while remained with his head buried in his arms.

He got up at last, wild-eyed, stumbling, bewildered. And again taking his arm I led him into the next room which had become a nursery. The baby had woken up alone while the nurse was downstairs, and had propped herself up into a sitting posture in her cradle. All one could see of her was her head, as her eyes turned to look at us in surprise.

"Here's your little girl," I said . . .

[HENRI ALAIN-FOURNIER, from *Le Grand Meaulnes*]

A novel that, unusual in modern French literature, keeps alive the strand of romantic love and loss with its upheavals so unlike the flat terrain in which the story is set. Here is the strange power of woman as romantic personification and the devastating effect it has on two men's lives.

11th September

The cloud-backed heron will not move:
He stares into the stream.
He stands unfaltering, while the gulls
And oyster-catchers scream.
He does not hear, he cannot see
The great white horses of the sea,
But fixes eyes on stillness
Below their flying team.

How long will he remain, how long
Have the grey woods been green?
The sky and the reflected sky,
Their glass he has not seen,
But silent as a speck of sand
Interpreting the sea and land,
His fall pulls down the fabric
Of all that windy scene.

Sailing with clouds and woods behind,
Pausing in leisured flight,
He stepped, alighting on a stone,
Dropped from the stars of night.
He stood there unconcerned with day,
Deaf to the tumult of the bay,
Watching a stone in water,
A fish's hidden light.

Sharp rocks drive back the breaking waves,
Confusing sea with air.
Bundles of spray blown mountain-high
Have left the shingle bare.
A shipwrecked anchor wedged by rocks,
Loosed by the thundering equinox,
Divides the herded waters
The stallion and his mare.

Yet no distraction breaks the watch
Of that time-killing bird.
He stands unmoving on the stone;
Since dawn he has not stirred.
Calamity about him cries,
But he has fixed his golden eyes
On water's crooked tablet,
On light's reflected word.

[VERNON WATKINS, from *The Heron*]

Whenever I see a nearby heron, it is always standing on a stone in the river. It is the Chinese ideogram for 'reflection'.

12th September

When those elements of dignity, order, reason, and intelligibility are prominent in human experience, we may reasonably describe as humanistic the outlook which ensues. This humanism will be much nearer to the type I have described as 'scientific' than to the 'literary' humanism, but I believe that this must be our starting point in any study of the central period of the Middle Ages.

The starting point is important because the subject has been confused by the tendency to start with the humanism of the Renaissance. This has given the love of ancient literature and the ability to imitate the style of ancient authors an exaggerated importance in judging medieval humanism. If we start with the concepts of natural nobility and of reason and intelligible order in the universe, the whole subject takes on a different appearance.

We may at once say that there is little evidence that these concepts played an important part in medieval experience before about 1050. In the main tradition of the early Middle Ages nearly all the order and dignity in the world was closely associated with supernatural power. There was order in symbolism and ritual, and order in worship and sacrament, and both of them were very elaborate and impressive. Man's links with the supernatural gave his life a framework of order and dignity: but in the natural order the chaos was almost complete. Almost nothing was known about secondary causes in natural events. Rational procedures in law, in government, in medicine, in argument were scarcely understood or practised even in the most elementary way. Man chiefly knew himself as a vehicle for divine activity. There was a profound sense of the littleness and sinfulness of man. Both physically and mentally human life had narrow limits: only in prayer and penance, in clinging to the saints, was there any enlargement. Man was an abject being, except when he was clad in symbolic garments, performing symbolic and sacramental acts, and holding in his hands the earthly remains of those who already belonged to the spiritual world ...

[R. W. SOUTHERN, from *Medieval Humanism and Other Studies*]

Here is the kind of authority that comes from knowing a subject supremely well. And humanism does matter. You can see that it does if you understand how very different our world is from that before 1050 – though you can argue that this century has seen a reversal.

13th September

By rejecting any definitive doctrinal expression of its Christian faith, the Society of Friends undid the distortion of Christianity through the influence of Greek philosophy, at least to a considerable extent. The effect is to shift the expression of Christianity from theory to practice. "By their fruits ye shall know them" becomes the accepted rule. Faith no longer means the acceptance of an established creed or the assent to an authoritative system of doctrine. It recovers its original meaning of trust and fearless confidence; and this spirit of faith is expressed in a way of living which cares for one another and for the needs of all men ...

This overcoming of the theoretical bias of traditional Christianity amongst us is not, however, complete. The unreality of Idealism and even of Sentimentalism still, on occasion, distorts our worship. But more important is the individualism which is an inevitable concomitant of the dualism which gives rise to the emphasis on theory and belief. In action we are in living contact with the world outside us; while for our spiritual or theoretical activities, we retire into ourselves, and into a world of ideas. This world in ourselves is an imaginary world, whose validity depends wholly upon a current reference to the material world – the world in which we act. It is only in action that we meet anyone but ourselves; and it is only in meeting others that we find ourselves and our own reality. We are not individuals in our own right; and in ourselves we have no value at all, since we are meaningless. Our human being is our relations to other human beings and our value lies in the quality of these relations. Our relation to God is itself real only as it shows itself in our relation to our neighbour. So the scriptures say, "If any man says he loves God, and loves not his brother, he is a liar; the truth is not in him." This is that 'likeness' between the two great commandments of which Jesus spoke. Individualism, therefore, is an error. The truth is that we are human beings only by being members of a community.

[JOHN MACMURRAY, from *Search for Reality in Religion*]

John MacMurray came back from the First World War sickened by organized Christianity. He kept the churches at arm's length but did join the Society of Friends. He did not insist on 100% perfection because to do this puts you out of touch with everyone else, but he did hammer away all his life at the significance of the personal.

14th September

So Swann was not mistaken in believing that the phrase of the sonata did, really, exist. Human as it was from this point of view, it belonged, none the less, to an order of supernatural creatures whom we have never seen, but whom, in spite of that, we recognize and acclaim with rapture when some explorer of the unseen contrives to coax one forth, to bring it down from that divine world to which he has access to shine for a brief moment in the firmament of ours. This was what Vinteuil had done for the little phrase. Swann felt that the composer had been content (with the musical instruments at his disposal) to draw aside its veil, to make it visible, following and respecting its outlines with a hand so loving, so prudent, so delicate and so sure, that the sound altered at every moment, blunting itself to indicate a shadow, springing back into life when it must follow the curve of some more bold projection. And one proof that Swann was not mistaken when he believed in the real existence of this phrase, was that anyone with an ear at all delicate for music would at once have detected the imposture had Vinteuil, endowed with less power to see and to render its forms, sought to dissemble (by adding, here and there, a line of his own invention) the dimness of his vision or the feebleness of his hand.

. . . (The phrase) reappeared, but this time to remain poised in the air, and to sport there for a moment only, as though immobile, and shortly to expire. And so Swann lost nothing of the precious time for which it lingered. It was still there, like an iridescent bubble that floats for a while unbroken. As a rainbow, when its brightness fades, seems to subside, then soars again and, before it is extinguished, is glorified with greater splendour than it has ever shown; so to the two colours which the phrase had hitherto allowed to appear it added others now, chords shot through with every hue in the prism, and made them sing. Swann dared not move, and would have liked to compel all the other people in the room to remain still also, as if the slightest movement might embarrass the magic presence, supernatural, delicious, frail, that would so easily vanish.

[MARCEL PROUST, from *Swann's Way*]

Like Marx, Proust was prepared to spend a lifetime doing one thing. And this whole novel shows a concern for the authentic in human relationships, across the sexes and the generations, in society and in the arts – here in music.

15th September

We saw one first and thought it was the only one,
For beauty made this flower seem to be alone
As stars born each alone in gulfs of time and space.
And opening distance like a star, with sunset face
Broken through earth as angels part the clouds, it made appear
The grass a firmament, confusing far and near.

As the evening star was not and is suddenly
On the fresh lawn of heaven, the clear unbroken sea –
Not made with hands, not born, it shines, not says "I am" –
So the one flower seemed in the grass, the shell-heart flame.

But the night ripens and another star
Takes body where none seemed in the ghost laden air;
And summoned to men's sight, exorcized to lay down
Invisibility, they crowd our vision,
Thicker than birds or bees, than clover leaves or stones;
And hands of children gather these solitary ones.

For most alone is most accompanied.
I watched the ballet dancer's lonely, floating steps and head
Proud, meek as one unborn, and wondering saw that she
Was compassed with her solitary kind, a galaxy.

So walking through the dunes the second day, we found
Another cranesbill flower, a world sprung from the ground;
And there a third and fourth, and further on the source,
The blood-tipped seeds, the opened rosy flowers,
There risen in time, a freshet flooding; strange and hard to see
As if they had been always known, yet could not be.

[E. J. SCOVELL, *Bloody Cranesbill on the Downs*]

*The poet sees the particular, and then recognizes that the particularity is not
lost by being part of a galaxy.*

16th September

Hence the absurdity of considering free competition as being the final
development of human liberty, and the negation of free competition as
being the negation of individual liberty and of social production founded
on individual liberty. It is only free development on a limited foundation – that of the dominion of capital.

This kind of individual liberty is thus at the same time the most
complete suppression of all individual liberty and total subjugation of
individuality to social conditions which take the form of material
forces and even of all-powerful objects that are independent of the
individuals relating to them.

The only rational answer to the deification of free competition by the
middle-class prophets or its diabolization by the socialists, lies in its own
development. If it is said that within the limits of free competition,
individuals by following their pure self-interest realize their social, or
rather their general interest, this means merely that they exert pressure
upon one another under the conditions of capitalist production, and that

this clash between them can only give rise to the conditions under which their interaction took place. Moreover, once the illusion that competition is the supposedly absolute form of free individuality disappears, this proves that the conditions of competition, i.e. of production founded on capital, are already felt and thought of as a barrier, that they indeed already are such and will increasingly become so. The assertion that free competition is the final form of the development of productive forces and thus of human freedom, means only that the domination of the middle class is the end of the world's history – of course quite a pleasant thought for yesterday's parvenus!

[KARL MARX, from *Grundrisse*]

David McLellan edited this work of Marx, which is six times the length of Das Kapital. *This passage, from 1857, is a summary of how to regard Marxism. For there is no system in sight. He wrote* The Communist Manifesto *for friends whom he left six months later. He scoffed at parties. Lenin was the one who turned his thought into a system. And that thinking will come back, not as an ideology wreaking havoc, but – if we are humble enough – by de-throning ideologies, not least the Stock Market, which will fall. Some things are bound to come to pass! Only truth can save you. Therefore you can afford to be patient. You don't have to dam the stream. You can let the current flow. For if you go against the divine intention for 'persons in community', you will fail. Sir Thomas Browne prayed, "Thy will be done, be it to my undoing."*

17th September

Hereto I come to view a voiceless ghost;
    Whither, O whither will its whim now draw me?
Up the cliff, down, till I'm lonely, lost,
    And the unseen waters' ejaculations awe me.
Where you will next be there's no knowing,
    Facing round about me everywhere,
      With your nut-coloured hair,
    And grey eyes, and rose-flush coming and going.

Yes: I have re-entered your olden haunts at last;
    Through the years, through the dead scenes I have tracked you;
What have you now found to say of our past –
    Scanned across the dark space wherein I have lacked you –
Summer gave us sweets, but autumn wrought division?
    Things were not lastly as firstly well

With us twain, you tell?
But all's closed now, despite Time's derision.

I see what you are doing: you are leading me on
　　To the spots we knew when we haunted here together,
The waterfall, above which the mist-bow shone
　　At the then fair hour in the then fair weather,
And the cave just under, with a voice still so hollow
　　That it seems to call out to me from forty years ago,
　　　　When you were all aglow,
　　And not the thin ghost that I now frailly follow!

Ignorant of what there is flitting here to see,
　　The waked birds preen and the seals flop lazily;
Soon you will have, Dear, to vanish from me,
　　For the stars close their shutters and the dawn whitens hazily.
Trust me, I mind not, though life lours,
　　The bringing me here; nay, bring me here again!
　　　　I am just the same as when
　　Our days were a joy, and our paths through flowers.

[THOMAS HARDY, *After a Journey*]

So often Hardy goes back to incidents of his early life. The fourth line of the third stanza sums up so much of his later life. It isn't regret. It is a tender remembering. And the memories are not barren: they are sustaining, once freed from blame and anger.

18th September

The casual glimpses which the ordinary population bestowed upon that wondrous world of sap and leaves called the Hintock Woods had been with these two, Giles and Marty, a clear gaze. They had been possessed of its finer mysteries as of commonplace knowledge; had been able to read its hieroglyphics as ordinary writing; to them the sights any sounds of night, winter, wind, storm, amid those dense boughs which had to Grace a touch of the uncanny, and even of the supernatural, were simple occurrences whose origin, continuance and laws they foreknew. They had planted together, and together they had felled; together they had, with the run of the years, mentally collected those remoter signs and symbols which seen in few were of runic obscurity, but altogether made an alphabet . . .

"He ought to have married you, Marty, and nobody else in the world!" said Grace with conviction, after thinking in the above strain.

Marty shook her head. "In all our outdoor days and years together, ma'am," she replied, "the one thing he never spoke of to me was love; nor I to him."

"Yet you and he could speak in a tongue that nobody else knew – not even my father; though he came nearest knowing – the tongue of the trees and fruits and flowers themselves."

...

"Now, my own, own love," she whispered, "you are mine and only mine; for she has forgot 'ee at last, although for her you died! But I – whenever I get up I'll think of 'ee, and whenever I lie down, I'll think of 'ee again. Whenever I plant the young larches I'll think that none can plant as you planted; and whenever I split a gad and whenever I turn the cider wring, I'll say none could do it like you. If ever I forget your name let me forget home and heaven! . . . But no, no, no, my love, I can never forget 'ee; for you was a good man, and did good things."

[THOMAS HARDY, from *The Woodlanders*]

This relationship to the woodland is true Hardy and unique. From within it comes the possibility of the human. But he never flinched from those accidental twistings of human relationships.

19th September

My face is against the grass – the moorland grass is wet –
My eyes are shut against the grass, against my lips there are the
little blades,
Over my head the curlews call,
And nor there is the night wind in my hair;
My heart is against the grass and the sweet earth; – it has gone
still at last.
It does not want to beat any more,
And why should it beat?
This is the end of the journey;
The Thing is found.

This is the end of all the roads –
Over the grass there is the night dew
And the wind that drives up from the sea along the moorland roads;
I hear a curlew start out from the heath

But fly off, calling through the dusk,
The wild, long, rippling call.
The Thing is found and I am quiet with the earth.
Perhaps the earth will hold it, or the wind, or that bird's cry,
But it is not for long in any life I know. This cannot stay,
Not now, not yet, not in a dying world, with me, for very long.
I leave it here;
And one day the wet grass may give it back –
One day the quiet earth may give it back –
The calling birds may give it back as they go by –
To someone walking on the moor who starves for love and will not
know
Who gave it to all these to give away;
Or, if I come and ask for it again,
Oh! then, to me.

[CHARLOTTE MEW, *Moorland Night*]

I can hear the curlews calling as I lie in bed at night. I am not sure what the poet has found, but I know she has found it!

20th September

That is the first duty of historical scholarship, criticism, again criticism, and criticism once more. A hard duty at times, for it may bring us into seeming collision with other duties and loyalties. But in reality by being true in this respect, we are true to the highest values of our civilization, that is to say, to our noblest traditions, to what we owe before every-thing to our own people and our nationality.

Without allowing ourselves to be misled by current views we should search fearlessly for the reality behind conventional terms, behind nationalistic or party phrases ... to look at the facts dispassionately, and unafraid, to use common sense. To train us in this exercise is one of the great gains that the study of history holds out for us, and I do not mean for the individual historian only, but for the community to which he belongs. It is salutary that there should be a group of men schooled in that discipline by which the dangerous clouds of fine-sounding words and of thoughtless repetition, of romanticism and mental laziness, can be dispelled ...

I lay so much stress on this aspect because some of the effects of the deceitful and crafty propaganda carried on by National Socialism against the true scholarly spirit, against criticism, against the intellect, are still with us . . . the most cold-blooded despotism and terrorism that have ever reigned, and the most terrible danger of destruction that has ever threatened European civilization, were made possible by a systematic extolling of instinct and passion above reason, by detestation and contempt of criticism. Reason and criticism are among the bulwarks of Western civilization.

And this is not all . . . no less needful is a sense for tradition, love for what has grown, love for what is distinctively ours, or to put it more briefly, love and respect . . . it, too, is a precious feature of the civilization that has helped to shape us, to which we belong, and which after the brutal outrages of revolution and fanaticism we must patiently try to nurse and to develop.

Reason and criticism are factors we cannot do without, but they are not enough. Even he who stands up for the rights of reason and criticism and, more, maintains that they belong to our most valuable cultural possessions, will know nowadays, that the great creative forces of life, of society and civilization, lie elsewhere.

Rationalists such as flourished in the 18th and 19th centuries are an extinct species. Nobody will nowadays regard the world as a mechanism driven by reason alone and to be controlled by reason. How shall we name these great creative forces? How shall we approach them?

[PIETER GEYL, from *Encounters with History*]

If you look at historians, their assessments are clearly coloured by their own points of view as well as their being convinced that their assessment is right. Hence this plea for criticism!

21st September

In late September the harvest was over. Elizabeth counted her money and surveyed the family's gleanings. She tidied the house for normal life to be resumed, and paid her small debts. Shoes must be bought for the three children, patterns for herself, and some unbleached calico, stout and cheap and warm – you could make almost any garment with it, if you must. Joseph was a wage-earner now; he had left school. You could be proud of him in a field, the tall, rosy, shapely lad, talking and laughing with everyone, quick at the work. Offers of permanent 'places' for him had been made; his new status must be marked. So Elizabeth and Joseph went to Banbury to do the shopping together. Seats were bespoken on the carrier's cart for the return, but eightpence would be saved by walking the outward journey – nine miles of field-paths to follow, crossing metalled roads only at two points. It was luxurious at first to walk through stubble or grass without rake or sickle in hand, with no heavy sheaves or aching back. Other families had the same errand, and groups passed or were passed by mother and son. When they were within a mile of Banbury, Elizabeth made a little speech. "Joe, I've been reckoning; I've brought thirty shillings with me. The shoes and calico will never cost all that. You've had to leave school, and we can't help it, but you have money to spend on books. Here be three shillings. You've read all I've got. It'll do you good to have some new. You shall choose 'em; I won't interfere, my boy."

Nine miles were a long and tiring way, but the astonishing sight of Banbury rapt Joseph out of all his other sensations. Around the Horse Fair and the markets, and Bridge Street and Sheep Street, wherever the streets broadened out, or houses stood back behind a little space, and in the inn-yards, stood rows of carriers' carts, hundreds of them, with their hinged shafts turned skywards to make close setting possible. "Nijni Novgorod!" breathed Joseph as the sight burst upon him. (His last school reading-book had contained a rich collection of descriptions of the world's oddities. There he had read of a giant fair in the Russian city.)

[M. H. ASHBY, from *Joseph Ashby of Tysoe*]

This book gives us a marvellous picture of agricultural life and conditions in Warwickshire a generation after Tolpuddle in Dorset. (And I too read of the Russian fair as a small boy.)

22nd September

Approach, for what we seek is here.
Alight, and sparely sup and wait
For rest in this outbuilding near;
Then cross the sward and reach that gate;
Knock, pass the wicket! Thou art come
To the Carthusians' world-famed home.

The silent courts, where night and day
Into their stone-carved basins cold
The splashing icy fountains play,
The humid corridors behold,
Where ghostlike in the deepening night
Cowled forms brush by in gleaming white.

The chapel, where no organ's peal
Invests the stern and naked prayer,
With penitential cries they kneel
And wrestle; rising then, with bare
And white uplifted faces stand,
Passing the Host from hand to hand.

Each takes; and then his visage wan
Is buried in his cowl once more.
The cells – the Suffering Son of Man
Upon the wall! the knee-worn floor!
And where they sleep, that wooden bed,
Which shall their coffin be, when dead.

The library, where tract and tome
Not to feed priestly pride are there,
To hymn the conquering march of Rome,
Nor yet to amuse, as ours are;
They paint of souls the inner strife,
Their drops of blood, their death in life.

The garden, overgrown – yet mild.
Those fragrant herbs are flowering there!
Strong children of the Alpine wild
Whose culture is the brethren's care;
Of human tasks their only one,
And cheerful works beneath the sun . . .

[MATTHEW ARNOLD, from *The Grande Chartreuse*]

From his very different place in life Arnold was sensitive to the importance of the Carthusians. He always struggled not to be provincial. And he was aware of the noise and bustle sweeping over us. But at the end of the poem one of the monks tells him that they have nothing directly to give him.

23rd September

Since brass, nor stone, nor earth, nor boundless sea,
But sad mortality o'ersways their power,
How with this rage shall beauty hold a plea
Whose action is not stronger than a flower?
O! how shall summer's honey breath hold out
Against the wrackful siege of battering days,

When rocks impregnable are not so stout,
Nor gates of steel so strong, but Time decays?
O fearful meditation! Where, alack,
Shall Time's best jewel from Time's crest lie hid?
Or what strong hand can hold his swift foot back?
Or who his spoil of beauty can forbid?
   O! none, unless this miracle have might,
   That in black ink my love may still shine bright.

[WILLIAM SHAKESPEARE, *Sonnet LXV*]

Lines 3 & 4 are a memorable couplet for me. And it is not just rage but a madness that overtakes us – the French 'rage'. How does beauty contend with this? And is the 'ink' about the artifice of composing a sonnet as an exercise or a genuine expression of an experience?

24th September

O wild West Wind, thou breath of Autumn's being,
   Thou from whose unseen presence the leaves dead
Are driven like ghosts from an enchanter fleeing,

   Yellow, and black, and pale, and hectic red,
Pestilence-stricken multitudes! O thou
Who chariotest to their dark wintry bed

The winged seeds, where they lie cold and low,
   Each like a corpse within its grave, until
Thine azure sister of the Spring shall blow

Her clarion o'er the dreaming earth, and fill
   (Driving sweet buds like flocks to feed in air)
With living hues and odours plain and hill;

Wild Spirit, which art moving everywhere;
Destroyer and preserver; hear, O hear!

   ...

Make me thy lyre, even as the forest is:
   What if my leaves are falling like its own?
The tumult of thy mighty harmonies

   Will take from both a deep autumnal tone
Sweet though in sadness. Be thou, Spirit fierce,

My spirit! Be thou me, impetuous one!
Drive my dead thoughts over the universe,
    Like wither'd leaves to quicken a new birth;
And by the incantation of this verse,

    Scatter, as from an unextinguish'd hearth
Ashes and sparks, my words among mankind
    Be through my lips to unawakened earth

The trumpet of a prophecy! O Wind,
If Winter comes, can Spring be far behind?

[P. B. SHELLEY, from *Ode to the West Wind*]

*Those two lines that start, 'Drive my dead thoughts . . .' describe what poetry is
for. But let this extract stand on its own!*

25th September

It is our very familiarity with God's expression of himself in the institutions of society, in the moral law, in the language and inner life of
Christians, in our own consciences, that helps to blind us to its divinity,
and emboldens us to claim the right to please ourselves unabashed by
its presence. Yet if thus, by refusing to recognize it, we turn the light
that is in us to darkness, how great is that darkness . . . If it becomes so
perverted in us that, having ceased to look for a God outside us, we will
not recognize Him in ourselves and in that which our conscience reveals
to us, we are committing the true sin against the Holy Ghost – a sin
unpardonable, in the sense that it shuts us out from the higher life – the
life of correlative self-reverence and self-abasement, of self-sacrifice and
self-development – the life of faith.
    . . . our danger (is) from the slow sap of an undermining indifference
which does not deny God and duty, but ignores them; which does not
care to trouble itself about them, and finds in our acknowledged
inability to know them, as we know matters of fact, a new excuse for
putting them aside . . .
    . . . The assertion that (God) exists cannot be verified like any other
matter of fact. But what if that be not because He is so far off, but
because He is so near? You cannot know Him as you know a particular
fact related to you, but neither can you so know yourself; and it is yourself – not as you are but as in seeking Him you become – that is His
revelation . . . The Word of God is very nigh thee, even in thy mouth and

in thy heart. It is the Word that has been made man; that has been
uttering in all the high endeavour, the long-suffering love, the devoted
search for the truth, which have so far moralized mankind, and that
now speaks in your conscience. It is the God in you which strives for
communication with God.

[T. H. GREEN, from *Sermon on Faith*]

*This is part of a long sermon which was preached to people who were prepared
to sit and who knew how to listen! And it is still worth hearing.*

26th September

    "Issues from the hand of God, the simple soul"
To a flat world of changing lights and noise,
To light, dark, dry or damp, chilly or warm;
Moving between the legs of tables and of chairs,
Rising or falling, grasping at kisses and toys,
Advancing boldly, sudden to take alarm,
Retreating to the corner of arm and knee,
Eager to be reassured, taking pleasure
In the fragrant brilliance of the Christmas tree,
Pleasure in the wind, the sunlight and the sea;
Studies the sunlit pattern on the floor
And running stags around a silver tray;
Confounds the actual and the fanciful,
Content with playing cards and kings and queens,
What the fairies do and what the servants say.
The heavy burden of the growing soul
Perplexes and offends more, day by day;
Week by week, offends and perplexes more
With the imperatives of 'is' and 'seems'
And may and may not desire and control.
The pain of living and the drug of dreams
Curl up the small soul in the window seat
Behind the *Encyclopaedia Britannica*.
Issues from the hand of time the simple soul
Irresolute and selfish, misshapen, lame,
Unable to fare forward or retreat,
Fearing the warm reality, the offered good,
Denying the importunity of the blood,
Shadow of its own shadows, spectre in its own gloom,

Leaving disordered papers in a dusty room;
Living first in the silence after the viaticum.

Pray for Guiterriez, avid of speed and power
For Boudin, blown to pieces,
For this one who made a great fortune,
And that one who went his own way.

Pray for Floret, by the boarhound slain between the yew trees,
Pray for us now and at the hour of our birth.

[T. S. ELIOT, *Animula*]

An extraordinary picture of childhood. I recall seeing a child at his grand-mother's funeral. He was looking up at the adult faces and seemed to be saying, "This is unintelligible to me, baffling, and is it the world I have to grow into?"

[*Eliot was born on this day in 1888. As a young man I was asked by the Catholic Crusade to respond to a talk Eliot gave at the Oxford School of Sociology. He was saying that you cannot afford to let people say what they want to say. I thought otherwise! I have such mixed feelings about him. I think he is too literary – though I know he was agonising personally. He was unable to emancipate himself from his acquaintance with too many works of literature. So there are only flashes of the authentic.*]

27th September

We begin to understand the Gospel only when we move on the frontiers of human life, face to face with that which goes beyond normal intellectual, ethical or political categories.

... Theologians and preachers have forgotten that it is their responsibility to take up the never-ending struggle – a struggle indeed – positive and critical – for a new reality ... If we shut ourselves up in our churches, if we hide – as it was said – in a ghetto, in closed circles, will we not go into intellectual decline? The life of thought and our moral life – will they not wither away, and our responsibility fade for those who are called by history to carry the heavy burdens of political and social duty?

... Few Communists or Christians know how to look beneath the surface of daily life or to keep themselves from being disorientated by the atmosphere of propaganda, vulgar atheism, or ecclesiastical prejudices about the impossibility of serious dialogue ...

[JOSEPH HROMADKA, from *Thoughts of a Czech Pastor*]

I talked with Hromadka in Vienna in 1952. It was a rare and humbling occasion. He had made up his mind in 1949 to go back to Czechoslovakia and face the grim situation there with his own people.

28th September

You could define art . . . as a passionate desire for accuracy, and the essentially aesthetic emotion as the excitement which is generated by direct communication. Ordinary language communicates nothing of the individuality and freshness of things. As far as that quality goes we live separated from each other. The excitement of Art comes from this rare and unique communication.

Creation of imagery is needed to force language to convey over this freshness of impression. The particular kind of art we are concerned with here, at any rate, can be defined as an attempt to convey over something which ordinary language and ordinary expression lets slip through. The emotion conveyed by an art in this case, then, is the exhilaration produced by the direct and unusual communication of this fresh impression. To take an example: What is the source of the kind of pleasure which is given to us by the stanza from Keats' *Pot of Basil*, which contains the line, "And she forgot the blue above the trees"? I do not put forward the explanation I give here as being, as a matter of fact, the right one, for Keats might have had to put trees for the sake of the rhyme, but I suppose for the sake of illustration that he put what he liked. Why then did he put 'blue above the trees' and not 'sky'? 'Sky' is just as attractive an expression. Simply for this reason, that he instinctively felt that the word 'sky' would not convey over the vividness and the actuality of the kind of feeling he wanted to express. The choice of right detail, the blue above the trees, forces that vividness on you and is the cause of the kind of thrill it gives you.

[T. E. HULME, from *Speculations*]

A North Staffordshire man, killed on this day in 1917, who had been to my school. We were never told about him! He had the makings of a first-class philosopher who did think ahead to a world after the First World War, with its clash between Fascism and an irresolute democracy which it did not have the strength to overcome in its early days. Here is an illustration of his determination to be accurate in the use of words.

29th September

What a clever moggie to tread only
    in the keys of G Minor and D Minor,
but then the gifted walk with care and flair
    as if on hot bricks; their bloodless
sleepwalking looks like exodus
    and the daggers are such dashing
footnotes. I chatted up a puss about Scarlatti
    but he had his Mason's secrets
and all I got was whiskers. Worthy men
    were walking by the gothic tulips,
sparrows purloined ears, so obviously
    the world was wired for sound.
Before you make your poem seem too twee
    I'll warn you, said the cat,
it's knowing when to stretto, how to keep
    your counter-subjects simple,
what to do when grandeur blows your mind –
    also, you'll notice that my fur
lies one way, so please don't brush it backwards
    and call the act experiment.
That sour cat was dead against our century
    and I was so ambitious,
I bought a cosmological notebook,
    Zinoviev's new machine
and a glossary of the German terms in Joyce –
    I'm in retirement till I make
my violent masterpiece: it's about a cat
    bigger than Bulgakov's, east
of Geoffrey in the night sky of the Lord;
    it stalks like plague along the grass,
fathering history on our post-diluvial age –
    named Jesus at the whole Jerusalem,
the Day of Modernism dawns; professors touched
    by wings fly purring to the moon.
These are its juvenilia and in Horatian
    retrospect I see the cat
restored to its domestic stalking one salt
    Iberian morning in the light
when genius saddened at the cold keyboard
    is jacked with white and black –

again our dainty-footed man's companion
strikes a balance with the dust
and props the world against its weary gravity.

[PETER PORTER, *Cat's Fugue*]

*Bulgakov's cat represents Stalin; Geoffrey was Christopher Smart's. What is
needed now in literature is something greater. Nothing has yet touched the
events of the middle years of this century. (I chose the phrase 'the night sky of the
Lord' as a title for a book I wrote about the seeming inability to come to terms
with the Holocaust.)*

30th September

Love is, precisely, the miracle of a person, a human body, that has
become wholly meaningful, and of a desire that branches out beyond all
limits. For, whether it be kept down or flattered, desire remains the
motive power of love: it is always the being who is most desired who
will be the most illuminating and mediating . . .

The truth is that every human being deserves to be looked at in this
way at least once in a lifetime – loved and venerated for what is authenti-
cally divine in him or her. And every human being is called to this.
It does seem, in fact, that where this discriminatory perception prevails
it is not the most beautiful people, nor even the youngest, who offer the
finest material in love, but rather those whose nature is rich, who have
'temperament', whose body and soul are gifted with a fine vitality.
Perfect beauties can be discouraging, like souls dedicated to calm; they
offer little purchase to the activity of loving, they leave it little to do.
Graceless bodies and souls, which give it too much to do, are also discouraging. Plato – in spite of the Greek fascination for bodily beauty –
regarded the love of a beautiful body as a stage lower than the love of a
"gentle soul in a body whose flowering is not brilliant."

. . . The only way in which the art of love in human beings can
genuinely progress is towards an always greater awareness: it is a long
elucidation of the spirit. But such a purification does not fit in with the
brevity of desire; it demands the long, the infinite patience of true love.
All the wiles of modern eroticism – which is, to my mind, already dated
– remain inefficient at satisfying our real thirst, which is spiritual.

[SUSANNE LILAR, from *Aspects of Love in Western Society*]

This is the best book I know on human sexuality and love. It examines what love has meant in the western world. The great failure is that we have not yet made love 'conjugal', where the sexes relate and do not stop merely with contact, and made this the texture and framework of our society. What might it mean so to 'conjugate'?

OCTOBER

1st October

Hatred of priests is one of the most profound human emotions, and among the least clearly understood. Doubtless it is as old as humanity. If the present age has contrived to raise it to an almost magic level of subtle efficacy, that is because the abasement or disappearance of other powers has made of the priest, apparently so closely related to the very structure of our society, a being more eccentric, harder to classify, than any of those magic greybeards whom the ancient world kept sequestered in temples, in close commerce only with the gods.

Today the priest is all the more strange and hard to classify, in that he will not admit that he is exceptional, nearly always the dupe of gross surface appearances, fooled by the ironic respect of some, the servile championship of others. But in the measure in which this contradiction, in any case more political than religious, from which their pride has so long drawn its sustenance, gets resolved by degrees into a kind of malicious indifference, the priest's ever-increasing sense of solitude impels him unarmed into the midst of social conflicts which the clergy fondly boasts it can solve with texts. But what does it matter? The hour is close upon us when, on the ruins of what is still left of our ancient Christian social order, the new order will be set up, that which will really be the rule of this world, the government of the Prince of this world, the prince whose kingdom is of this world. And then under the harsh law of necessity this pride of churchmen, sustained so long by mere convention outlasting belief, will have lost even its own purpose – and beggars' feet will make the earth quake again . . .

[GEORGES BERNANOS, from *The Open Mind*]

Hatred of the priest in France, contempt in England? Bernanos writes a quite outstanding description of the encounter with evil. He was convinced that there was indeed an epoch of hideous evil upon us – he saw so much, not just of Franco and Hitler, but of what Frenchmen did to Frenchmen in the war. And he saw how in a small village there was enough evil to be of concern to the priest whose job it is to confront it. I think the analysis is correct.

2nd October

It is eighteen years ago, almost to the day –
A sunny day with the leaves just turning,
The touch-lines new ruled – since I watched you play
Your first game of football, then, like a satellite
Wrenched from its orbit, go drifting away

Behind a scatter of boys. I can see
You walking away from me towards the school
With the pathos of a half-fledged thing set free
Into a wilderness, the gait of one
Who finds no path where the path should be.

That hesitant figure, eddying away
Like a winged seed loosened from its parent stem,
Has something I never quite grasp to convey
About nature's give-and-take – the small, the scorching
Ordeals which fire one's irresolute clay.

I have had worse partings, but none that so
Gnaws at my mind still. Perhaps it is roughly
Saying what God alone could perfectly show –
How selfhood begins with a walking away,
And love is proved in the letting go.

[C. DAY-LEWIS, *Walking Away*]

*An extraordinary simplicity in which something very significant is discerned
about small ordeals and love's letting go. If I had written an autobiography, I
would have called it* Firing the Clay.

3rd October

The near-drawn stone-smooth sky, closed in and grey,
  Broods on the garden, and the turf is still.
The dim lake shines, oppressed the fountains play,
  And shadowless weight lies on the wooded hill.

The patient trees rise separate, as if deep
  They listened dreaming through the hollow ground,
Each in a single and divided sleep,
  While few sad leaves fall heedless with no sound.

The marble cherubs in the wavering lake
    Stand up more still, as if they kept all there,
The trees, the plots, in thrall. Their shadows make
    The water clear and hollow as the air.

The silent afternoon draws in, and dark
    The trees rise now, grown heavier is the ground,
And breaking through the silence of the park
    Farther a hidden fountain flings its sound.

[EDWIN MUIR, *October at Hellbrunn*]

This poem is always connected in my mind with the film, Last Year in Marien-bad. Hellbrunn was a park and house in Czechoslovakia, and Muir is facing the fact that Nazism has wiped out everything human in the place. What is left is this landscape frozen into stillness. There is an atmosphere of mystery, but there are no human beings here. At best they are ghostly presences. And the poem is an extraordinary achievement in sound.

4th October

As time went on I merely learned that even those who were better than the rest could not keep themselves nowadays from killing or letting others kill, because such is the logic by which they live; and that we can't stir a finger in this world without the risk of bringing death to somebody.

Yes, I've been alarmed ever since I have realized that we all have plague, and I have lost my peace. And today, I am still trying to find it, still trying to understand all those others and not to be the mortal enemy of anyone. I only know that one must do what one can to cease being plague-stricken, and that's the only way in which we can hope for some peace, or, failing that, a decent death.

This, and only this, can bring relief to men, and, if not save them, at least do them the least possible harm and even sometimes a little good. So that is why I resolved to have no truck with anything which, directly or indirectly, for good reasons or for bad, brings death to anyone, or justifies putting him to death. That too, is why this epidemic has taught me nothing new, except that I must fight it at your side. I know posi-tively – yes, Rieux, I can say I know the world inside out as you may see – that each of us has the plague within him; no one, no one on earth is free from it. And I know too, that we must keep endless watch on ourselves lest in careless moment we breathe in somebody's face and fasten the infection on him.

[ALBERT CAMUS, from *The Plague*]

Few novels portray our European world so vividly. We are all infected and there is a struggle between cruelty and fear on the one hand and watchfulness and understanding and service on the other. A saintliness emerges in a few. And now AIDS.

5th October

Turning and turning in the widening gyre
The falcon cannot hear the falconer;
Things fall apart; the centre cannot hold;
Mere anarchy is loosed upon the world,
The blood-dimmed tide is loosed, and everywhere
The ceremony of innocence is drowned;
The best lack all conviction, while the worst
Are full of passionate intensity.

Surely some revelation is at hand;
Surely the Second Coming is at hand.
The Second Coming! Hardly are those words out
When a vast image out of Spiritus Mundi
Troubles my sight: somewhere in the sands of the desert
A shape with lion body and the head of a man,
A gaze blank and pitiless as the sun,
Is moving its slow thighs, while all about it
Reel shadows of the indignant desert birds.
The darkness drops again; but now I know
That twenty centuries of stony sleep
Were vexed to nightmare by a rocking cradle,
And what rough beast, its hour come round at last,
Slouches towards Bethlehem to be born?

[W. B. YEATS, *The Second Coming*]

We would all recognize and warm to the first section. The 'intensity' is in the market at the moment, not in tanks, but they are not far apart. As to the second section, what was going on in Yeats's mind? His own life was tortuous at the time, and we have only the words that came because of (or in spite of?) it.

6th October

All history is the history of thought.

But how does the historian discern the thoughts which he is trying to discover? There is only one way in which it can be done: by rethinking them in his own mind. The historian of philosophy, reading Plato, is trying to know what Plato thought when he expressed himself in certain words. The only way in which he can do this is by thinking it for himself. This, in fact, is what we mean when we speak of 'understanding' the words. So the historian of politics or warfare, presented with an account of certain actions done by Julius Caesar, tries to understand these actions, that is, to discover what thoughts in Caesar's mind determined him to do them. This implies envisaging for himself the situation in which Caesar stood, and thinking for himself what Caesar thought about the situation and the possible ways of dealing with it. The history of thought, and therefore all history, is the re-enactment of past thought in the historian's own mind.

This re-enactment is only accomplished, in the case of Plato and Caesar respectively, so far as the historian brings to bear on the problem all the powers of his own mind and all his knowledge of philosophy and politics. It is not a passive surrender to the spell of another's mind; it is a labour of active and therefore critical thinking. The historian not only re-enacts past thought, he re-enacts it in the context of his own knowledge, and therefore, in re-enacting it, criticizes it, forms his own judgment of its value, corrects whatever errors he can discern in it. This criticism of the thought whose history he traces is not something secondary to tracing the history of it. It is an indispensable condition of the historical knowledge itself. Nothing could be a completer error concerning the history of thought than to suppose that the historian as such merely ascertains 'what so-and-so thought', leaving it to someone else to decide 'whether it was true'. All thinking is critical thinking; the thought which re-enacts past thoughts, therefore, criticizes them in re-enacting them.

[R. G. COLLINGWOOD, from *The Idea of History*]

One of the few historians in this country who asks what history is for. Colling-wood reckons it is about getting into the mind of people from the past, their motives and choices. Is this in fact possible? The Marxist would say that he forgets that a person can think only within the limits of the patterns which he lives in and have been shaping him. What then are the fragments of thought that are shaping our actions?

7th October

>   . . . Now I cease to glower
> My fit reverts to its original anxiety, and then
> Turns to destruction: I shout at you again,
> And as this leaves my lips I hear the cold echo
> Of a man left alone between these walls, and know
> How much I love you: suddenly, like a pulled tendon, taut
> Runs the touched nerve. I can see that you are hurt,
> And yet I will not humble me: as I pass by
> Silent, withdrawn, my belly heaves, my heart gives a sigh,
> My body wrestles like a captive in a net,
> Heart, mind, compassion fight me strenuously, yet.
> I dare not let them free until you lift the phone,
> And I must plead for amnesty. Bruised, in a stun
> Our day goes by, then the return of trust
> Restores romantic softness, that rise away to lust.
>
> I watched the water spring this morning wondering
> At its continual fullness as each ripple ring
> Spread from the source, at the continual wave
> That wells restoring by such waterlights. The peace you gave
> Flows thus back round our home: in this fresh lake
> Our children dance, the blue kingfisher streaks, the
>   waterflowers awake.

> [DAVID HOLBROOK, from *The Return*]

Few have put so well this experience within marriage.

8th October

> When Jesus walked into the wilderness
> he carried a man on his back,
> at least it had the form of a man,
> a fisherman perhaps with a wet nose,
> a baker perhaps with flour in his eyes.
> The man was dead it seems
> and yet he was unkillable.
> Jesus carried many men
> yet there was only one man –
> if indeed it was a man.

...

For forty days, for forty nights
Jesus put one foot in front of the other
and the man he carried,
if it was a man,
became heavier and heavier.
He was carrying all the trees of the world
which are one tree.
He was carrying forty moons
which are one moon.
He was carrying all the boots
of all the men in the world
which are one boot.
He was carrying our blood.
One blood.

To pray, Jesus knew,
is to be a man carrying a man.

[ANNE SEXTON, from *The Death Notebooks*]

The weight of prayer, the burden-bearing, the endurance. "If I be lifted up I will draw all men unto me." All? What meaning has this in multi-religious cities? This is a new phenomenon, Christianity as one among many faiths. What do we do now with the symbolism of the Cross? Is the weakening preparatory to a new widening?

9th October

Religious doctrines are not so much the causes of conversion as the consequences, and the poems that are the cause of such an experience in the reader are also the consequence of a similar experience in the writer. The converted man or the poet finds that he cannot adequately describe his experience, with all its reality and value, without using the language of religion or poetry.

Psychology no more replaces that language than botany replaces Wordsworth's *Daffodils*. We can only force it into service if we give to psychological terms an emotional weight and a range of implications that will destroy their scientific value.

Similarly, we may speak of prayer, as we can speak of conversion, in psychological terms; but it is effective only if, in the act of praying, we think of it as a reality, a transaction with an unseen power. It is the fact of prayer which makes the language of religion necessary, and it is prayer that distinguishes religion from moral, philosophical or aesthetic sentiment. It is the daily counterpart of conversion: we may say that it is an act of supreme mental honesty, reaching beyond the conscious mind to the world of hidden motives; that it allows us to realize our deepest and most lasting desires and to set in order the contradictions and confusions within ourselves; that it involves at the one moment the most strenuous effort of honesty and the most complete relaxation. But we cannot describe it adequately unless we speak of it as a communion with something beyond ourselves:

Church-bells beyond the starres heard, the soul's blood,
The land of spices, something understood.

This sense of an access of strength, and of a voice wiser than our conscious selves, is the core of religion and worship, and makes all definitions of God in terms of metaphysical absolutes seem irrelevant and useless.

[MICHAEL ROBERTS, from *The Modern Mind*]

I joined Michael Roberts once at a WEA school at Aspatria. I find this passage on prayer worthwhile because of its emphasis on honesty.

10th October

The salvation that Jesus offered was dismissed . . . because of our praxis, the age-old yet ever new praxis of man and society, which sweeps away whatever or whoever does not fit into the pattern of things. The offer of religious salvation is – paradoxically enough – the condition of its potential rejection. Only thus was that rejection made manifest in its religious implication and only thus did it acquire an ethical depth that cannot be plumbed or measured. We rightly speak of a demonic strain in our history which, despite amelioration here and there, appears over and over again; a fundamental human impotence dogs our best intentions and achievements. The hard facts of history do not in themselves offer any guarantee or hope that ultimate shalom and reconciliation are possible. We humans are good at making our history on this earth go wrong or allowing it to do so. Shalom, universal meaning and reconciliation, can therefore only be articulated, given our negative contrast experiences, in parables and eschatological symbols, in images of promise and admonition, finally of God's Kingdom or God's rule, of forgiveness and metanoia. The rejection of proffered salvation is not theoretically explicable, because evil in all its depths is in the last analysis not amenable to understanding and eludes every theory; it will not fit into any system of ontological unity or identity-philosophy; and the only adequate response is via a practical exercise of resistance to evil, not a theory about it. Believing in a universal meaning to history therefore cannot be thematized in a 'universal history', philosophically interpreted; it only validates itself in a course of action that tries to overcome evil and suffering in the strength of the religious affirmation that things can be otherwise. Evil and suffering are the dark stain upon our history to which no one can offer a solution and which we cannot reconcile with a theodicy or ever wipe away with a social critique and the praxis resulting from it (however necessary they may be).

[EDWARD SCHILLEBEECKX, from *Jesus*]

This puts yesterday's questioning to all religious traditions and challenges Christianity as we have known it.

11th October

It may not appear very striking to say that *Paradise Lost* is about punishment. But it is a striking fact, and it is worth our while to remember that punishment, in the old tributary and retributive sense, is not only *not* an integral part of Christianity as stated by Christ, but that his main purpose was to supersede it. Two thousand years of 'Christian' history have consisted largely of intellectual and practical manifestations that human beings in general cannot without great difficulty understand this simple and profound revolution. The many gentle and mystical interpretations of the ideas of sacrifice and atonement must not mislead us. When we start to formulate our ideas about human nature and about man's place in the universe, we are predominantly liable to talk in fact about our own most primitive fears and passions, the shadows of which we dimly perceive and try to objectify. As a result, our theology, by whatever name we call it, reveals itself as still tied to the God of Wrath; patriarchal, aggressive, tense, aware of danger within and without, particularly aware of the danger of love, and deeply pre-occupied with payment of a more or less material kind, which ranges from out-and-out simony to merely telling one's beads, or to the various neurotic compulsions.

Preoccupation with sin, one's own and other people's, also has the mechanical quality which subsumes it under payment in kind. For the belief in original sin is psychologically a tribute, a mechanical confession that we are incurable and that therefore we must pay endlessly in order to be allowed to live.

One may readily understand how St Paul and the early theologians of the Church became dominated by the death of Christ and saw it out of due proportion to his life; but one should not fail to note how this negative interpretation, with its emphasis on sin, hatred of sexual life (which means in practice Hate), and punishment, has foisted itself on the whole of explicit theology since. When we build intellectual structures, we all drive more and more towards the crudely mechanical and away from the life of the imagination and experience.

[KATHLEEN NOTT, from *The Emperor's Clothes*]

This book is a refreshing blast against the religious gurus of her time – C. S. Lewis, T. S. Eliot, Dorothy Sayers. Why has the Church fastened on this incubus and why have we not seen it?

12th October

First of the first,
Such I pronounce Pompilia, then as now
Perfect in whiteness – stoop down, my child,
Give one good moment to the poor old Pope,
Heart-sick at having all his world to blame –
Let me look at thee in the flesh as erst,
Let me enjoy the old clean linen garb,
Not the new splendid vesture! Armed and crowned,
Would Michael, yonder, be, nor crowned nor armed,
The less pre-eminent angel? Everywhere
I see in the world the intellect of man,
That sword, the energy his subtle spear,
The knowledge which defends him like a shield –
Everywhere; but they make not up, I think,
The marvel of a soul like thine, earth's flower
She holds up to the softened gaze of God!
It was not given Pompilia to know much,
Speak much, to write a book, to move mankind,
Be memorized by who records my time.
Yet if in purity and patience, if
In faith held fast despite the plucking fiend,

Safe like the signet-stone with the new name
That saints are known by – if in right returned
For wrong, most pardon for worst injury,
If there be any virtue, any praise –
Then will this woman-child have proved – who knows? –
Just the one prize vouchsafed unworthy me . . .
It was authentic to the experienced ear
O' the good and faithful servant. Go past me
And get thy praise, – and be not far to seek
Presently when I follow if I may!

[ROBERT BROWNING, from *The Ring and the Book*]

The Pope is saying that this woman brought the grace of God near to him for she had acted as truly as God would want her to act: she simply embodied the right thing.

13th October

Son Martin, take care – it is I who have sown in you this bitterness. It is with me and in me and by my ordinance that you suffer from the wretched state of my Church. Don't presume upon this suffering to my face. Others who love me a thousand times better than you are capable of loving me don't feel it to the same degree, or hardly feel it at all. What revolts your conscience seems to them no more than a bad dream and they turn their thoughts away from it . . .

But your place is firmly marked out in this world, – I have seen to that – and I have made you a carnal man, solid and heavy. I shall pit you against other men just as carnal as yourself, formed of the same matter, so that they shall feel the force of your blows, because it is through you, if you keep faith with me, that I have decided to break their pride and to avenge my people whose souls they are putting up for auction.

But don't deceive yourself, brother Martin, this is neither the greatest nor the noblest task I could give you: it is simply the task made to your measure. I have given you health and strength and popular eloquence and a genius for controversy almost equal to that of my son Augustine. But these are not the favourite weapons of our saints, you will only find them good for tearing up, sweeping away, and uprooting the corrupted stock. Think of my apostle Paul whom you are so fond of. He too was a carnal man, violent, rash, argumentative: what a business I had to soften and unstiffen his soul . . .

From the beginning my Church has been what it is today, and will be
to the end of time, a scandal to the strong, a disappointment to the
weak, the ordeal and consolation of those interior souls who seek in it
nothing but myself. Yes, brother Martin, whoever looks for Me there
will find Me there, but he will have to look, and I am better hidden
than people think or certain of my priests would have you believe. I am
still more difficult to discover than I was in the little stable at Bethlehem
for those who will not approach me humbly in the footsteps of the
shepherds and the Magi ... but if you want to find me, the thing to do is
to do what they did on the old road in Judaea, buried under the snow,
and ask for the one thing you need, a star and a pure heart.

[GEORGES BERNANOS, from *Bernanos par lui-même*]

*Writing on Martin Luther, Bernanos appeals to us because the action of God is
brought into human history. God raises up particular persons, no better than
others, some of whom we approve of, some not, but they are the tools with which
God acts. Compared with this, most of what I have chosen in this anthology is
frivolous. I have had a comfortable life – and that is a minority life on this
earth.*

14th October

The most valuable insights into the human situation have been gained
not through patient introspection or systematic scrutiny, but rather
through the surprise and shock of dramatic failures. Indeed it is usually
in the wake of frustration, in moments of crisis and self-disillusionment,
and rarely out of astonishment at man's glorious achievements, that
radical reflection comes to pass.

This is an age in which it is impossible to think about the human
situation without shame, anguish, and disgust, in which it is impossible
to experience enjoyment without grief and unending heartache, to
observe personal triumphs without pangs of embarrassment. Why do
we ask the question about man? Because the knowledge about man
which we had accepted as self-evident has proved to be a mass of
bubbles bursting at the slightest increase of temperature. Some of us
live in dismay caused by what man has revealed about himself. The
sickness of our age is the failure of conscience rather than the failure of
nerve. Our conscience is not the same. Stultified by its own bankruptcy, staggered by the immense complexity of the challenge, it
becomes subject to automation. Pride in our immediate past would be

callousness, just as optimism about the immediate future would be stupidity. In the period of the Enlightenment a major concern of philosophy was to emancipate man from the clutches of the past. Today our concern seems to be to protect ourselves against the abyss of the future.

[ABRAHAM HESCHEL, from *Who is Man?*]

Heschel is indeed a man of radical reflection. How often today do we hear people talk of conscience?

15th October

To sit in the Throne of God is to inhabit Eternity. To reign there is to be pleased with all Things in Heaven and Earth from Everlasting to Everlasting, as if we had the Sovereign Disposal of them. For He is to Dwell in us, and We in Him, because He liveth in our Knowledge and We in His. His Will is to be our Will, since our Will is to be His Will, so that both being joyned and becoming one, we are pleased in all His Works as He is, and herein the Image of God perfectly consisteth. No Artist maketh a throne too wide for the Person. God is the Greatest and Divinest Artist.

[THOMAS TRAHERNE, from *Centuries of Meditation*]

So many of the Centuries *are wonderful in rush and gush. But I wanted to know where the man himself was as a human being. Here he writes in a straightforward working way. Elsewhere he says he has decided to live on £10 a year. This meant wearing leather clothes because they never wear out.*

16th October

> Christ is the language which we speak to God
> And also God, so that we speak in truth;
> He in us, we in him, speaking
> In one another, to him, the city of God.

   I Such a fool as I am you had better ignore.
      Tongue twist, malevolent, fat mouthed,
      I have no language but that other one,
      His the Devil's; no mouse I, creeping out of the cheese
      With a peaked cap scanning the distance

Looking for truth.
Words when I have them, come out, the Devil
Encouraging, grinning from the other side of the street,
And my tears
Streaming, a blubbered face, when I am not laughing.
Where in all this
Is calm, measure,
Exactness,
The Lord's peace?

VI   So speech is treasured, for the things it gives
Which I can not have, for I speak too plain
Yet not so plain as to be understood.
It is confusion and a madman's tongue.
Where drops the reason, there is no one by.
Torture my mind: and so swim through the night,
As envy cannot touch you, or myself.
Sleep comes, and let her, warm at my side, like death.
The Holy Spirit and the Holy One
Of Israel be my guide. So among tombs
Truth may be sought, and found, if we rejoice
With Ham and Shem and Japhet in the dark.
The ark rolls onward over a wide sea.
Come sleep, come lightning, comes the dove at last.

[C. H. SISSON, from *The Usk*]

*The poem is a series of six comments on the first statement. Here are the first and
the sixth. Speech twisted yet treasured!*

17th October

They shut the road through the woods
Seventy years ago.
Weather and rain have undone it again,
And now you would never know
There was once a road through the woods
Before they planted the trees.
It is underneath the coppice and heath
And the thin anemones.
Only the keeper sees
That, where the ring-dove broods,

And the badgers roll at ease,
There was once a road through the woods.

Yet, if you enter the woods
Of a summer evening late,
When the night-air cools on the trout-ringed pools
Where the otter whistles his mate,
(They fear not men in the woods,
Because they see so few.)
You will hear the beat of a horse's feet,
And the swish of a skirt in the dew,
Steadily cantering through
The misty solitudes,
As though they perfectly knew
The old lost road through the woods . . .
But there is no road through the woods.

[RUDYARD KIPLING, *The Way through the Woods*]

As a youngster wandering through the woods where the road had grown over (it was called Whisper Lane), I became aware of worlds that are lost – not only a road, but a patch of dead trees.

18th October

Calling all butterflies of every race
From source unknown but from no special place
They ever will return to all their lives,
Because unlike the bees they have no hives,
The milkweed brings up to my very door
The theme of wanton waste in peace and war
As it has never been to me before.
And so it seems a flower's coming out
That should if not be talked then sung about.
The countless wings that from the infinite
Make such a noiseless tumult over it
Do no doubt with their colour compensate
For what the drab weed lacks of the ornate.
For drab it is its fondest must admit.
And yes, although it is a flower that flows
With milk and honey, it is bitter milk,
As anyone who ever broke its stem

And dared to taste the wound a little knows.
It tastes as if it might be opiate.
But whatsoever else it may secrete,
Its flowers' distilled honey is so sweet
It makes the butterflies intemperate.
There is no slumber in its juice for them.
One knocks another all from where he clings.
They knock the dyestuff off each other's wings –
With thirst on hunger to the point of lust . . .

But waste was of the essence of the scheme.
And all the good they did for man or god
To all those flowers they passionately trod
Was leave as their posterity one pod
With an inheritance of restless dream.
He hangs on upside down with talon feet
In an inquisitive position odd
As any Guatemalan parakeet.
Something eludes him. Is it food to eat?
Or some dim secret of the good of waste?
He almost has it in his talon clutch.
Where have those flowers and butterflies all gone
That science may have staked the future on?
He seems to say the reason why so much
Should come to nothing must be fairly faced.

[ROBERT FROST, from *Pod of the Milkweed*]

And shall be in due course.

19th October

I marked when the weather changed,
    And the panes began to quake
And the winds rose up and ranged
    That night, lying half-awake.

Dead leaves blew into my room
    And alighted upon my bed,
And a tree declared to the gloom
    Its sorrow that they were shed.

> One leaf of them touched my head,
> And I thought that it was you,
> There stood as you used to stand,
> And saying at last you knew.

[THOMAS HARDY, *A Night in November*]

The touch of the leaf – it sends a shudder through you. Hardy so often recalls, through something from the natural world, an ordinary moment which unlocks a recognition, a recollection of human relationships that were of supreme importance. And you carry it with you as part of your spiritual food. It is what human memory is for.

20th October

If I were to think that my wife's devotion to me is nothing more than the simple expression of a necessity to love somebody, that there is nothing in me which justifies such devotion, I should be miserable. Rather, I take it, is the love of woman to man a revelation of the relationship in which God stands to him – of what ought to be, in fact. In the love of a woman to the man who is of no account, God has provided us with a true testimony of what is in His own heart . . . The love of a woman is, in other words, a living witness, never failing of an actuality in God which otherwise we should never know.

[MARK RUTHERFORD, from *Deliverance*]

A man sensitive to suffering, to the horrors done to the poor, and to the depth of love.

21st October

When at last *Huckleberry Finn* was completed and published and widely loved, Mark Twain became somewhat aware of what he had accomplished with the book that had begun as journeywork and depreciated, postponed, threatened with destruction. It is his masterpiece and perhaps he learned to know that. But he could scarcely have estimated it for what it is, one of the world's great books and one of the central documents of American culture.

Wherein does its greatness lie? Primarily in its power of telling the truth . . . No-one, as he well knew, sets a higher value on truth than a boy. Truth is the whole of a boy's conscious demand upon the world of adults. He is likely to believe that the adult world is in a conspiracy to lie to him, and it is this belief, by no means unfounded, that arouses Tom and Huck and all boys to their moral sensitivity, their everlasting concern for justice, which they call fairness. At the same time it often makes them skilful and profound liars in their own defence, yet they do not tell the ultimate lie of adults: they do not lie to themselves. That is why Mark Twain felt that it was impossible to carry Tom Sawyer beyond boyhood – in maturity "he would lie just like all the other one-horse men of literature and the reader would conceive a hearty contempt for him."

. . . The truth of *Huckleberry Finn* is of a different kind from that of *Tom Sawyer*. It is a more intense truth, fiercer and more complex. *Tom Sawyer* has the truth of honesty – what it says about things and feelings is never false and always both adequate and beautiful. *Huckleberry Finn* has this kind of truth too, but it also has the truth of moral passion; it deals directly with the virtue and depravity of man's heart . . .

. . . *Huckleberry Finn* is a great book because it is about a god – about, that is, a power which seems to have a mind and will of its own, and which to men of moral imagination appears to embody a great idea.

[LIONEL TRILLING, from *The Liberal Imagination*]

I would concur with this estimate of Huckleberry Finn. *Mark Twain illustrates how it was possible for some Americans to re-discover what moral choice really means. For they were in a new situation, innocent of Europe. And Twain was free of camp-fire evangelism and Jeffersonian liberalism. He was neither cultured nor a moralist, but he stumbled through as a human being to a knowledge of moral imagination.*

22nd October

When a building threatens to fall one begins by rescuing those whom it may bury. If they, at least, remain alive, they will rebuild it if they take any heed. It was a question of saving conscience first, the true tabernacle of the living God. There exists one universal truth for man, dazzling in its clarity, and which has no need of compromise. Whoever rejects it makes an attack on man. Christians possess this truth – but not only Christians, for it has penetrated humanity for centuries; only, they should possess it more clearly than others. The Church respects it from habit, without knowing fully what it says, and they themselves feel a proprietary right in their souls, although they scarcely pause to consider the real nature of this truth which belongs to them. They are no longer able to produce it before the demands of the century; and the century cries its need aloud . . . Both ironical and pitiful, it brings to light all the contradictions, and Christians can only rub their eyes and say: "Is that my truth?" They feel that it is impossible to live this truth as it is, above all in such a period of upheaval. That is why they have no wish to see it naked, but rather adorned with those material possessions and the social consideration which attach themselves to ideas when they grow complex. In former days, the Christian truth was proud and unyielding in its purity: growing old, it becomes lax through fear of being soon abandoned. It is true that it is still paid court to; but will this last much longer? Nothing could be less sure. It has already abandoned much: and its splendid remnants, which barely hold together any longer, will soon betray it. Christians feel themselves falling into the grip of fear.

[PIERRE EMMANUEL, from *The Universal Singular*]

Why cannot religious people recognize that conscience is wider than the Church? Newman suggested that "conscience is like a clock: you have to remember to wind it up."

23rd October

That time of year thou mayst in me behold
When yellow leaves, or none, or few, do hang
Upon those boughs which shake against the cold,
Bare ruin'd choirs, where late the sweet birds sang.
In me thou see'st the twilight of such day
As after sunset fadeth in the west;
Which by and by black night doth take away,
Death's second self, that seals up all in rest.
In me thou see'st the glowing of such fire,
That on the ashes of his youth doth lie,
As the deathbed whereon it must expire,
Consum'd with that which it was nourish'd by.
　　This thou perceiv'st, which makes thy love more strong,
　　To love that well which thou must leave ere long.

[WILLIAM SHAKESPEARE, *Sonnet LXXIII*]

Autumnal and unforgettable. Whether an awareness of the limitations of age or of time – it is fruitless to regret the decay and the endings – the only question is whether or not this leads you to love more or to betray yourself by neglecting to love.

24th October

. . . The balance, fortuitously rather than deliberately achieved, between the State and the subordinate centres of authority, between centralization and localism, between compulsion and free choice, which had served sufficiently well for the fifties and most of the sixties, was being upset. It would be inexact to say that the transition was from greater to less freedom; for many people, married women, for example and tenant-farmers, it was towards much greater freedom. What was fading, rather, was a certain concept of freedom, based on that "preservation of an inner sphere exempt from State power" in which, in Acton's opinion, all liberty, *in radice*, consisted. The 'inner sphere' had never been as extensive as most contemporaries imagined and its preservation had been much more dependent upon authority and the accidents of rank and wealth than they admitted. But it, or the illusions entertained about it, had given a particular strength and unity to the mid-Victorian generation. It had enabled them to see complex problems in simple – often in dangerously simple – terms, to be reasonably confident that the qualities of manliness, independence and energy by which they set such store would produce a satisfactory synthesis, to accept the present with a good deal of contentment and to face the future in attitudes which range from rather fatuous hope to stoical equanimity. It had not prevented them, subtle and prudent as they liked to see themselves, from being content with specious generalizations and with much that was superficial, with seeing the result rather than investigating the cause; but it had given them a standard, that of the responsibility, to God and Man, of a sane adult for the foreseeable consequences of his actions, which enabled them to take many wrongs and many evils in their robust stride.

[J. L. BURN, from *The Age of Equipoise*]

Just what is the sphere of freedom? The Thatcher years made us ask that again. If you simplify because you cannot cope with all the details, what are you sacrificing? How can you maintain human values when faced with a unique amount and pace of change? Where do 'free market' and 'social cohesion' come into this?

25th October

Angelo	Your brother is a forfeit of the law,
	And you but waste your words.
Isabella	Alas, Alas!
	Why, all the souls that were, were forfeit once,
	And He that might the vantage best have took
	Found out the remedy. How would you be
	If He, which is the top of judgment, should
	But judge you as you are? O, think on that,
	And mercy then will breathe within your lips,
	Like man new made.
Angelo	Be you content, fair maid;
	It is the law, not I, condemn your brother;
	Were he my kinsman, brother, or my son,
	It should be thus with him. He must die tomorrow.
. . .	
Isabella	O, 'tis excellent,
	To have a giant's strength, but it is tyrannous
	To use it like a giant.
Lucio	(To Isabella) That's well said.
Isabella	Could great men thunder
	As Jove himself does, Jove would ne'er be quiet,
	For every pelting petty officer
	Would use his heaven for thunder; nothing but thunder.
	Merciful Heaven,
	Thou rather with thy sharp and sulphurous bolt
	Splits the unwedgeable and gnarled oak,
	Than the soft myrtle. But man, proud man,
	Dress'd in a little brief authority,
	Most ignorant of what he's most assur'd –
	His glassy essence – like an angry ape
	Plays such fantastic tricks before high heaven
	As makes the angels weep; who, with our spleens,
	Would all themselves laugh mortal.

[WILLIAM SHAKESPEARE, from *Measure for Measure*]

This as an observation of our times: the power of the one in authority to prolong his will and yet be so ignorant. So often is our power out of all proportion to our moral integrity. No one is good enough to be the master of another – and you do not realize it until you are·in such a position. Measure for Measure *is a*

comedy which resolves matters at one level, but it is only a temporary respite.
The underlying issues are left unresolved.

26th October

I remember stopping for a long time one day to look at a little plaque
on the wall of a house in the Via degli Artisti, representing the Annunciation. An angel and a young girl, their bodies inclined towards each
other, their knees bent as if they were overcome by love, 'tutto tremente',
gazed upon each other like Dante's pair; and that representation of a
human love so intense that it could not reach further seemed the perfect
earthly symbol of the love that passes understanding. A religion that
dared to show forth such a mystery for everyone to see would have
shocked the congregations of the north, would have seemed a sort of
blasphemy, perhaps even an indecency. But here it was publicly shown,
as Christ showed himself on earth.

That these images should appear everywhere, reminding everyone of
the Incarnation, seemed to me natural and right, just as it was right that
my Italian friends should step out frankly into life. This open declaration
was to me the very mark of Christianity, distinguishing it from the older
religions. For although the pagan gods had visited the earth and con-
versed with men, they did not assume the burden of our flesh, live our
life and die our death, but after their intervention withdrew into their
impenetrable privacy. There is a church in Assisi built above an older
one, reputed once to have been dedicated to the ancient gods. In the
lower church all is darkness and mystery: in the upper one, all clear
colour and light; and ascending to it is like passing into another age . . .

. . . I think that if anyone examines his life, he will find that most good
has come to him from a few loyalties, and a few discoveries made many
generations before he was born, which must always be made anew.
These too may sometimes appear to come by chance, but in the infinite
web of things and events chance must be something different from what
we think it to be. To comprehend that which is not given to us, and to
think of it is to recognize a mystery, and to acknowledge the necessity of
faith. As I look back on the part of the mystery which is my own life, my
own fable, what I am most aware of is that we receive more than we can
ever give; we receive it from the past, on which we draw with every
breath, but also – and this is the point of faith – from the Source of the
mystery itself, by the means which religious people call Grace.

[EDWIN MUIR, from *An Autobiography*]

The first part of this quotation – it is wonderful for the Northener to be presented with the Incarnation! And the second – Muir's sense of enrichment by what has come to him from the past.

27th October

It was my thirtieth year to heaven
Woke to my hearing from harbour and neighbouring wood
    And the mussel pooled and the heron
        Priested shore
    The morning beckon
With water praying and call of seagull and rook
And the knock of sailing boats on the net webbed wall
    Myself to set foot
        That second
    In the still sleeping town and set forth.

My birthday began with the water –
Birds and the birds of the winged trees flying my name
    Above the farms and the white horses
        And I rose
    In rainy autumn
And walked abroad in a shower of all my days.
High tide and the heron dived when I took the road
    Over the border
        And the gates
    Of the town closed as the town awoke.

A springful of larks in a rolling
Cloud and the roadside bushes brimming with whistling
    Blackbirds and the sun of October
        Summery
    On the hill's shoulder,
Here were fond climates and sweet singers suddenly
Come in the morning where I wandered and listened
    To the rain wringing
        Wind blow cold
    In the wood faraway under me.
. . .

And there could I marvel my birthday
Away but the weather turned around. And the true

Joy of the long dead child sang burning
    In the sun.
It was my thirtieth
Year to heaven stood there then in the summer noon
Though the town below lay leaved with October blood.
    O may my heart's truth
        Still be sung
On this high hill in a year's turning.

[DYLAN THOMAS, from *Poem in October*]

All a lyrical rush! How did *he maintain it? Hopkins could manage it only for the length of a sonnet!*

28th October

It is a curious fact that the most important debate in English political history took place not in the House of Commons but in the fifteenth century parish church of St Mary in Putney. There, on 28th October 1647, and for the next two weeks, a group of about forty men met in informal conclave, and proceeded to invent modern politics – to invent, in fact, the public framework of the world in which nearly 3000 million now live. There was no significance in the choice of the church; it was simply convenient. The men sat or stood around the bare communion table and kept their hats on, as Englishmen had learnt to do in the Commons House. The meeting was officially styled the General Council of the New Model Army, the force which had recently annihilated the armies of King Charles and was now the effective master of the whole country . . . It was a very representative gathering of Englishmen, covering all classes save the highest, and a wide variety of peace-time trades and callings . . . Every major political concept known to us today, all the assumptions which underlie the thoughts of men in the White House, or the Kremlin, or Downing Street, or in presidential mansions or senates or parliaments through five continents, were expressed or adumbrated in the little church of St Mary.

[PAUL JOHNSON, from *The Offshore Islanders*]

(Paul Johnson quotes from the verbatim record of that meeting these words of one William Rainborough: "For really I think that the poorest he that is in England hath a life to live, as the greatest he; and therefore truly, sir, I think it's clear that every man that is to live under a govern-

ment ought first by his own consent to put himself under that government, and I do think that the poorest man in England is not at all
bound in a strict sense to that government that he hath not had a voice
to put himself under.")

*At certain moments in history the lid comes off and human beings have to face
one another with whatever integrity they have. History has brought them to this
moment, and now is disclosed what is really at issue.*

29th October

Nevertheless, he reflected, sitting alone in the little office when she had
gone, the idiotic sentimentality about 'gardening and the future' was
right in its general line. Over the years he had built up a life encom-
passed by simple immediate duties and recreations – an ordered
present; but an ordered present demanded at least the fiction of an
immediate future with simple duties and recreations to be planned.
Only such a life, he had come to believe, could allow one to cross the
shapeless tract of human existence with grace and with gentleness; if
the path was a meaningless progress to the grave, then the more
necessary to take each step as a deliberate progress to the next; he
could see no other way of preserving the fiction of civilization, and
nothing to recommend the indulgence of exposing it. Now in this cruel
November, prelude to Gordon's last few wintry months of life, careful
ordering of the future had become more than ever his aim. The present
was only a matter of giving the very little to Gordon of all that he
would have wished to give, and more still of keeping from Gordon all
the things that he and others, in indulgence of their affection, might
have imposed. It was as an aid to this discipline of emotions, his own and
others', that planning and attention to the coming year's duties and
routines proved so valuable. If it meant an outrage of his own feelings in
dwelling on the time when Gordon would be dead, that must be
nothing if in result it assisted Gordon to be free of vexation. Pain, the
great enormity, only the doctors could in some measure ease, but added
vexation it was his task to remove. The one compensation in this crisis of
his life was that his way of living proved of value. He had thought once
that it was one which, by small example and through long stretches of
time, might yet 'save humanity' from the grosser absurdities of self-
destruction; this was a dream he had now rejected . . .
    He had been lucky perhaps that this love, and the object of his love,
had declared, so openly and once for all, that loneliness was the condition

of man, a loneliness to be endured and fulfilled in the constant disguise of human contact. It was so simple a truth, but so many lives – Meg's for instance – seemed shaped to hide it. If the whole discipline of his days, then, was designed to accept this reality, he could at least congratulate himself on his luck rather than on his superior wisdom and so preserve his self-effacement. He smiled with anticipatory pleasure when he thought of the amusement he would give to Gordon in telling him the smug conclusion of all this self-inquiry.

[ANGUS WILSON, from *The Middle Age of Mrs Eliot*]

The narrator is Mrs Eliot's brother. It is his friend Gordon who is dying and he accepts the loneliness of the one who is left. In the novel this acceptance is contrasted with his sister Meg. Her husband was killed while travelling, and she is needy of another relationship.

30th October

The whole aim of the 'selfless revolutionary' as defined by Steve above, 'the liberation not only of the oppressed but also of the oppressor', presupposes not only that the oppressor can be brought to a state of repentance for what he has done, but also that at that moment he is embraced, and so liberated by the forgiveness extended to him by the oppressed. I personally cannot pray for the forgiveness of those responsible for his death. I can and do pray for their repentance, which will then make possible and efficacious their forgiveness. The real miracle of the Gospel, as Coleridge saw, is not forgiveness but repentance.

Steve did give an unbreakable substance to the hope he had already implanted in our breasts, the hope of freedom in South Africa. That is what he lived for, in fact one can truly say that is what he lived. He was himself a living embodiment of the hope he proclaimed by word and deed. That is why I call this little personal memoir 'Martyr of Hope'. Martyr means witness. He was in his person a witness to the hope that all men, women, and children in South Africa, the oppressed and oppressor alike, could be free.

[AELRED STUBBS, from *Martyr of Hope*]

Steve Biko died in prison in South Africa in 1977. There is this sense of dismay when you hear of the murder of a Biko or a Gandhi or a Lumumba. We recklessly throw out the ones the Spirit is using to try and help us.

31st October

Christ clearly taught that there is no final and absolute authority in the will and ideology of parents, and they have no rights over the child in the face of real values. Christ did not hesitate to transcend family ties, and did not regard them as the ultimate arbiters of the individual's fate and development. Parents are the guardians but not the property owners of the child's personality, and the Christian faith has stood for the innate and eternal value of every individual soul of man. That is not only a charter of freedom against the mass tyranny of the political dictator who would hold the lives of individual human beings cheap and claim the right to liquidate them at will if they refuse to submit to his pattern. It is equally the charter of freedom that gives every child an unchallenged right to become a true individual in his own right, and not just an enforced copy of his parents . . .

. . . It is a plain matter of fact that the religious experience and faith of a mature person gives the most comprehensive and invulnerable security, and the largest sense of self-realization possible to man. I do not say that that proves the objective truth of religion. I note it as a psychological fact. The best of parents cannot guarantee to us, or enable us to reach, full maturity and peace of mind. They can lay a sound foundation but we still have to erect our own building on it, and to make of life something that is fully meaningful and satisfying to us. They may enable us to orient stably to one another on a finite human plane in our basic emotional relationships, and that will always content many. Nevertheless, life can embrace more than that and the spirit of man does not remain merely earthbound. The fullest maturity involves an adjustment to the whole as well as to its parts. It does not involve any specific theology or philosophy, but it does involve an essentially religious way of experiencing life.

[HARRY GUNTRIP, from *Mental Pain and the Cure of Souls*]

We have hammered away at "Honour thy father and mother" and ignored "Who is my father?" Even with the best of intentions we never know what we are doing to a vulnerable youngster.

NOVEMBER

1st November

So to Him passed over, so I must believe, him therefore, O sister most dear, him to whom once you clung in the union of the flesh and now in that stronger fiercer bond of the divine affection, with whom and under whom you have long served the Lord; him, I say, in your place or as another you, hath Christ taken to His breast to comfort him, and there shall keep him, till at the coming of the Lord, the voice of the archangel and the trump of God descending, He shall restore him to your heart again.

[PETER OF CLUNY to HÉLOÏSE]

The human element, 'romantic' love at this pitch, was beginning to break through in history – and an old monk affirms its value. It is remarkable for its time and is a milestone in the story of human relationships.

2nd November

They were alone together on the sands, children once more; but Eustace knew that it was the visit he had been denying himself for so long, and he knew also that never in actuality or in memory had the pang of pleasure been as keen as this. For his sense of union with Hilda was absolute; he tasted the pure essence of the experience and as they began to dig, every association the sands possessed seemed to run up his spade and tingle through his body.

Inexhaustible, the confluent streams descended from the pools above; unbreakable, the thick retaining walls received their offering; unruffled, the rock-girt pond gave back the cloudless sky. They did not speak, for they knew each other's thoughts and wishes; they did not hurry, for time had ceased to count; they did not look at each other, for each had an assurance of the other's presence beyond the power of sight to amplify. Indeed, they must not look or speak, for fear of losing each other.

How long this went on Eustace could not tell, but suddenly he forgot, and spoke to Hilda. She did not answer. He looked up, but she was not there; he was alone on the sands.

"She must have gone home," he thought, and at once he knew that it was very late and the air was darkening round him. So he set off towards the cliffs, which now seemed extraordinarily high and dangerous, too high to climb, too dangerous to approach. He stopped and called "Hilda!" – and this time he thought she answered him in the cry of a sea-mew, and he followed in the direction of the cry. "Where are you?" he called, and the answer came back, "Here!" But when he looked he only saw a seaweed-coated rock standing in a pool. But he recognized the rock, and knew what he would find there.

The white plumose anemone was stroking the water with its feelers. The same anemone as before, without a doubt, but there was no shrimp in its mouth. "It will die of hunger," thought Eustace, "I must find it something to eat," and he bent down and scanned the pool. Shrimps were disporting themselves in the shallows; but they slipped out of his cupped hands, and fled away into the dark recesses under the eaves of the rock, where the crabs lurked. Then he knew what he must do. Taking off his shoes and socks, he waded into the water. The water was bitterly cold; but colder still were the lips of the anemone as they closed round his finger. "I shall wake up now," thought Eustace, who had wakened from many dreams.

But the cold crept onwards and he did not wake.

[L. P. HARTLEY, from *Eustace and Hilda*]

The last page of a trilogy! Eustace dreams as he is dying of his childhood with his sister Hilda, back on the seashore near Hunstanton.

3rd November

2

Have you built your ship of death, O have you?
O build your ship of death, for you will need it.
The grim frost is at hand, when the apples will fall
thick, almost thunderous, on the hardened earth.

3

And death is on the air, like a smell of ashes!
Ah, can't you smell it?

And in the bruized body, the frightened soul
finds itself shrinking, wincing from the cold
that blows upon it through the orifices.

4

O let us talk of quiet that we know,
that we can know, the deep and lovely quiet
of a strong heart at peace!

And can we this, our own quietus, make?

5

Build then the ship of death, for you must take
the longest journey to oblivion.

And die the death, the long and painful death
that lies between the old self and the new.
Already our bodies are fallen, bruized, badly bruized,
Already our souls are oozing through the exit
of the cruel bruize.

Already the dark and endless ocean of the end
is washing in through the breaches of our wounds,
already the flood is upon us.

O build your ship of death, your little ark
and furnish it with food, with little cakes and wine
for the dark flight down oblivion . . .

[D. H. LAWRENCE, from *The Ship of Death*]

*Not many poems address themselves to the fact of dying. This one is outside the
Christian frame and taps the pagan sentiment of burying with the dead things
deemed needful for the journey. And within the Christian frame what is the
content of our stock phrases, like 'Meeting our Maker'?*

4th November

To the south an immense archangel, black as thunder beat up from the
Pacific. And yet, after all, the storm contained its own secret calm . . .
His passion for Yvonne (whether or not she'd ever been much good as
an actress was beside the point, he'd told her the truth when he said she
would have been more than good in any film he made) had brought

back to his heart, in a way he could not have explained, the first time that alone, walking over the meadows from Saint Près, the sleepy French village of backwaters and locks and grey disused water mills where he was lodging, he had seen, rising slowly and wonderfully and with boundless beauty above the stubble fields blowing with wild-flowers, slowly rising into the sunlight, as centuries before the pilgrims straying over those same fields had watched them rise, the twin spires of Chartres Cathedral. His love had brought a peace, for all too short a while, that was strangely like the enchantment, the spell, of Chartres itself, long ago, where every side-street he had come to love and every café where he could gaze at the Cathedral eternally sailing against the clouds, the spell not even the fact he was scandalously in debt there could break. M. Laurelle walked on swiftly towards the Palace. Nor had any remorse for the Consul's plight broken that other spell fifteen years later here in Quauhnahuac! For that matter, M. Laurelle reflected, what had re-united the Consul and himself for a time, even after Yvonne left, was not on either side, remorse. It was perhaps, partly, more the desire for that illusory comfort, about as satisfying as biting on an aching tooth, to be derived from the mutual unspoken pretence that Yvonne was still there.

  – Ah, but all these things might have seemed a good enough reason for putting the whole earth between themselves and Quauhnahuac. Yet neither had done so. And now M. Laurelle could feel their burden pressing upon him from outside, as if somehow it had been transferred to those purple mountains all around him, so mysterious, with their secret mines of silver, so withdrawn, yet so close, so still, and from these mountains emanated a strange melancholy force that tried to hold him here bodily, which was its weight, the weight of many things, but mostly that of sorrow.

[MALCOLM LOWRY, from Under the Volcano]

In the reviewing of the life he has lived, a consul in Mexico, now a hopeless drunkard, senses a great sorrow that he will never get to grips with his life and make something of it.

5th November

Dear friends, you will allow me at the opening of this magnificent meeting to recall a personal memory. My father who lived in Barcelona was an animal painter. He loved to depict birds and particularly doves. As his life was waning, he began to allow me to use his paint brushes, and used to ask me to paint in the feet of the doves for him, a very delicate work which he could no longer do. When he found out that I could do it fairly well, he gave his paint brushes to me, and I have succeeded him in the family of painters.

What joy he would feel if he were still alive to see that my too humble doves have circled the world.

In this way I have contributed, within my powers and with the same conviction which I have put into my art, to the struggle for the finest and most just of all causes.

I am for life against death, for peace against war.

[PABLO PICASSO, Speech at Sheffield City Hall, 1950]

A peace conference had been planned with people attending from all over the world. Attlee, as Prime Minister at the time, refused many of the visas and half the people invited never arrived. Only one meeting was held in Sheffield. The next day we all went over to Warsaw where everybody was able to gather for the actual conference. But Picasso came to Sheffield and spoke in Spanish. This translation was made at the time and given to me.

6th November

And who are these twelve labouring men?
I do not understand your words:
I taught you speech, we named the birds.
You marked their big migrations then
Like any child. So turn again
To silence from the place of crowds.
"I am my own and not my own."

Why are you sullen when I speak?
Here are your tools, the saw and knife
And hammer on your bench. Your life
Is measured here in week and week
Planed as the furniture you make,
And I will teach you like a wife
To be my own and all my own.

Who like an arrogant wind blown
Where he may please, needs no content?
Yet I remember how you went
To speak with scholars in furred gown.

I hear an outcry in the town;
Who carries that dark instrument?
"One all his own and not his own."

Treading the green and nimble sward
I stare at a strange shadow thrown.
Are you the boy I bore alone
No doctor near to cut the cord?
I cannot reach to call you, Lord,
Answer me as my only son.
"I am my own and not my own."

[THOM GUNN, from *Jesus and His Mother*]

It is the refrain here that particularly draws me. Christian devotion was once securely locked into the figure of the mother at the foot of the Cross. And there is something there not to be lost – only the mother who knows the pangs of birth has the right to say the refrain. Men cannot.

7th November

"He had to go his way. He had his trouble and he's gone. He was young, he was bright, he was beautiful, we expected great things of him – but he's gone away from us now and it's us will have to make the great things happen. I believe I know how terrible some of you feel. I know how terrible I feel – ain't nothing I can say going to take away that ache, not right away. But that boy was one of the best men I ever met, and I been around awhile. I ain't going to try to judge him. That ain't for us to do. You know, a lot of people say that a man who takes his own life oughtn't to be buried in holy ground. I don't know nothing about that. All *I* know, God made every bit of ground I ever walked on and everything God made is holy. And don't none of us know what goes on in the heart of someone, don't many of us know what's going on in our own hearts for the matter of that, and so can't none of us say why he did what he did. Ain't none of us been there and so don't none of us know. We got to pray that the Lord will receive him like we pray that the Lord's going to receive us. That's all. That's *all*. And I tell you something else, so don't none of you forget it! I know a lot of people done took their own lives and they're walking up and down the streets today and some of them is preaching the gospel and some is sitting in the seats of the mighty. Now, you remember that. If the world wasn't so full of dead folks maybe those of us that's trying to live wouldn't have to suffer so bad...

". . . But don't lose heart, dear ones – don't lose heart. Don't let it make you bitter. Try to understand. Try to understand. The world's already bitter enough, we got to try to be better than the world."

He looked down, then, over to the front row.

"You got to remember," he said, gently, "he was trying. Ain't many trying and all that tries must suffer. Be proud of him. You got a right to be proud. And that's all he ever wanted in this world."

[JAMES BALDWIN, from *Another Country*]

A cry of people who through such as Baldwin find a voice. On this day in 1989 *were elected the first black Mayor of New York and the first black Governor of Virginia. And in Britain?*

8th November

On one of these occasions, when they had both been perfectly quiet for a long time, and Mr Dombey only knew that the child was awake by occasionally glancing at his eye where the bright fire was sparkling like a jewel, little Paul broke silence thus:

"Papa! What's money?"

. . . "Gold, and silver, and copper. Guineas, shillings, half-pence. You know what they are."

"Oh yes, I know what they are," said Paul. "I don't mean that, papa. I mean what's money after all?"

"What is money after all," said Mr Dombey, backing his chair a little, that he might the better gaze in sheer amazement at the presumptuous atom that propounded such an inquiry.

"I mean, papa, what can it do?" returned Paul, folding his arms (though they were hardly long enough to fold) and looking at the fire, and up at him, and at the fire, and up at him again.

Mr Dombey drew his chair back to its former place, and patted him on the head. "Money, Paul, can do anything." He took hold of the little hand, and beat it softly against one of his own, as he said so. But Paul got his hand free as soon as he could; and rubbing it gently to and fro on the elbow of his chair, as if his wit were in the palm, and he were sharpening it – and looking at the fire again, as though the fire had been his adviser and prompter – repeated, after a short pause:

"Anything, papa?"

"Yes. Anything – almost," said Mr Dombey.

"Anything means everything, don't it, papa?" asked his son: observing, or possibly not understanding, the qualification.

"It includes it: yes," said Mr Dombey.

"Why didn't money save my mama?" returned the child. "It isn't cruel, is it?"

"Cruel?" said Mr Dombey, settling his neckcloth, and seeming to resent the idea. "No, a good thing can't be cruel."

"If it's a good thing, and can do anything." said the little fellow, thoughtfully, as he looked back at the fire, "I wonder why it didn't save my mama."

[CHARLES DICKENS, from *Dombey and Son*]

I could have chosen so much from Dickens, but I selected this one for our age, more blatant than ever about money, what with the endless financial reports on the radio. (A.D. for Mr Dombey meant 'Anno Dombeii'.) Dickens is at his best when he gets children in the picture.

9th November

November sunlight floats and falls
Like soapsuds on the castle walls.
Where broken groins are slanted west
The bubbles touch the stone and burst,
And the moist shadows dribble down
And slime the sandy red with brown.
        . . .

Still the moated dungeons hide
Legends of poverty and pride,
And murdered skulls are stuffed with lore
Of pillage, plunder, famine, fear,
And dirk has carved upon the bone:
"Blood will not show on the red stone."

The damp autumnal sunlight drips
On chimneys, pit-shafts, rubble-tips.
Centuries of feudal weight
Have made men stoop towards their feet.
They climb no rocks nor stare around,
But dig their castles in the ground.

Castles in the red ore made
Are buttressed, tunnelled, turretted,
And like a moat turned inside out
The pit-heaps trap the sieging light,
With lantern-flints the miners spark
And gouge their windows in the dark.

Here in the hollows the men store,
Rich as rubies, the red ore;
And rock and bones are broken both
When the stone spine is theft from earth.
The crime defiles like a red mud
The ore, the sandstone, and the blood.

But the robbed earth will claim its own
And break the mines and castles down
When Gabriel from heaven sent
Blows the Horn of Egremont,
Tabulates the tenants' needs
And reassumes the title-deeds.

[NORMAN NICHOLSON, from *Egremont*]

Egremont is a small town not far from where I live, and I tried to memorize this poem as I passed through on the bus. There is a pub there called The Horn of Egremont. *The poem is important for me because I came first to West Cumbria in the last days of the mining of iron ore. It was a murderous industry: so many men I buried whose chests were worn through with iron ore dust.*

10th November

. . . that we . . . should see so few really great, convincing Christians amongst us . . . is, I venture to say, due to one simple but sufficient cause: we are not human enough to be saints. No, right from the outset, from an utterly false notion of piety, we dare not let ourselves become human beings. A human being is made not born. We don't let our children grow up into real, healthy men and women, we wish them to be simply and solely Christians – and forget that grace needs a deep, reliable, healthy, natural ground if it is to take root and bear a hundred-fold; that otherwise the 'supernatural' remains in the air, is unnatural a phantom without strength or life-blood, and will therefore disappear before the first onslaught of a real power, springing from strong, natural roots.

... Visit the Galleries in Munich and Basle and see the saints depicted by the medieval painters. Look at the gay, robust figures of Lochner, Dürer, Holbein and Hans Baldung Grien and the many nameless painters. See how, for all the halo of unearthly glamour which invests them, they stand against the landscape of their own country, 'with strong and sturdy limbs planted on firm and enduring soil' – men of flesh and blood, in recognizable costumes of Nuremberg, Cologne, Bruges or Florence. And then go across and look at the saints of El Greco, clad in timeless 'garments' floating in vague cloudy regions, with shadowy greenish features and emaciated hands which could hold neither weapon nor distaff; bathed in weird light, stiff, or writhing in feverish ecstasy – their gaze ravished into Nowhere. These, indeed, are no longer men ... they are gruesome chimeras, arbitrarily put together, with bodies hung on them like ghostly sheaths already withered and falling, never created by God ...

And Elizabeth? The essence of her humanity is that she is a great lover, a generous heart of incomparable capacity for self-giving. And the essence of her Christianity is that she is a saint – and that means literally the same thing, a great lover, a heart with an incomparable capacity for self-giving.

... Not 'love' then, of the idyllic, pathetic and 'poetical' sort, but that great love in which passion burns, unmeasured, dangerous. A loving soul: that means that in her love there lived that spiritual element which raises it, so to speak, to a higher dimension, and gives it a new quality of danger and finality, because it lifts it into the sphere of the permanent, indestructible, irrevocable, inalienable. Do you begin to feel how perilous it is, what courage is needed to risk such love?

[IDA COUDENHOVE, from *The Nature of Sanctity*]

My wife's birthday. We both enjoyed this book about Elizabeth of Hungary.

11th November

So, it seems, this tight-rope of a life, this altogether too difficult business of living (like giving a child of five logarithms to do ...) is drawing to an end. And, to press the simile a little further the rope is definitely getting steeper. It was always difficult to keep a balance but now there is fatigue as well. You get definitely tired and desirous of peace and quiet – and there is none to be had. There is no place to which, like a retired seaman, you can go and sit and contemplate your sweet youth and watch the admirable doings of your contemporaries. You have sown the wind and are indeed reaping the whirlwind. We shall have to make up our minds to perish in the storm.

But facing death – that is the chief business of living after all. The soldier, the sailor, the mountaineer and such-like foolhardy persons, miners and air-plane pilots, see death as the normal risk of their trades. But for ordinary people death is not a risk; it is a certainty. Perhaps my forty years as a monumental mason have made this fact uncommonly clear. Perhaps my upbringing as the son of a non-conformist parson gave me a good hold on this thought even earlier. But the grand rush of the modern world to destruction makes it impossible, even if you would, to put the thought aside. How are we going to face up to that? Is death merely the end of all things or is it indeed, truly, surely, certainly, and, so to say, visibly and not merely in the conventionally accepted theory, the gate of life? In the former case the less said about it the better, and even the less thought about it; but in the latter . . .

The thing about Christianity, the thing about the Cross, about Calvary, is that it is true to man . . . the person known to himself and to God, the creature who knows and wills and loves, master of his acts (however much he be hindered by and subject to heredity and circumstance), therefore responsible. That is the creature who desires happiness and by the very nature of things, by his own nature, cannot find it except in God. That is why death is the gate of life.

[ERIC GILL, from *Autobiography*]

I heard Eric Gill in Maryport when he came to talk to the unemployed. He spoke directly about work as a sacrament. He was passionately concerned about a just society. He once carved a frieze of Christ driving the money changers out of the Temple on a war memorial for Leeds University. The commercial city did not like it. Sexually, much of his life was disastrous. His intentions were good – not to deny the sexual nor to triumph over it – but it was his trip wire.

12th November

There is much comfort in high hills
   and a great easing of the heart.
We look upon them and our nature fills
   with loftier images from their life apart.
They set our feet on curves of freedom, bent
   to snap the circles of our discontent.

> Mountains are moods; of larger rhythms and line,
>   moving between the eternal mode and mine.
> Moments of thought, of which I too am part,
>   I lose in them my instant of brief ills.
> There is a great easing of the heart,
>   And cumulance of comfort on high hills.
>
> [G. W. YOUNG, *High Hills*]

Mountains gave Wordsworth quietness and a larger mood. He was never querulous. Walking the fells gave me a sense of breadth, a place which is not cramped. The high hills suggest this wider dimension. Perhaps some respond and some do not. And in the twenties very few people walked the Lakeland fells: there were no jets flying below you then, no Sellafield, no erosion of the paths.

13th November

> Darling, this is goodbye. The words are ordinary
> But love is rare. So let it go tenderly
> as the sound of violins into silence.
>
> Parting is sad for us, because something is over,
> But for the thing we have ended, it is a beginning –
> Let love go like a young bird flying from the nest,
>
> Like a new star, airborne into the evening,
> Watched out of sight, or let fall gently as a tear,
> Let our love go out of the world, like the prayer for a
>   soul's rest.

Let the roses go, that you fastened in my hair
One summer night in a garden, and the song
That we heard from another house, where a piano was playing:
The shadow a street lamp cast through the net of a curtain,
The river at night, smooth silent Thames, flowing through London.

For two years Ullswater was silver with my love of you,
The golden birch-leaves were holy, the wild cherry was sweet
On the fell-sides, scenting the spring for you.
The bees, drunk with the lime-flowers, dropped like grapes on the
                                                              road,
And the silence was yours, over all Westmorland at night.

I raised the mountains for you, and set the streams
Running down the hills for love. I saw the moss grow
And the ferns unroll their croziers for love of you,
The snowdrops, the primrose, the heron, the martin, the sheep on
          the fells.
. . .

Yours, too, was the anteroom of the angels,
When I could hear a pin drop, or a drop of rain,
Or the creak of a beam, or a butterfly caught in the rafters.
I wrestled with angels for you, and in my body
Endured the entire blessing of love's pain.

All this is true. These things, my dear, are a life
Lived for love of you. The fire in the heart, the fire on the hearth,
And children's stories in the evening, even hope's death
Were precious for you. Precious all things in time
And outside time. The poem I know, and the wisdom
That is not mine, the poem that can never be written . . .

       [KATHLEEN RAINE, from *Parting*]

A marvellous passionate love poem with its outstanding gathering of particularities.

14th November

  When that prime heroine of our nation, Alice,
  Climbing courageously in through the Palace
  Of Looking Glass, found it inhabited
  By chessboard personages, white and red,
  Involved in never-ending tournament,
  She being of a speculative bent
  Had long foreshadowed something of the kind,
  Asking herself: "Suppose I stood behind
  And viewed the fireplace of their drawing-room
  From hearth-rug level, why must I assume
  That what I'd see would need to correspond
  With what I now see? And the rooms beyond? . . .
  For Alice though a child could understand
  That neither did this chance-discovered land
  Make nohow or contrariwise the clean

Dull round of mid-Victorian routine,
Nor did Victoria's golden rule extend
Beyond the glass: it came to the dead end
Where empty hearses turn about; thereafter
Begins that lubberland of dream and laughter,
The red-and-white-flower-spangled hedge, the grass
Where Apuleius pastured his Gold Ass,
Where young Gargantua made whole holiday . . .
But further from our heroine not to stray,
Let us observe with what uncommon sense –
Though a secure and easy reference
Between Red Queen and kitten could be found –
She made no false assumption on that ground
(A trap in which the scientist would fall)
That queens and kittens are identical.

[ROBERT GRAVES, from *Alice*]

I like good humour in poetry, and it's rare!

15th November

Worship of the Prince of this world, worship of temporal power: how
appallingly has God's Church, the Bride of Christ, fallen into this
temptation, and following her all that has sprung from her impure
womb – the national Orthodox and Protestant churches, the heirs of the
French Revolution, the totalitarian states of the first half of this century,
and finally the world Communist movement. How well he has been
served, but how many of us have ears to hear what Bernanos calls "the
laugh, the incomprehensible joy of Satan"?

Let us enumerate his victories. The conversion of Constantine which
subjected the Eastern Church to the imperial power; the spurious
Donation of Constantine which made the Papacy itself a temporal
power; the legitimation of persecution, the raising of the flesh to the
rank of the Devil himself as the enemy of man, and the inhuman doctrine of predestination which the great Augustine bequeathed to the
Western Church; the great schism between East and West; the dis-
sensions and corruption of medieval Christendom; the religious wars of
the sixteenth and seventeenth centuries; the rejection of Christianity by
the French Revolution; the tyranny of Bonaparte and his insane wars,
prefiguring the far worse tyrannies and bloodbaths of this century; the

perversion of Communism almost at its birth; and last but not least the conversion of the American ideal of liberty into the most crassly materialist, soulless civilization the world has ever seen. It is not the Galilean who has conquered but Satan, under whose noonday sun "we live and move and have our being."

. . . To corrupt what is itself good, this is his favourite weapon, for he is not only a murderer but a liar and deceiver. In the last two hundred years he has had it all his own way: he has murdered and lied with complete impunity. His element, of course, is war, since war is simply murder and lying exalted as the highest national virtue.

. . . It is ridiculous to suppose that we are in control of our own affairs: collectively as well as individually we are up against "not flesh and blood" but against "principalities, against powers, against the rulers of the darkness of this world, against spiritual wickedness in high places."

Of course, this sounds hopelessly old-fashioned, for who believes in Satan today? That is his triumph, for when no one believes in him he has it all his own way. Of modern writers only two have been seriously interested in him, and these, you will scarcely be suprised to hear, were novelists, not theologians – Dostoevsky and Bernanos . . . Both have represented Satan in human form, and in both of them he appears so ordinary, so unassuming, so apparently benevolent . . .

[R. C. ZAEHNER, from *Concordant Discord*]

The title, a quotation from St Francis de Sales, is of the Gifford Lectures 1967–69

16th November

Katherine   Sir, I desire you do me right and justice,
And to bestow pity on me; for
I am a most poor woman, and a stranger,
Born out of your dominions, having here
No judge indifferent, nor no more assurance
Of equal friendship and proceeding. Alas, sir,
In what have I offended you? What cause
Hath my behaviour given to your displeasure,
That thus you should proceed to put me off,
And take your good grace from me? Heaven witness,
I have been to you a true and humble wife,
At all times to your will conformable,
Even in fear to kindle your dislike,

Yea, subject to your countenance, glad or sorry,
As I saw it inclin'd. When was the hour
I ever contradicted your desire
Or made it not mine too? Or which of your friends
Have I not strove to love, although I knew
He were mine enemy? What friend of mine
That had to him deriv'd your anger, did I
Continue in my liking? nay, gave notice
He was from thence discharg'd? Sir, call to mind
That I have been your wife in this obedience
Upward of twenty years, and have been blest
With many children by you. If in the course
And process of this time you can report,
And prove it too, against my honour aught,
My bond to wedlock, or my love and duty
Against your sacred person; in God's name
Turn me away, and let the foul'st contempt
Shut door upon me, and so give me up
To the sharp'st kind of justice . . .

[WILLIAM SHAKESPEARE, from *Henry VIII*]

One of the most moving speeches Shakespeare ever wrote – steely, supple, tender.

17th November

One quite general, yet very helpful preparation towards the practice of sobriety in prayer . . . is admirably preached and practised by Jean Nicholas Grou. This fine classical scholar, and deeply spiritual writer and leader of souls, urges the importance of the soul's possession and cultivation of two levels and kinds of action and interest – a wholesome natural interest and action, and a deep supernatural interest and action. The soul will then possess and will cultivate a genuine interest in politics or economics, in language or history, in natural science or philosophy – in these, as part of its bread-winning or as quite freely chosen studies. And we will thus, when in dryness or even in anticipation of it, possess a most useful range of interest to which to turn, as our disporting ground, in relief of the dreariness or the strain of our directly religious life . . .

. . . If then spiritual dryness is indeed inevitable in the life of prayer, we will be much helped to bear these desert stretches, by persistent recognition – hence also, indeed especially, in our times of fervour – of the normality and the necessity of such desolation . . . And if the desolation is more acute, we will act as the Arab caravans behave in the face of a blinding sandstorm in the desert. The men dismount, throw themselves upon their faces in the sand; and there they remain, patient and uncomplaining, till the storm passes, and until, with their wonted patient endurance, they can and do continue on their way.

There are generally a weakness and an error at work within us, at such times, which considerably prolong the trouble, and largely neutralize the growth this very trouble would otherwise bring to our souls. The weakness lies in that we let our imagination and sensitiveness be directly absorbed in our trouble. We contemplate, and further enlarge, the trouble, present in ourselves, instead of firmly and faithfully looking away, either at the great abiding realities of the spiritual world, or, if this is momentarily impossible for us, at some other, natural or human, wholesome fact or law. And the error lies in our lurking suspicions that, for such trials to purify us, we must feel them fully in their tryingness – that is, we must face and fathom them directly and completely. Such a view completely overlooks the fact that such trials are sent us for the purpose of de-occupying us with our smaller selves; and again, it ignores the experiences of God's saints across the ages, that, precisely in proportion as we can get away from direct occupation with our troubles to the thought and love of God, to the presence of Him who permits all this, in the same proportion do and will these trials purify our souls.

[F. von Hügel, from *Essays and Addresses II*]

He has such good things to say about the real difficulties of prayer. True spiritual health is much more straightforward than the complexities of many writers on prayer. Simple plod and common sense, common endurance and common fulness – these are much more significant than miracles.

18th November

Bright star, would I were steadfast as thou art –
   Not in lone splendour hung aloft the night
And watching, with eternal lids apart,
   Like nature's patient, sleepless Eremite,
The moving waters at their priestlike task
   Of pure ablution round earth's human shores,
Or gazing on the new soft-fallen mask

Of snow upon the mountains and the moors –
No – yet still steadfast, still unchangeable,
Pillow'd upon my fair love's ripening breast,
To feel for ever its soft fall and swell,
Awake for ever in a sweet unrest,
Still, still to her her tender-taken breath,
And so live ever – or else swoon to death.

[JOHN KEATS, *Written on a Blank Page in Shakespeare's Poems*]

Aware of both the beauty of the stars and his relation to a human being. Keats is
seeking for the validity of both experiences. Unlike the Russians, he has so little
to sustain him, so little in his experience. And he is so conscious of his mortality.
The ordeal you go through leaves you with but one or two perceptions that
matter.

19th November

Where is there an end to it the river of women,
Walking proudly through time on their high-heeled shoes,
On their shoulders for a space the weight of being human
The tale of their being here will never close.

They step into their births and put on sorrow
Like a purple vest, a mantle of dark green.
Then the bow is drawn, the string shoots forth the arrow
And they follow its course to a target that cannot be seen.

The sound of the music of their movement
Sweetens with praise the dull hammer blows of time
Through the intricate metres of their slow advancement,
God, through his daughters here, is taking aim.

And it unfolds the steel petals of the rose of their being
And scented like the rose in an expanding tense
They walk with light feet over the apotheosis of ruin
Obeying the far gone conductor of the intolerable dance.

Where is there an end to it, the river of women
Walking proudly through their dust through devious ways,
The high keen merriment of their passing
All that is not dust must continually praise.

[THOMAS BLACKBURN, *Luna*]

*This delights me beyond words – an extraordinary revelation. I know no
greater tribute from a man to women. 'Kairos' is the Greek word originally
meaning 'the groove in the arrow that fits into the string of the bow', and so
comes to mean 'the critical moment'.*

20th November

He did not stop on the steps either, but went quickly down: his soul,
overflowing with rapture, yearned for freedom, space, openness, The
vault of heaven, full of soft, shining stars, stretched vast and fathomless
above him. The Milky Way ran in two pale streams from the zenith to
the horizon. The fresh, motionless, still night enfolded the earth. The
white towers and golden domes of the cathedral gleamed out against
the sapphire sky. The gorgeous autumn flowers, in the beds round the
house, were slumbering till the morning. The silence of earth seemed to
melt into the silence of the heavens. The mystery of earth was one with
the mystery of the stars . . .

Alyosha stood, gazed, and suddenly threw himself down on the earth.
He did not know why he embraced it. He could not have told why he
longed so irresistibly to kiss it, to kiss it all. But he kissed it weeping,
sobbing and watering it with his tears, and vowed passionately to love
it, to love it for ever and ever. "Water the earth with the tears of joy
and love those tears," echoed in his soul.

What was he weeping over?

Oh! in his rapture he was weeping over those stars which were
shining to him from the abyss of space, and "he was not ashamed of that
ecstasy". There seemed to be threads from all those innumerable
worlds of God, linking his soul to them, and it was trembling all over
"in contact with other worlds". He longed to forgive everyone and for
everything, and to beg forgiveness. Oh, not for himself, but for all men,
for all and for everything. "And others are praying for me too," echoed
again in his soul. But with every instant he felt clearly and, as it were,
tangibly, that something firm and unshakeable as that vault of heaven
had entered into his soul. It was as though some idea had seized the
sovereignty of his mind – and it was for all his life and for ever and ever.
He had fallen on the earth a weak boy, but he rose up a resolute cham-
pion, and he knew and felt it suddenly at the very moment of his
ecstasy. And never, never, all his life long, could Alyosha forget that
minute.

"Someone visited my soul in that hour," he used to say afterwards,
with implicit faith in his words.

Within three days he left the monastery in accordance with the words of his elder, who had bidden him "sojourn in the world".

[FYODR DOSTOEVSKY, from *The Brothers Karamazov*]

Almost the best part of Russian literature is this overwhelming sense of the life of the earth, of incarnation and beatification. There is so much rapture in this description. And it is all so much more than anything to be found in the churches, however colourful the ikons.

21st November

. . . Shakespearean criticism can take one of two lines. It can investigate with increasing subtlety and knowledge the significance for Shakespeare of the age in which he lived: or it can try to study Shakespeare as a unique individual, not to be wholly explained by reference to any generalizations men have made about his epoch. Either approach may yield new knowledge and new insights, either approach developed alone is liable to cause misconceptions. The same two modes of criticism can be applied to other periods and other people. In the past, even sometimes today, writers were prepared to apply to all the people who flourished between 1837 and 1901 the common adjective 'Victorian'. Recently more and more people have come to reflect that that period is, in modern terms, a long one and that Britain was in that period a complex community which was changing very rapidly, and so they have divided the period up at least into 'late', 'middle', and 'early' Victorian and have marked the great differences in the habits and ways of thought of different sections of the population in each of the different periods. All this revision has no doubt added to the better understanding of those human beings who lived at that time, but it cannot fully explain any one of them. No one can have been a middle-class early Victorian and nothing more: he will also have been a man and have hidden in his heart the complexities and inscrutabilities common to all men. Even if it is impossible to learn much about him it will be important to re-member the difference between the human being and the label, for it is important to remember the difference between the facts upon which history is based and the concepts which men have created to explain history . . .

Take the various styles in architectures – such as romanesque, gothic, renaissance, baroque. Each of these is firmly rooted in a particular period. It was developed in that period, it can only be studied through it.

The general historical criticism which can throw light on that period throws light on the artistic patterns it developed, while the contemplation of individual examples of each style may teach something which no generalization can teach. But the style itself can survive the period that produced it. It can linger on into later ages of which it is in no way typical. It can be reproduced in an age which is separated by centuries from the era in which it first appeared. It is something which has appeared in history, and to the understanding of which a sense of period probably should contribute but which involves something which is in its way independent of history.

[G. KITSON CLARK, from *The Critical Historian*]

An attempt to raise the quality of historical writing to a level adequate to its task – really to get into the mind of people from the past, their thought and feeling and style.

22nd November

The Kotzker would call upon us to be uneasy about our situation, to feel ashamed of our peace of mind, of our spiritual stagnation. One's integrity must be constantly examined. In his view, self-assurance, certainty of one's honesty, was as objectionable as brazen dishonesty. A moderately clean heart was like a moderately foul egg. Lukewarm Judaism would be as effective in purging our character as a lukewarm furnace in melting steel. Gone for our time is the sweetness of faith. It has ceased to come to us as a gift. It requires "blood, sweat, and tears". We are frightened by a world that God may be ready to abandon. What a nightmare to live in a cosmic lie, in an absurdity that makes pretensions to beauty ...

The Kotzker could not anticipate the disaster that befell his people during the Holocaust. He did not deal with the political situation of the Jews or with the phenomenon of anti-Semitism. Nevertheless, he seems to have had a haunting awareness of the terrible danger of human cruelty. He may not have analyzed the dynamic nature of persecution, yet he was profoundly aware that in a world of lies the demonic had a free reign. Had he been alive in the 1940s the Holocaust would not have come as a surprise to his soul. Indeed, when human beings establish a *modus vivendi* on the basis of mendacity, the world can turn into a nightmare. This may explain the obsessive preoccupation with falsehood in the Kotzker's thinking. For the Holocaust did not take place suddenly. It was in the making for several generations. It had its origins in a lie:

that the Jews were responsible for all social ills, for all personal frustrations. Decimate the Jews and all problems would be solved.

The Holocaust was initiated by demonic thoughts, savage words. What is the state of mankind today? Has the mind been purged, have the words been cleansed of corrupt deceit? How shall we prevent genocide in the years to come? Has mankind become less cruel, less callous?

[ABRAHAM HESCHEL, from *A Passion for Truth*]

The Kotzker was the nineteenth century Rabbi Mendl of Kotzk. The writing here is strong and firm, leaving us with the questions still. Such genocide certainly threatens southern Africa. The whites have never been deterred by being a tiny minority and are ruthless enough to be allied with the Zulus against the rest.

23rd November

> "Most men are not wicked . . . they are
> sleep-walkers, not evil-doers."
> [KAFKA to G. JANOUGH]

Eve and her envy roving slammed me down
prone in discrepancy: I can't get things right:
the passion for secrets the passion worst of all,
the ultimate human, from Leonardo and Darwin

to the austere Viennese with the cigar
and Bohr a-musing: "The opposite of a true
statement is a false statement. But the opposite
of a profound truth may be another profound truth."

So now we see where we are, which is all-over
we're nowhere, son, and suffering we know it,
rapt in delusion, where weird particles
frantic and Ditheletic orbit our

revolutionary natures. She snaked out a soft
small willing hand, curved her ivory fingers on
a new taste sensation, in reverie over
something other,
sank her teeth in, and offered him a bite.

I too find it delicious.

[JOHN BERRYMAN, *Gislebertus' Eve*]

The reference is to a sculpture over a doorway of Autun Cathedral. The idea here is not that of the tragedy of sin entering the world through Eve, but of the necessary offering to a man by a woman of something that only the woman has – a possibility to mankind which, yes, will be paid for: but man on his own is all confusion. Here then is an honest attempt to humanize theodicy. Job is wonderful but so male!

24th November

Miranda not only *is* the wonder, but her capacity for wonder, springing from her own youth, is her own special power, her virtue. For wonder wakes in her "the very virtue of compassion", a virtue which is connected to human potential.

> Miranda: If by your Art, my dearest father, you have
>   Put the wild waters in this roar, allay them . . .
>   . . . O I suffered
>   With those that I saw suffer! a brave vessel
>   (Who had, no doubt, some noble creature in her)
>   Dash'd all to pieces.

Over and over again in this play we are made to witness this wonderful compassion, this instinct towards limitless human possibilities which, at the same time, is often dangerously innocent and naïve, and yet is always necessary if there is to be any room for renewal and rebirth . . .

. . . Wonder which springs from innocent life is fecund, but not enough to manage alone the art of creation. Nature must be nurtured. Even as Miranda's compassion controls Prosper's powers, so his power shapes her grace . . .

It is the shaping imagination, art, which produces harmonies, music, grace and nobility, human civilization itself. It is art, but an art which nature makes, an imagined order, but an order with consonances in the world; it is no figment, but founded on deep natural bonds.

> Mark how one string, sweet husband to another,
> Strikes each in each my mutual ordering,
> Resembling sire and child and happy mother,
> Who, all in one, one pleasing note do sing.

. . . Imagination is a way to the fulness of experience, and to its harmony and order. And because it is a way to order, to a design and epic of being beyond mere contingency and presence, imagination shares in creation. For man is a creation of the orders in which he participates, the orders that raise his creatureliness to humanity and set the stage on which his nobility can be enacted.

[DAVID HOROWITZ, from *Shakespeare, an Existential View*]

The high-water mark of Shakespeare's romaticism. And this passage is a good introduction to what he was doing in The Tempest.

25th November

> I am – yet what I am, none cares or knows;
>   My friends forsake me like a memory lost:
> I am the self-consumer of my woes –
>   They rise and vanish in oblivion's host,
> Like shadows in love frenzied stifled throes
>   And yet I am, and live – like vapours tost
>
> Into the nothingness of scorn and noise,
>   Into the living sea of waking dreams,
> Where there is neither sense of life or joys,
>   But the vast shipwreck of my life's esteems;
> Even the dearest that I love the best
>   Are strange – nay, rather stranger than the rest.
>
> I long for scenes where man hath never trod
>   A place where woman never smiled or wept,
> There to abide with my Creator God,
>   And sleep as I in childhood sweetly slept,
> Untroubling and untroubled where I lie
>   The grass below, above, the vaulted sky.

[JOHN CLARE, *I am*]

The most tragic poem that Clare wrote. It is a brave and vivid realization of his increasing isolation as he became insane. It is controlled enough not to be raving.

26th November

. . . It would be a great injustice . . . not to insist on (the) beauty (of the Pont du Gard) – a kind of manly beauty, that of an object constructed not to please but to serve, and impressive simply from the scale on which it carries out this intention. The number of arches in each tier is different; they are smaller and more numerous as they ascend. The preservation of the thing is extraordinary; nothing has crumbled or collapsed; every feature remains, and the huge blocks of stone, of brownish yellow (as if they had been baked by the Provençal sun for eighteen centuries), pile themselves, without mortar or cement, as evenly as the day they were laid together. All this to carry the water of a couple of springs to a little provincial city! The conduit on the top has retained its shape and traces of the cement with which it was lined. When the vague twilight began to gather, the lonely valley seemed to fill itself with the shadow of the Roman name, as if the mighty empire were still as erect as the supports of the aqueduct; and it was open to believe that no people has ever been, or ever will be as great as that, measured, as we measure the greatness of an individual, by the push they gave to what they undertook. The Pont du Gard is one of the three or four deepest impressions they have left; it speaks of them in a manner with which they might have been satisfied.

[HENRY JAMES, from *A Little Tour in France*]

I do so enjoy the Pont du Gard! And this sense of a bygone culture, brutal in many ways, but giving this part of what is now France some sense of dignity and social purpose.

27th November

The conversation of prayers about to be said
By the child going to bed and the man on the stairs
Who climbs to his dying love in her high room,
The one not caring to whom in his sleep he will move
And the other full of tears that she will be dead,

Turns in the dark on the sound they know will arise
Into the answering skies from the green ground,
From the man on the stairs and the child by his bed,
The sound about to be said in the two prayers
For sleep in a safe land and the love who dies

Will be the same grief flying, Whom shall they calm?
Shall the child sleep unharmed or the man be crying?
The conversation of prayers about to be said
Turns on the quick and the dead, and the man on the stairs
Tonight shall find no dying but alive and warm

In the fire of his care his love in the high room.
And the child not caring to whom he climbs for prayer
Shall drown in a grief as deep as his true grave,
And mark the darkeyed wave through the eyes of sleep,
Dragging him up the stairs to one who lies dead.

[DYLAN THOMAS, *The Conversation of Prayer*]

Certainly a poet who gained full value from the repetition of phrases. I wanted to find a poet on prayer that takes us beyond George Herbert. (This has the sinuous movement that Herbert refers to in his catalogue of phrases describing prayer.) Thomas has the human element. Prayer is in movement and is interwoven with such human concerns.

28th November

We are in a low vaulted room; vaulted, not with arches, but with small cupolas starred with gold, and chequered with gloomy figures; in the centre is a bronze font charged with rich bas-reliefs, a small figure of the Baptist standing above it in a single ray of light that glances across the narrow room, dying as it falls from a window high in the wall, and the first thing that it strikes, and the only thing that it strikes brightly, is a tomb. We hardly know if it be a tomb indeed; for it is like a narrow couch set beside the window, low-roofed and curtained, so that it might seem, but that it is some height above the pavement, to have been drawn towards the window, that the sleeper might be wakened early; – and only there are two angels who have drawn the curtain back, and are looking down upon him. Let us look also and thank that gentle ligh t that rests upon his forehead for ever, and dies away upon his breast . . .

Through the heavy door whose bronze network closes the place of his rest, let us enter the church itself. It is lost in still deeper twilight, to which the eye must be accustomed for some moments before the form of the building can be traced; and then there opens before us a vast cave, hewn out into the form of a Cross, and divided into shadowy aisles by many pillars. Round the domes of its roof the light enters only through narrow apertures like large stars; and here and there a ray or two from some far away casement wanders into the darkness and casts a narrow phosphoric stream upon the waves of marble that heave and fall in a thousand colours along the floor. What else there is of light is from torches, or silver lamps, burning ceaselessly in the recesses of the chapels; the roof sheeted with gold, and the polished walls covered with alabaster, give back at every curve and angle some feeble gleaming to the flames; and the glories round the heads of the sculptured saints flash out upon us as we pass them, and sink again into the gloom.

[JOHN RUSKIN, from *The Stones of Venice*]

Voluptuous writing! It is my own memory of St Mark's in Venice – the gloom and the light coming from God knows where. Ruskin was a pioneer in discerning a sense of the spirit of buildings which pays attention to their detail.

29th November

He sniffed all the holes over again one quick one, to get the smells down good, then suddenly froze still with one paw lifted and his head tilted, listening. I listened too, but I couldn't hear anything except the popping of the window shade. I listened for a long time. Then, from a long way off, I heard a high, laughing gabble, faint and coming closer. Canada honkers going south for the winter. I remembered all the hunting and belly-crawling I'd ever done trying to kill a honker and that I'd never got one.

I tried to look where the dog was looking to see if I could find the flock, but it was too dark. The honking came closer and closer till it seemed like they must be flying right through the dorm, right over my head. Then they crossed the moon – a black, weaving necklace drawn into a V by that lead goose. For an instant that lead goose was right in the centre, bigger than the others, a black cross opening and closing, then he pulled his V out of sight into the sky once more.

I listened to them fade away till all I could hear was my memory of the sound. The dog could still hear them a long time after me. He was still standing with his paw up; he hadn't moved or barked when they flew over. When he couldn't hear them any more either, he commenced to lope off in the direction they had gone, toward the highway, loping steady and solemn like he had an appointment. I held my breath and I could hear the flap of his big paws on the grass as he loped; then I could hear a car speed up out of a turn. The headlights loomed over the rise and peered ahead down the highway. I watched the dog and the car making for the same spot of pavement.

[KEN KESEY, from *One Flew Over the Cuckoo's Nest*]

Each spring I hear the sound of geese and see them in V-formation flying over Gosforth.

30th November

Something has ceased to come along with me;
Something like a person: something very like one.
And there was no nobility in it
Or anything like that.

Something was there like a one year
Old house, dumb as stone. While the near buildings
Sang like birds and laughed
Understanding the pact

They were to have with silence. But he
Neither sang nor laughed. He did not bless silence
Like bread, with words.
He did not forsake silence.

But rather, like a house in mourning
Kept the eye turned in to watch the silence while
The other houses
Sang around him.

And the breathing silence neither
Moved nor was still.

I have seen stones: I have seen brick
But this house was made up of neither bricks nor stone
But a house of flesh and blood
With flesh of stone

And bricks for blood. A house
Of stones and blood in breathing silence with the other
Birds singing crazy on its chimneys,
But this was silence,

This was something else, this was
Hearing and speaking though he was a house drawn
Into silence, this was
Something religious in his silence,

Something shining in his quiet,
This was different this was altogether something else:
Though he never spoke, this
Was something to do with death.

And then slowly the eye stopped looking
Inward. The silence rose and became still.
The look turned to the outer place and stopped,
    With the birds still shrilling around him,
        As if he could speak

He turned over on his side with his one year
    Red as a wound
He turned over as if he could be sorry for this
And out of his eyes two great tears rolled, like stones,
    And he died.

                    [JON SILKIN, *Death of a Son*]

His son died in a mental hospital, aged one. You can only be silent after reading such a poem.

DECEMBER

1st December

> Be sad, be cool, be kind,
> remembering those now dreamdust
> hallowed in the ruts and gullies,
> solemn bones under the smooth blue sea,
> faces warblown in a falling rain.
>
> Be a brother, if so can be,
> to those beyond battle fatigue
> each in his own corner of earth
>   or forty fathoms undersea
>   beyond all boom of guns,
>   beyond any bong of a great bell,
>   each with a bosom and number,
>   each with a pack of secrets,
> each with a personal dream and doorway
> and over them now the long endless winds
>   with the low healing song of time,
>   the hush and sleep murmur of time.
>
>   ...
>
> Be sad, be kind, be cool,
> remembering under God, a dreamdust
> hallowed in the ruts and gullies,
> solemn bones under the smooth blue sea,
> faces warblown in a falling rain.
> Sing low, sing high, sing wide.
> Make your wit a guard and cover,
> Let your laughter come free
> like a help and a brace of comfort.
>   The earth laughs, the sun laughs
> over every wise harvest of man,
> over man looking toward peace

by the light of the hard old teaching:
"We must disenthrall ourselves."

[CARL SANDBURG, from *The Long Shadow of Lincoln*]

"We can succeed only by concert . . . The dogmas of the quiet past are inadequate to the stormy present. The occasion is piled high with difficulty; and we must rise with the occasion. As our case is new so we must think anew and act anew. We must disenthrall ourselves."

[ABRAHAM LINCOLN, 1st December 1862]

That phrase of Lincoln was so true of him. He was conscious of enthralment, not only of slavery in the South, but everywhere, not least our mental chains.

2nd December

John Brown's body lies a-mouldering in the grave.
Spread over it the bloodstained flag of his song,
For the sun to bleach, the wind and the birds to tear,
The snow to cover over with a pure fleece
And the New England cloud to work upon
With the grey absolution of its slow, most lilac-smelling rain,
Until there is nothing there
That ever knew a master or a slave
Or, brooding on the symbol of a wrong,
Threw down the irons in the field of peace.
John Brown is dead, he will not come again,
A stray ghost-walker with a ghostly gun.
Let the strong metal rust
In the enclosing dust
And the consuming coal
That was the furious soul
And still like iron groans,
Anointed with the earth,
Grow colder than the stones
While the white roots of grass and little weeds
Suck the last hollow wildfire from the singing bones.

. . .

And with these things, bury the purple dream
Of the America we have not been,

The tropic empire, seeking the warm sea,
The last foray of aristocracy
Based not on dollars or initiative
Or any blood for what that blood was worth
But on a certain code, a manner of birth,
A certain manner of knowing how to live,
The pastoral rebellion of the earth
Against machines, against the Age of Steam,
The Hamiltonian extremes against the Franklin mean,
The genius of the land
Against the metal hand,
The great, slave-driven bark,
Full-oared upon the dark,
With gilded figurehead
With fetters for the crew
And spices for the few,
The passion that is dead,
The pomp we never knew,
Bury this too.

[STEPHEN VINCENT BENET, from *John Brown's Body*]

John Brown was hanged on 2nd December 1859. This poem is one of the best lyrical comments on the American Civil War. It was still possible then to see a war as a drama in which human motives were revealed. The wars of this century have been on too vast a scale for that.

3rd December

In practical life we cannot content ourselves with piling up motives and noting the inextricably complex inter-relationships of things; we have to decide and act, and in our action we have to depend on other people, to co-operate with them at least temporarily, even if what they do is not always in accord with our own ideals. This is usually where tragedy enters our existence, and everyone has to suffer from it, and the more determined a man is to act honestly, vigorously, fruitfully and with love, the more he will suffer, even if not to the extent that Jesus did on Calvary. But the opaqueness, the impossibility of knowing all the consequences of our actions and desires, is what makes us human: it demands from us the strength to hope again, even though hope has been pushed aside or disappointed or destroyed dozens of times, not to give up, not to fall into cynicism and despair, but to believe, to hope even when one is rejected, misunderstood, and unloved. "Then Peter came up and said, 'Lord, how often shall my brother sin against me and I forgive him? As many as seven times?' Jesus said to him, 'I do not say to you seven times, but seventy times seven.'" The real question today is not whether someone takes the name of Jesus on his lips, especially in a traditional churchy-religious way, but whether he lives out the principles of the Good Samaritan that Jesus put before us. More and more areas of our personal and social lives today become the object of scientific research and technical control. New nations enter the stage of world history, from sources quite different from those of traditional European culture. In this situation, what does the requirement really and truly to help 'one's neighbour' mean? Although Jesus's message has almost merged with European Western civilization and culture, can one leave it in the hands of those to whom the saying perhaps applies, "Leave the dead to bury their own dead."

[MILA MACHOVEC, from *A Marxist Looks at Jesus*]

A challenge to Christians – have you really got it clear, have you made your point? What is the relationship between what you are saying and what is being unfolded in research and technology now?

4th December

> Nothing is lost.
> We are too sad to know that, or too blind;
> Only in visited moments do we understand:
> It is not that the dead return –
> They are about us always, though unguessed.
>
> This pencilled Latin verse
> You dying wrote me, ten years past and more,
> Brings you as much alive to me as the self you wrote it for,
> Dear father, as I read your words
> With no word but Alas.
>
> Lines in a letter, lines in a face
> Are faithful currents of life: the boy has written
> His parents across his forehead, and as we burn
> Our bodies up each seven years,
> His own past self has left no plainer trace.

Nothing dies.
The cells pass on their secrets, we betray them
Unknowingly: in a freckle, in the way
   We walk, we recall some ancestor,
   And Adam in the colour of our eyes.

Yes, on the face of the new born,
Before the soul has taken full possession,
There pass, as over a screen, in succession
   The images of other beings:
   Face after face looks out, and then is gone.

Nothing is lost, for all in love survive.
I lay my cheek against his sleeping limbs
To feel if he is warm, and touch in him
   Those children whom no shawl could warm,
   No arms, no grief, no longing could revive.

Thus what we see, or know,
Is only a tiny portion, at the best,
Of the life in which we share; an iceberg's crest
   Our sunlit present, our partial sense,
   With deep supporting multitudes below.

[ANNE RIDLER, *Nothing is Lost*]

I am struck by her relationship with her father and by the reference to inherited
patterns.

5th December

But are there not errors in existence today, too, and do not these errors
have to be fought? It is precisely the Church, ruled as she is by the Lord's
abiding truth, who has no need to get excited over the often swiftly
changing opinions of men or to lose patience with them; she can meet
the errors of the day and rise calmly above them. "At the outset of the
Second Vatican Council, it is evident as always that the truth of the Lord
will remain forever. We see, in fact, as one age succeeds the other, that
the opinions of men follow one another and exclude each other, and
often errors vanish as quickly as they arise, like fog before the sun." In
any case, in the present situation a different kind of combat against error
is called for, not the method of condemnatory severity but that of helpful compassion: "Ever since the Church opposed these errors, frequently

she has condemned them with the greatest severity. Nowadays, however, the spouse of Christ prefers to make use of the medicine of mercy
rather than that of severity. She considers that she meets the needs of
the present day by demonstrating the validity of her teaching rather
than by condemnations." And when men themselves already perceive
that these things are errors, it is not necessary for the Church to let herself go in repeated condemnations and moralizing admonitions: "Not,
certainly, that there is a lack of fallacious teaching, opinions and dangerous concepts to be guarded against and dissipated, but they are so
evidently in contrast with the right norm of honesty, and have produced such lethal fruits, that by now it would seem that men of themselves are inclined to condemn them, particularly those ways of life
which despise God and his law, excessive confidence in technical progress, and well-being based exclusively on the comforts of life." It is
precisely by following this course of mercy and not severity that the
Church can show herself as ecumenical in breadth: "That being so, the
Catholic Church, raising the torch of religious truth by means of this
Ecumenical Council, desires to show herself to be the loving mother of
all, benign, patient, full of mercy and goodness toward all the children
separated from her." The speech, striking a note of hope throughout its
length, came to climax in a call for unity among Christians and all men.

> [HANS KÜNG, from *The Living Church*, quoting Pope John XXIII's
> opening speech at the Second Vatican Council]

*I believe the Second Vatican Council was very important, though it has been
difficult for many people to understand its significance. And the battle has gone
on since!*

6th December

I have walked and prayed for this young child an hour
And heard the sea-wind scream upon the tower,
And under the arches of the bridge, and scream
In the elms above the flooded stream;
Imagining in excited reverie
That the future years had come,
Dancing to a frenzied drum
Out of the murderous innocence of the sea.

May she be granted beauty and yet not
Beauty to make a stranger's eye distraught,

Or hers before a looking-glass, for such,
Being made beautiful overmuch,
Consider beauty a sufficient end,
Lose natural kindness and maybe
The heart-revealing intimacy
That chooses right, and never find a friend . . .

The courtesy I'd have her chiefly learned;
Hearts are not had as a gift but hearts are earned
By those that are not entirely beautiful;
Yet many, that have played the fool
For beauty's very self, has charm made wise,
And many a poor man that has roved,
Loved and thought himself beloved,
From a glad kindness cannot take his eyes.

May she become a flourishing hidden tree
That all her thoughts may like the linnet be,
And have no business but dispensing round
Their magnanimities of sound,
Nor but in merriment begin a chase,
Nor but in merriment a quarrel.
O may she live like some green laurel
Rooted in one dear perpetual place . . .

[W. B. YEATS, from *A Prayer for my Daughter*]

Here is the desire that a human being should have a natural growing and flowering, without self-consciousness or distortion – a wistful hope that her very presence will contribute something that men cannot possibly make.

7th December

For one day as I leant over a gate that led into a field, the rhythm stopped: the rhymes and the hummings, the nonsense and the poetry. A space was cleared in my mind . . .

The scene beneath me withered. It was like the eclipse when the sun went out and left the earth, flourishing in full summer foliage, withered, brittle, false. Also I saw on a winding road in a dust dance the groups we had made, how they came together, how they ate together, how they met in this room or that. I saw my own indefatigable busyness – how I had rushed from one to the other, fetched and carried, travelled and returned, joined this group and that, here kissed, here withdrawn; always kept hard at it by some extraordinary purpose, with my nose to the ground like a dog on the scent; with an occasional toss of the head, an occasional cry of amazement, despair, and then back again with my nose on the scent. What a litter – what a confusion; with here birth, here death, succulence and sweetness; effort and anguish; and myself always running hither and thither. Now it was done with. I had not more appetites to glut; no more stings in me with which to poison people, no more sharp teeth and clutching hands or desire to feel the pear and grape and the sun beating down on the orchard wall.

The woods had vanished; the earth was a waste of shadow. No sound broke the silence of the wintry landscape. No cock crowed; no smoke rose; no train moved. A man without a self, I said. A heavy body leaning on a gate. A dead man. With dispassionate despair, with entire dis-illusionment, I surveyed the dust dance; my life, my friends' lives, and those fabulous presences, men with brooms, women writing, the willow tree by the river – clouds of phantoms made of dust too, of dust that changed, as clouds lose and gain and take gold or red and lose their summits and billow this way and that, mutable, vain. I, carrying a note-book, making phrases, had recorded merely changes; a shadow, I had been sedulous to take note of shadows. How can I proceed now, I said, without a self, weightless and visionless, through a world weightless, without illusion?

[VIRGINIA WOOLF, from *The Waves*]

Such a packed book, wave after wave, ceaselessly! She makes each character show a glimpse of each wave before it falls. She was filled with a sense of what each successive moment can give us.

8th December

Christ's reference to his own blood occurred at the supper which cele-brated the Passover, normally a feast of thanksgiving for deliverance. For two centuries after his death, the Eucharist was celebrated as an Agape, or Love-Feast. However much Christ's view of the Last Supper was dominated by his premonition of his own death, we may reasonably conclude that the more positive and living symbolism of the Bread and Wine, the idea of sharing one's substance with the brothers and the beloved, was not obliterated from his mind any more than from those of his disciples. Such a poetic awareness of life continuing and circu-

lating is more in consonance with the gospel of love than later interpretations have been, however orthodox.

The efforts of reformers in religion have usually been directed towards recovering the truth of Christianity, the actual meaning of
Christ's words behind the current theological misinterpretations. But
they have repeatedly failed and have stopped short at some new justification of the hatred of opponents, in their more abstract theory, and
some rationalization of their own guilt, as far as their practical precepts
are concerned.

The most unarguable meaning that Christ's words have is the biological observation that "we must love one another or die", but this is
seldom marked in any new outbreak of orthodoxy. As I continue to
point out, our most recent orthodox are far more concerned with
establishing codes of behaviour and belief than with helping any of us to
live in the actual world around us. It may be that they know, as we all
do, that to love one another at present, as heretofore, appears impossible. But it may still be necessary for survival that we should learn to do
so and it serves nothing to offer people instead mere talismans of
salvation.

[KATHLEEN NOTT, from *The Emperor's Clothes*]

*She may or may not be right, but she throws out a challenge with a clear and
unusual voice. Why don't you respond to essentials?*

9th December

"This year she has changed greatly"
                    – meaning you –
My sanguine friends agree,
And hope thereby to reassure me.

No, child, you never change; neither do I.
Indeed all our lives long
We are still fated to do wrong,
Too fast caught by care of humankind.
Each easily vexed and grieved,
Foolishly flattered and deceived.

And yet each knows that change-less other
Must love and pardon still,
Be the new error what it will;

Assured by that some glint death-lessness
Which neither can surprise
In any other pair of eyes.

[ROBERT GRAVES, *Change*]

*This poem was sent to me on a postcard by someone whose wife was mentally ill
and who is now dead. It portrays human life in its raw reality.*

10th December

I have lately had a sudden conception of the true nobility of men and
women. It is well enough to say that they walk like chickens or like
monkeys, except when they are fat and look like hippopotamuses. But
the zoological point of view is not a happy one; and merely from the
desire to think well of men and women I have suddenly seen the very
elementary truth (which I had *never* seen before) that their nobility
does not lie in what they look like but in what they endure and in the
manner in which they endure it. For instance, everybody except a child
appreciates that 'things are not what they seem', and the result of
disillusion might be fatal to content, if it were not for courage, good will
and the like. The mind is the arena of life. Men and women must be
judged, to be judged truly, by the valour of their spirits, by their conquest of the natural being, and by their victories in philosophy. I feel as
if I had made a long step in advance: as if I had discovered for myself
why life is called noble and why people set a value on it, abstractly.

[WALLACE STEVENS, from *Letter to Elsie Moll*]

*We may be shabby, awkward, garrulous, or whatever, but think of what people
have to weather without being bitter or despairing.*

11th December

Woman much missed, how you call to me, call to me,
Saying that now you are not as you were
When you had changed from the one who was all to me,
But as at first, when our day was fair.

Can it be you that I hear? Let me view you then,
Standing as when I drew near to the town,

Where you would wait for me: yes, as I knew you then,
Even to the original air-blue gown!

Or is it only the breeze, in its listlessness
Travelling across the wet mead to me here,
You being ever dissolved to wan wistlessness,
Heard no more again far or near?

    Thus I; faltering forward,
    Leaves around me falling,
Wind oozing thin through the thorn from norward
    And the woman calling.

               [THOMAS HARDY, *The Voice*]

*Again, the woman who is much missed. This is the kind of poetry that helps to
build up memory of personal relationships, memory being the process of recovering and going forward with a profound meaning, not losing, but sifting
and enriching, paying attention, deepening awareness, understanding what we
did not understand at the time. It is a kind of invocation of what needs to be
voiced. We do not let them die.*

12th December

Whenever the writer of this Study reads this masterpiece of Gibbon's
art (*The History of the Decline and Fall of the Roman Empire*), there rises up
before his mind a vision of the Connecticut Valley as he once saw it late
in the Fall, on a visit to Amherst. As he drove through the woods in the
valley bottom, every leaf was still intact in its place, and every leaf had
turned pure crimson or pure gold. Nor did the course of his journey
prevent him from seeing the wood from the trees, for as the car began
to climb the hills by which the valley is bounded, the widening horizon
showed that the beauty of detail was trivial compared with the beauty
of the whole. As we paused at the highest point, we looked back over
miles and miles of golden and crimson woodland spread out below us.
The sky was clear blue, without a cloud; the sun was in power and
glory, the air was bathed in a golden light; and it seemed to be passing
on this gift to the leaves, though these hardly needed any enhancement
of their natural brilliance. The whole landscape made an overwhelming impression of tranquil splendour. Here, surely, was 'a thing of
beauty' which could not pass but was destined to remain to be 'a joy
for ever'...

But my companion's native eyes were not deceived by the beauty
that had dazzled mine. He knew that this was not the summer and not
the spring *a fortiori*. It was the 'Indian summer' whose brief splendour
celebrates not the Promethean élan of life, but the inexorable onset of
Mortality. 'Morituri te salutamus' was the silent declaration of the
leaves which now wore those brilliant colours in place of the living
green. Under sentence of death, they hung on their boughs but hung by
a thread. One breath of wind, one touch of frost, and they would drop
blackened and crumpled to the ground. With my inexperienced eye I
had not understood the true meaning of the spectacle which had taken
my breath away and captivated my imagination.

[ARNOLD TOYNBEE, from *A Study of History*]

*I know Toynbee is out of favour as a historian, but this is a rare purple passage
from his long study.*

13th December

'Tis the year's midnight, and it is the day's,
Lucy's, who scarce seven hours herself unmasks;
    The sun is spent, and now his flasks
    Send forth light squibs, no constant rays;
        The world's whole sap is sunk;
The general balm th'hydroptic earth hath drunk,
Whither, as to the bed's feet, life is shrunk,
Dead and interr'd; yet all these seem to laugh,
Compared with me, who am their epitaph.

Study me then, you who shall lovers be
At the next world, that is, at the next spring;
    For I am every dead thing,
    In whom Love wrought new alchemy.
        For his art did express
A quintessence even from nothingness,
From dull privations, and lean emptiness;
He ruin'd me, and I am re-begot
Of absence, darkness, death – things which are not.

All others, from all things, draw all that's good,
Life, soul, form, spirit, whence they being have;
    I, by love's limbeck, am the grave

Of all, that's nothing. Oft a flood
   Have we two wept, and so
Drown'd the whole world, us two; oft did we grow
To be two Chaoses, when we did show
Care to aught else; and often absences
Withdrew our souls, and made us carcasses.

But I am by her death – which word wrongs her –
Of the first nothing the elixir grown;
   Were I a man, that I were one
   I needs must know; I should prefer,
     If I were any beast,
Some ends, some means; yea plants, yea stones detest,
And love; all, all some properties invest,
If I an ordinary nothing were,
As shadow, a light, and body must be here.

But I am none; nor will my sun renew.
You lovers, for whose sake the lesser sun
   At this time to the Goat is run
   To fetch new lust, and give it you,
     Enjoy your summer all,
Since she enjoys her long night's festival.
Let me prepare towards her, and let me call
This hour her vigil, and her eve, since this
Both the year's and the day's deep midnight is.

[JOHN DONNE, *A Nocturnal upon St Lucy's Day*]

I like the poem for the phrase "the year's midnight" – the time of the solstice, of night, death, and doubt (St Thomas's Day, 21st December). And though Donne shows he is haunted by death, St Lucy stands for 'light'.

14th December

History is essentially necessary to religion, if only as a corrective'
probably the sole efficient corrective, against the delusions of a false
mysticism. For false mysticism has not been satisfied with denying mere
clock-time and proclaiming simultaneity and action as what ultimate
reality already fully is, and as to what we ourselves may hope in a
future form of existence, to possess, according to our creaturely degree,
in predominance and with clearness. But it has generally ignored or

denied the profoundly important element of duration; and, still worse, has attempted to reduce the simultaneity to a mere empty point of blank unity. Now these two errors are inter-related; and history, and the acceptance of history as necessary to religion, effectually suppresses them both. Because there is so rich a variety of constituents to harmonize, with every constituent, as far as possible, itself an organism deriving its fuller self-expression from its function in that larger organization; therefore we poor little human organizers require duration till our organizing task be fulfilled. And because this harmonization and integration – not of dead things into a dead mosaic, but of living forces into a great equilibrium of, at least preponderantly, simultaneous action of the richest, most unified and efficacious kind – is our end and ideal; therefore history has got a true final meaning, and therefore will that simultaneity in no way abolish even the least of the valuable resultants of the succession in history, or be in any sharp anatagonism with what now looks like mere process, but which, to be truly historical, is even now something more than such mere succession.

[F. von Hügel, from *Essays and Addresses*]

It is always 'both-and' with von Hügel. Here is a corrective to those who are uncritically enthusiastic about the mystical.

15th December

Cold in the earth, and the deep snow piled above thee!
Far, far removed, cold in the dreary grave!
Have I forgot, my only Love, to love thee,
Severed at last by Time's all-wearing wave?

Now, when alone, do my thoughts no longer hover
Over the mountains, on that northern shore,
Resting their wings where heath and fern-leaves cover
Thy noble heart for ever, ever more?

Cold in the earth, and fifteen wild Decembers
From those brown hills have melted into Spring –
Faithful, indeed, is the spirit that remembers
After such years of change and suffering!

Sweet Love of youth, forgive if I forget thee
While the World's tide is bearing me along:

Sterner desires and darker hopes beset me,
Hopes which obscure, but cannot do thee wrong.

No other sun has lightened up my heaven;
No other star has ever shone for me:
All my life's bliss from thy dear life was given –
All my life's bliss is in the grave with thee.

But, when the days of golden dreams had perished
And even Despair was powerless to destroy,
Then did I learn how existence could be cherished,
Straightened and fed without the aid of joy;

Then did I check the tears of useless passion,
Weaned my young soul from yearning after thine;
Sternly denied its burning wish to hasten
Down to that tomb already more than mine!

And even yet, I dare not let it languish,
Dare not indulge in Memory's rapturous pain;
Once drinking deep of that divinest anguish,
How could I seek the empty world again?

[EMILY BRONTË, *Remembrance*]

It is the way Emily Brontë here expresses an intense yet controlled passion that is so marvellous.

16th December

Lifting up a word and putting a space round it has been the conscious enterprise of serious French poetry since Baudelaire and Rimbaud. With this 'alchemy' poetry dissolves traditional preconceptions and brings one face to face with existence and with inspiration as a fact . . .

Poetry as verbal alchemy is a *way* of experiencing, never the expression or illustration of a philosophy. It neither begins with ideas nor ends with them. Its magic consists in getting along without the guidance of generalizations, which is the most difficult thing in the world.

[HAROLD ROSENBERG, from *The Tradition of the New*]

A book which enabled me to look afresh at so much. And thinking of the sheer torrent of words on the media - how is it possible for there to be a silence round words?

17th December

Here is the ancient floor.
Footworn and hollowed and thin,
Here was the former door
Where the dead feet walked in.

She sat here in her chair,
Smiling into the fire;
He who played stood there
Bowing it higher and higher.

Childlike, I danced in a dream;
Blessing emblazoned that day;
Everything glowed with a gleam;
Yet we were looking away!

[THOMAS HARDY, *The Self-Unseeing*]

So extraordinary simple! You may not see at the time, but you can recover it. It is what the Arts are for.

18th December

Complacencies of the peignoir, and late
Coffee and oranges in a sunny chair,
And the green freedom of a cockatoo
Upon a rug mingle to dissipate
The holy rush of ancient sacrifice.
She dreams a little, and she feels the dark
Encroachment of that old catastrophe,
As a calm darkens among water-lights.
The pungent oranges and bright green wings
Seem things in some procession of the dead,
Winding across wide water, without sound,
The day is like wide water, without sound,
Stilled for the passing of her dreaming feet
Over the seas, to silent Palestine,
Dominion of the blood and sepulchre.

Why should she give her bounty to the dead?
What is divinity if it can come
Only in silent shadows and in dreams?

Shall she not find in comforts of the sun,
In pungent fruit and bright green wings, or else
In any balm or beauty of the earth,
Things to be cherished like the thought of heaven?
Divinity must live within herself.
Passions of rain, or moods in falling snow;
Grievings in loneliness, or unsubdued
Elations when the forest blooms: gusty
Emotions on wet roads on autumn nights:
All pleasures and all pains, remembering
The bough of summer and the winter branch.
These are the measures destined for her soul.

[WALLACE STEVENS, from *Sunday Morning*]

Wallace Stevens attracted a lot of critical attention. He was a businessman whose poetry was sometimes sharp and clear though often over-long and complex. Here he describes a different Sunday morning from the celebration of what happened in silent Palestine. What can such a morning be when it is removed from its setting in the continuities of Europe?

19th December

But as yet most people, when they must choose between integration on a low human level and intolerable inner strain, will probably take the first and forego the second to regain peace. Yet there is much truth in the saying that the peace that reigns under tyranny is not the peace of human existence, but the peace of death.

And this may turn out to be a reassuring thought. I have stated my conviction before. As in all other great revolutions in the history of mankind, so too in this technological, industrial and social revolution we live in: after some delay man will once again develop the requisite inner structures, and the great ability to achieve inner integration, that must go with our new conditions of life . . .

If these views seem too optimistic, those who cannot share them may take some comfort from what happened in the Hitler state where some of its victims dug their own graves and laid themselves into them or walked on their own to the gas chambers. All of them were the vanguard of a walk toward death, toward the peace of death I have just spoken of. Men are not ants. They embrace death rather than an antlike existence. That is a further meaning of these victims of the SS walking to

their death. That the SS killed them is of less import than the fact that
they marched themselves into death, choosing to give up a life that was
no longer human.

In times of great crisis, of inner and outer revolutions in all phases of
life, situations may occur in which men have only the choice between
such a giving up of life and the achieving of a higher integration. Because
we have not yet achieved the latter is no proof we are going to choose
the former. If I read the signs of our times correctly, we have taken the
first steps toward mastering the new conditions of life in an age of
atomic power. But let us not fool ourselves either: the struggle will be
long and hard, taxing all our mental and moral powers, if we do not
want a brave new world but an age of reason and humanity.

[BRUNO BETTELHEIM, from *The Informed Heart*]

*An appalling book which should be frequently read. He states factually what
happened to people under the Nazis. How he could write it and preserve his
sanity I don't know.*

20th December

It was nearly midnight on the eve of St Thomas's, the shortest day in the
year. A desolating wind wandered from the north over the hill whereon
Oak had watched the yellow wagon and its occupant in the sunshine of a
few days earlier.

Norcombe Hill – forming part of Norcombe Ewelease – was one of the
spots which suggest to a passer-by that he is in the presence of a shape
approaching the indestructible as nearly as any to be found on earth.
It was a featureless convexity of chalk and soil – an ordinary specimen of
those smoothly outlined protuberances of the globe which may remain
undisturbed on some great day of confusion, when far grander heights
and dizzy precipices topple down...

The sky was clear – remarkably clear – and the twinkling of all the
stars seemed to be but throbs of one body, timed by a common pulse.
The North Star was directly in the wind's eye, and since evening the
Bear had swung round it outwardly to the east, till he was now at a right
angle with the meridian. A difference of colour in the stars – oftener read
of than seen in England – was really perceptible here. The kingly
brilliancy of Sirius pierced the eye with a steely glitter, the star called
Capella was yellow, Aldebaran and Betelgueux shone with a fiery red.

To persons standing alone on a hill during a clear midnight such as this, the roll of the world eastward is almost a palpable movement. The sensation may be caused by the panoramic glide of the stars past earthly objects, which is perceptible in a few minutes of stillness, or by the better outlook upon space that a hill affords, or by the wind, or by the solitude; but whatever be its origin, the impression of riding along is vivid and abiding. The poetry of motion is a phrase much in use, and to enjoy the epic form of that gratification it is necessary to stand on a hill at a small hour of the night, and, having first expanded with a sense of difference from the mass of civilized mankind, who are horizontal and disregardful of all such proceedings at this time, long and quietly watch your stately progress through the stars. After such a nocturnal reconnoitre among those astral clusters, aloft from the customary haunts of thought and vision, some men may feel raised to a capability for eternity at once.

[THOMAS HARDY, from *Far from the Madding Crowd*]

Hardy was so conscious of the great cycles of movement in nature. I wanted this extract for the Solstice.

21st December

At four o'clock the building enters harbour.
All day it seems that we have been at sea.
Now, having lurched through the last of the water,
We lie, stone-safe, beside the jumping quay.
The stiff waves propped against the class-room window,
The razor-back of cliffs we never pass,
The question-mark of green coiling behind us,
Have all turned into cabbages, slates, grass.

Up the slow hill a squabble of children wanders
As silence dries the valley like a drought,
When suddenly that speechless cry is raging
Once more round these four walls to be let out.
Like playing cards the Delabole slates flutter,
The founding stone is shaken in its mine,
The faultless evening light begins to stutter
As the cry hurtles down the chimney-spine.

Packing my bags with useless bits of paper
I wonder, when the last word has been said,

If I'd prefer to find each sound was thudding
Not round the school, but just inside my head.
I watch where the street lamp with sodium finger
Touches the darkening voices as they fall.
Outside? Inside? Perhaps either condition's
Better than his who hears nothing at all.

And I recall another voice. A teacher
Long years ago, saying, "I think I know
Where all the children come from but the puzzle
To me is, as they grow up, where they go."
Love, wonder, marvellous hope. All these can wither
With crawling years like flowers on a stalk;
Or, to some Piper's tune, vanish for ever
As creatures murdered on a morning walk.

Though men may blow this building up with powder,
Drag its stone guts to knacker's yard, or tip,
Smash its huge heart to dust, and spread the shingle
By the strong sea, or sink it like a ship –
Listen. Through the clear shell of air the voices
Still strike like water from the mountain bed;
The cry of those who to a certain valley
Hungry and innocent came. And were not fed.

[CHARLES CAUSLEY, *School at four o'clock*]

The end of the school day in winter. I like this poem!

22nd December

"For there, against the sky, I saw the nearest pinnacle; and it was the
exact image of my prayer in stone. There was the uprush, the ornamen-
tation of side thoughts for others, then the rush of the heart, rising,
narrowing, piercing – and at the top, still carved in stone, the thing I had
felt as a flame of fire."

"That's how it was. You can still see the pinnacle if you turn your
head."

"If this seemed strange to my ignorance, my children, how shall I
describe the wonder of what happened next? For as I looked my understanding spread. It was as if the pinnacle had been a key to unlock a vast
book. It was as if I had acquired a new ear for hearing, a new eye to look

with. For the whole building spoke. 'We are labour,' said the walls. The ogival windows clasped their hands and said, 'We are prayer.' And the trinity of the triangular roof – but how shall I say it? I had tried to give away my house; and it had returned to me a thousand-fold."

"Even so!"

". . . and at the top, if top is the word, some mode, some gift that brought no pride of having. My body lay on the soft stones, changed in a moment, the twinkling of an eye, resurrected from daily life. The vision left me at last; and the memory of it, which I savoured as manna, shaped itself to the spire, fitted into a shape, the centre of the book, the crown, the ultimate prayer."

"It is an ungainly crumbling thing. Nothing like. Nothing at all."

"So at last I got to my feet. The candles still burned not a whit shorter, and the mass priests muttered; for this had been nothing but an instant as the world measures. I carried the image of the temple down the nave, in my eye. Do you know, my children? The spiritual is to the material, three times real! It was only when I was halfway to my house that I understood the true nature of the vision. As I turned to look once more, and bless, I saw there was something missing. The church was there; but the ultimate prayer, spiring upward from the centre – physically speaking did not exist at all. And from that moment I knew why God had brought me here, his unworthy servant."

[WILLIAM GOLDING, from *The Spire*]

The visually exact descriptions drew me to this piece. And I remember one time when I was preparing for the following morning's Holy Communion in the Lady Chapel at Wells Cathedral, I walked up and down the nave at night, alone in the body of the building. It can be built, it can cohere, but it can also be destroyed.

23rd December

The presence of nature in my winter room
With curtains drawn across the clouds and stars,
Lakes, fells, and green sweet meadows far away
Is fire, older and more wild than they.

Fire will outlast them all and take them all
For into fire the autumn woods must fall.
Spring blossoming is the slow combustion of the tree,
The phoenix fire that burns bird beast and flower away.

Once Troy and Dido's Carthaginian pyre
And Baldur's ships, and fabulous London burning,
Robes, wooden walls and crystal palaces
In their apotheosis were such flames as these.

Flames more fluent than water of a mountain stream,
Flames more delicate and swift than air,
Flames more impassable than walls of stone,
Destructive and irrevocable as time.

Essential fire is the unhindered spirit
That, laid upon the lips of prophecy
Frees all the shining elements of the soul;
Whose burning teaches love the way to die
And selves to undergo their ultimate destruction
Upon those flaming ramparts of the world
That rise between our fate, and the lost garden.

[KATHLEEN RAINE, *The Lost Garden*]

What a strange vision it is, the angel with the flaming sword at the entrance to the garden. Yet there is an unusual gentleness about fire through much of this poem. When I have made my fire, alone in winter, I am struck by this fluency of the flames, more vivid than flowing water.

24th December

Come out for a while and look from the outside in
At a room you know
As the firelight fitfully beats on the windowpane
An old heart sinking low,
And the whispering melting kisses of the snow
Soothe time from your brow.

It is Christmastide. Does the festival promise as fairly
As ever to you? "I feel
The numbness of one whose drifted years conceal
His original landmarks of good and ill.
For a heart weighed down by its own and the world's folly
This season has little appeal."

But tomorrow is Christmas Day. Can it really mean
Nothing to you? "It is hard

To see it as more than a time-worn tinsel routine
Or else a night incredibly starred,
Angels, oxen, a Babe – the recurrent dream
Of a Christmas card."

You must try again. Say "Christmas Eve". Now, quick,
What do you see?
"I see in a firelit room a child is awake
Mute with expectancy,
For the berried day, the presents, the Christmas cake,
Is he mine or me?"

He is you, and yours. Desiring for him tomorrow's
Feast – the crackers, the Tree, the piled
Presents – you lose your self in his yearning, and borrow
His eyes to behold
Your own young world again. Love's mystery is revealed
When the father becomes the child.

"Yet would it make those carolling angels weep
To think how Incarnate Love
Means such trival joys to us children of unbelief?"
No. It's a miracle great enough
If through centuries, clouded and dingy, this Day can keep
Expectation alive.

                                [CECIL DAY LEWIS, *Christmas Eve*]

*He takes up everything we experience about Christmas, turns it towards the
personal, and suggests that expectation at least is still alive.*

25th December

That night, before the storm died,
and the snows stopped drifting, He cried.
His breath smoked in His mother's face
before the late star caught the last trace
of the storm that met his birth.

Is it any birth? Apart from cold,
and lack of shelter, is it the old
pain and dread of making new flesh,
or a new womb making man afresh?
New snow over a new earth?

She blenched at the cold and tried to rest
the avid child at her avid breast.
Was it for more than the physical joy
she blessed God for the gift of the boy?
Did she see beyond His thirst?

That dawn, before anyone came,
and the sky was kindling its spare flame,
He slept. She stole out to watch it rise,
her body still aching with surprise;
The child asleep was her first.

[MAUD SAVILLE]

This poem was given to me by the poet herself after a chance encounter in Rydal Church. She gave me permission to use it with groups I was leading.

26th December

Beloved, we do not think of a martyr simply as a good Christian who has been killed because he is a Christian: for that would be solely to mourn. We do not think of him simply as a good Christian who has been elevated to the company of the Saints, for that would be simply to rejoice: and neither our mourning nor our rejoicing is as the world's is. A Christian martyrdom is no accident. Saints are not made by accident. Still less is a Christian martyrdom the effect of a man's will to become a saint, as a man by willing and contriving may become a ruler of men. Ambition fortifies the will of man to become ruler over other men: it operates with deception, cajolery, and violence, it is the action of impunity upon impunity. Not so in Heaven. A martyr, a saint, is always made by the design of God, for His love of men, to warn them and to teach them, to bring them back to His ways. A martyrdom is never the design of man; for the true martyr is he who has become the instrument of God, who has lost his will in the will of God, not lost it but found it, for he found freedom in submission to God. The martyr no longer desires anything for himself, not even the glory of martyrdom. So thus as on earth the Church mourns and rejoices at once, in a fashion that the world cannot understand; so in Heaven the Saints are most high, having made themselves most low, seeing themselves not as we see them, but in the light of the Godhead from which they draw their being.

[T. S. ELIOT, from *Murder in the Cathedral*]

This reading is for St Stephen's Day. The day on which we remember St Thomas of Canterbury is 29th December: it was the first available date after Christmas Day that he could be put in the English Calendar, since St Stephen, St John, and the Holy Innocents were already there.

27th December

The heart could never speak
But that the Word was spoken.
We hear the heart break
Here with hearts unbroken.
Time, teach us the art
That breaks and heals the heart.

Heart, you would be dumb
But that your Word was said
In time, and the Echoes come
Thronging from the dead.
Time, teach us the art
That resurrects the heart.

Tongue, you can only say
Syllables, joy and pain,
Till Time, having its way
Makes the Word live again.
Time, merciful Lord,
Help us to learn your Word.

[EDWIN MUIR, *The Heart Could Never Speak*]

For St John the Evangelist's Day – poet of the Word. R. P. Blackmur, an American literary critic, wrote this couplet:
Words verge on flesh and so we may
Someday be to ourselves the things we say.
The Incarnation edges its way in.

28th December

Be cheerful, sir.
Our revels now are ended. These our actors,
As I foretold you, were all spirits, and

Are melted into air, into thin air:
And, like the baseless fabric of this vision,
The cloud-capp'd towers, the gorgeous palaces,
The solemn temples, the great globe itself,
Yea, all which it inherit, shall dissolve,
And, like this insubstantial pageant faded,
Leave not a rack behind. We are such stuff
As dreams are made on; and our little life
Is rounded with a sleep.

[WILLIAM SHAKESPEARE, from *The Tempest*]

So too come to an end the Christmas revels!

29th December

And today, Henry, in the anthem, when they sang it, "When the Lord
turned the captivity of Zion, we were like them that dream," I thought,
yes, like them that dream, them that dream. And then it went, "They
that sow in tears shall reap in joy, and he that goeth forth and weepeth
shall doubtless come again with rejoicing, bringing his sheaves with
him." I looked up from the book and saw you. I was not surprised when
I saw you. I knew you would come, my dear, and saw the gold sunshine round your head.

[WILLIAM THACKERAY, from *The History of Henry Esmond*]

The book fascinated me as a youngster, though I no longer think it a great novel.
This passage illustrates what literature should be doing, alerting us to moments
of vision, even if we don't have many of our own.

30th December

Fear no more the heat o' th' sun,
    Nor the furious winter's rages;
Thou thy worldly task hast done,
    Home art gone and ta'en thy wages:
Golden lads and girls all must,
    As chimney-sweepers, come to dust.

Fear no more the frown o' th' great,
    Thou art past the tyrant's stroke;

Care no more to clothe and eat;
  To thee the reed is as the oak:
The sceptre, learning, physic, must
  All follow this, and come to dust.

Fear no more the lightning-flash,
  Nor th' all-dreaded thunder-stone;
Fear not slander, censure rash;
  Thou hast finished joy and moan:
All lovers young, all lovers must
  Consign to thee, and come to dust.

No exorcisor harm thee.
  Nor no witchcraft charm thee.
Ghost unlaid forbear thee.
  Nothing ill come near thee.
Quiet consummation have,
  And renowned be thy grave!

[WILLIAM SHAKESPEARE, from *Cymbeline*]

We are made of particles of dust, yes, but dust is not mean. It is part of the total creative drive. Why should we be afraid to be dust? (And it is worth looking at how Shakespeare ends his plays, The Tempest, Hamlet, King Lear.)

31st December

Ring out wild bells to the wild sky,
  The flying cloud, the frosty light:
  The year is dying in the night;
Ring out wild bells and let him die.

Ring out the old, ring in the new,
  Ring, happy bells, across the snow:
  The year is going, let him go;
Ring out the false, ring in the true.

Ring out the grief that saps the mind,
  For those that here we see no more;
  Ring out the feud of rich and poor,
Ring in redress to all mankind.

Ring out a slowly dying cause
  And ancient forms of party strife;

Ring in the nobler modes of life,
With sweeter manners, purer laws.

Ring out the want, the care, the sin,
The faithless coldness of the times;
Ring out, ring out, my mournful rhymes,
But ring the fuller minstrel in.

Ring out false pride in place and blood,
The civic slander and the spite;
Ring in the love of truth and right,
Ring in the common love of good.

Ring out the shapes of foul disease
Ring out the narrowing lust of gold;
Ring out the thousand wars of old,
Ring in the thousand years of peace.

Ring in the valiant man and free,
The larger heart, the kindlier hand;
Ring out the darkness of the land,
Ring in the Christ that is to be.

[ALFRED TENNYSON, from *In Memoriam*]

Farewell.

One tries at least
To say only what the heart says; do only
What the buds do, flower by conviction;
The inward mastery of the outward act.

[R. P. BLACKMUR]

References and Acknowledgments

Owing to Alan Ecclestone's death in December 1992, it has not been possible to trace every single reference in the detail the publisher would wish. Additional information would be gratefully received from readers of this anthology.

The publisher acknowledges permission to reproduce copyright material in this book; he apologises for any inadvertent omissions, which will be put right in any future edition.

ACTON, Lord. *A lecture on the study of history*, London, 1895; *History of freedom and other essays*, London, 1922.

ADAMS, Henry. *Mont-Saint-Michel and Chartres*, Constable, 1961; *The education of Henry Adams*, Constable, 1928.

ALAIN-FOURNIER, Henri. *Le Grand Meaulnes*, tr. Davison, Frank, *The Lost Domain*, OUP, 1959.

ARNOLD, Matthew. 'Thyrsis', *New Oxford book of English verse*, OUP, 1972; 'Essay on Heinrich Heine', *Essays literary and critical*, Dent, 1906; 'Memorial verses 1850', *Arnold: poetry and prose*, OUP, 1939; 'To a gypsy child by the sea-shore', *Poems*, Longman, 1965; 'The Grand Chartreuse', *Arnold: poetry and prose*, OUP, 1939.

ASHBY, M. H. *Joseph Ashby of Tysoe*, reprinted by permission of Cambridge University Press.

AUDEN, W. H. *For the time being*, Faber, 1944; 'Edward Lear', 'Look stranger', 'On this island', *Collected poems*, Faber, 1976; 'August for the people', *The English Auden*; reprinted by permission of Faber & Faber Ltd. *The Protestant mystics*, Freemantle, A., (ed.), Mentor Books, New York, 1965.

BALDWIN, James. *Another country*, Michael Joseph, 1963, reproduced by permission of Penguin Books Ltd.

BARTH, Karl. *Church dogmatics vol 3.3*, reprinted by permission of T. & T. Clark.

BELL, Daniel. *The coming of post-industrial society*, Peregrine Books, 1976, reprinted by permission of Daniel Bell.

BENET, S. V. *John Brown's body*, OUP, 1928.

BENNETT, Arnold. *Clayhanger*, London, 1925.

BERGER, John. *A painter of our time*, Secker & Warburg, 1958, reprinted by permission of the author.

BERNANOS, G. *The open mind*, Bodley Head, 1945.

BERRYMAN, John. 'Giselbertus' eve', *Collected poems 1937–1971*, reprinted by permission of Faber & Faber Ltd.

BETTELHEIM, Bruno. *The informed heart*, Thames & Hudson, 1961, reprinted by permission of Thames & Hudson Ltd.

BIKO, Steve. see Stubbs, Aelred.

BLACKBURN, Thomas. 'Luna', *Collected poems*, Hutchinson, 1975.

BLAKE, William. 'The Divine image', *New Oxford book of English verse*, OUP, 1972; 'Proverbs in Hell', *Poetry and prose of William Blake*, Nonesuch, 1946.

BORROW, George. *Romany rye*, Everyman, Dent, 1906.

BRIDGES, Robert. 'On a dead child', *New Oxford book of English verse*, OUP, 1972.

BRONOWSKI, J., and MAZLISH, B. *The western intellectual tradition*, Hutchinson, 1960, reprinted by permission of HarperCollins, Publishers, Inc.

BRONTË, Emily. 'Stanzas', *Complete poems*, Columbia University Press, 1941; 'Remembrance', *New Oxford book of English verse*, OUP, 1972.

BROWN, Norman O. *Love's body*, Random House, 1966.

BROWNING, Elizabeth Barrett. 'A musical instrument', *Complete works vol.6*, Thomas Crowell, New York, 1900.

BROWNING, Robert. 'Parleying with Gerard de Laurèse', 'By the fireside', 'Bishop Brougham's apology', 'The ring and the book', 'James Lee's wife', Everyman, Dent.

BUBER, Martin. *Between man and man*, Kegan Paul, 1947, reprinted by permission of Balkin Agency, Inc., agent for the Estate of Martin Buber; *I and thou*, T. & T. Clark, 1937, *Imitatio Deo* reprinted by permission of T. & T. Clark Ltd; An address at the third international educational conference, Heidelberg, August 1925; *Israel and the world*, Schocken Books, 1963; *Moses*, Harper Torch, 1958.

BURN, W. L. *The age of equipoise*, Allen & Unwin, 1964, reprinted by permission of HarperCollins Publishers Ltd.

BYATT, A. S. *Still life*, Chatto & Windus, 1985, reprinted by permission of Random House UK Ltd.

CAMUS, Albert. *The plague*, Penguin, 1960, reprinted by permission of Penguin Books Ltd.

CARY, Joyce. *Mister Johnson*, Gollancz, 1939, reproduced by permission of the J. L. A. Cary Estate.

CARROLL, Lewis. *Alice in wonderland*, London, 1896.

CAUSLEY, Charles. 'I am the great sun', 'School at four o'clock', *Collected poems*, reprinted by permission of David Higham Associates.
CLARE, John. 'I am', *New Oxford book of English verse*, OUP, 1972; 'Song'.
CLARK, G. Kitson. *The critical historian*, Heinemann, 1967.
COLERIDGE, S. T. 'Kubla Khan', 'The rime of the ancient mariner', *New Oxford book of English verse*, OUP, 1972.
COLLINGWOOD, R. G. *The idea of history*, Clarendon Press, 1946, reprinted by permission of Oxford University Press.
COLLINS, W. 'Ode to evening', *New Oxford book of English verse*, OUP, 1972.
COLLIS, Maurice. *Stanley Spencer*, Harvill Press, 1962.
CONDENHOVE, Ida. *The nature of sanctity*, Sheed and Ward, 1932.
CONRAD, J. *Under western eyes*, Dent, 1947; *Almayer's folly*, Dent, 1947; *Chance*, Dent, 1947.
CORNFORD, J. 'Huesca', in Sloan, P., (ed.), *John Cornford, a memoir*, Jonathan Cape, 1938.
CRANE, Hart. 'For the marriage of Faustus and Helen', *Complete Poems*, Bloodaxe, 1984.
CUMMINGS, E. E. 'I thank you, God', *Collected poems*, 1910–62, Granada, 1981.

DAVIES, Idris. 'One February evening', *Collected poems*, Llandysul, 1972, reprinted by permission of J. D. Lewis & Sons Ltd.
DAY LEWIS, Cecil. 'The Album', 'Birthday poem for Thomas Hardy', 'Statuette: late Minoan', 'Walking away', Penguin, 1969; 'On not saying everything', *The room and other poems*, Jonathan Cape, 1965; 'The heartsease', *Collected poems*, Jonathan Cape and Hogarth Press, 1977; 'Christmas eve', *Pegasus and other poems*, Jonathan Cape, 1957; reprinted by permission of Sinclair-Stevenson.
DE LA MARE, Walter. 'The scribe', 'Vain questioning', *Collected poems*, reproduced by permission of The Literary Trustees of Walter de la Mare and the Society of Authors as their representative.
DE MORGAN, W. *Joseph Vance*, OUP, World's Classics, 1954.
DE TAVERNIER, Johan. *Concilium* 1991(4), reprinted by permission of T. & T. Clark and Concilium.
DICKENS, Charles. *Dombey and son*.
DIX, Gregory. *The shape of the liturgy*, Dacre Press, 1945, reprinted by permission of A. & C. Black.
DODDS, E. R. 'When the ecstatic body grips', *Thirty-two poems*, Constable, 1979, reprinted by permission of Constable & Co. Ltd.
DONNE, John. 'Holy sonnet', 'The sun rising', 'A nocturnal upon St Lucy's day', *New Oxford book of English verse*, OUP, 1972.

DOSTOEVSKY, Fyodr. *The brothers Karamazov*, Everyman, Dent.

DRAYTON, Michael. 'Sonnets to Idea', *New Oxford book of English verse*, OUP, 1972.

DRUCKER, Peter. *The end of economic man*, Harper & Row, 1969.

DURRELL, Lawrence. *Reflections on a marine Venus*, Faber, 1953, reprinted by permission of Faber & Faber Ltd.

EBERHART, Richard. 'Formative mastership', *Collected poems 1930–86*, OUP, 1988.

EHRENZWEIG, Anton. *The hidden order of art*, Weidenfeld & Nicolson, 1967.

ELIOT, T. S. 'Journey of the Magi', 'Animula', *Collected poems*, Faber, 1963; *Murder in the cathedral*, Faber, 1935, reprinted by permission of Faber & Faber Ltd.

EMMANUEL, Pierre. *The universal singular*, Grey Walls Press, 1950.

EWART, Gavin. 'The late eighties', *Collected poems 1980–1990*, reprinted by permission of Random Century Group.

FAST, Howard. see Vanzetti, Bartolomeo.

FAUSSET, Hugh L'Anson. *Walt Whitman*, Jonathan Cape, 1942.

FERLINGHETTI, L. 'Sometime during eternity', *An eye on the world*, MacGibbon & Kee, 1967.

FITZGERALD, Edward. 'The Rubáiyát of Omar Khayam', *New Oxford book of English verse*, OUP, 1972.

FITZGERALD, Scott. *The great Gatsby*, Penguin, 1950.

FITZPATRICK, P. J. 'Turkish delight laced with incense', *The Independent*, 18 April 1987, reprinted by permission of The Independent.

FORSTER, E. M. *A room with a view*, Edward Arnold, 1908, reproduced by permission of King's College, Cambridge and The Society of Authors as the literary representatives of the E. M. Forster Estate; *Howard's End*, Penguin, 1975.

FRANKL, Victor. *The will to meaning*, Souvenir Press, 1971.

FREEDURG, S. J. *Painting in Italy 1500–1600*, Penguin, 1971, copyright Yale Pelican History of Art, reprinted by permission of Yale University Press.

FROST, Robert. *Pod of the milkweed*, The poetry of Robert Frost, Jonathan Cape, 1971.

FROUDE, James Anthony. *The history of England*, London, 1856–70.

GARDINER, S. R. *Oliver Cromwell*, Longman Green & Co., 1909.

GASCOYNE, David. 'Ecce homo', *Poems 1937–42*, Nicholson & Watson, 1943.

GEYL, Pieter. *Encounters in history*, Collins, 1963.

GIEDION, S. *Architecture, you and me*, Harvard University Press, 1958, reprinted by permission of Harvard University Press.

GILL, Eric. *Autobiography*, Jonathan Cape, 1940.

GOFFIN, Magdalen, in Bedoyère, M. (ed.). *The future of Catholic Christianity*, reprinted by permission of Constable & Co. Ltd.

GOLDING, William. *The spire*, reprinted by permission of Faber & Faber Ltd.

GRAVES, Robert. 'Alice', 'Change', *Collected poems*, Cassell, 1965, reprinted by permission of A. P. Watt Ltd on behalf of the Trustees of the Robert Graves Copyright Trust.

GREEN, Julian. *Diary 1928–57*, Collins and Harvill Press, 1964.

GREEN, T. H. 'Sermon on faith', *The witness of God and faith*, Longman Green & Co., 1889.

GUNN, Thom. 'My sad captains', 'In Santa Maria del popolo, 'Jesus and his mother', in *Selected poems 1950–1975*, reprinted by permission of Faber & Faber Ltd.

GUNTRIP, Harry. *Mental pain and the cure of souls*, Independent Press, 1956.

HARDY, Thomas. 'To meet, or otherwise', 'Wessex heights', 'The voice', 'The self unseeing', *Collected poems*, Macmillan, 1928; 'After a journey', 'A night in September', *Poems*, Folio Society, 1979; *Far from the madding crowd*, Osgood, McIlvaine & Co; *The woodlanders*, Macmillan, 1887.

HARTE, Bret. 'Tennessee's Partner', *Tales, poems, sketches*, Everyman, Dent, 1914.

HARTLEY, L. P. *The Go-Between*, Folio, 1975, reproduced by permission of Hamish Hamilton Ltd; *Eustace and Hilda*, Putnam, 1947, reprinted by permission of The Bodley Head.

HAUGHTON, Rosemary. *The passionate God*, DLT, 1981, reprinted by permission of Darton, Longman and Todd.

HELLER, Erich. *In the age of prose*, CUP, 1984, reprinted by permission; *Karl Kraus: the disinherited mind*, CUP, 1952, reprinted by permission of Cambridge University Press.

HERBERT, George. 'The flower', *New Oxford book of English verse*, OUP, 1972.

HERRICK, Robert. 'Fair daffodils', *New Oxford book of English verse*, OUP, 1972.

HERSEY, John. *A single pebble*, Hamilton, 1956.

HESCHEL, Abraham. *Who is man?*, Stanford University Press, 1966, reprinted by permission of Stanford University Press; *A passion for truth*, Secker & Warburg, 1974, reprinted by permission of Farrar, Straus & Giroux, Inc.

HILL, Geoffrey. 'Lachrimae Amantis', *Collected poems*, Penguin, 1985.

HODGES, H. A. *William Dilthey*, Kegan Paul, Trench, Trubner, 1944, reprinted by permission of Routledge & Kegan Paul.

HOLBROOK, David. 'The return', *Against the cruel frost*, Putnam, 1963, reprinted by permission of David Holbrook.

HOPKINS, G. M. 'Carrion comfort', *Gerard Manley Hopkins*, Penguin, 1953; 'The starlight night', *Selected poems*, Heinemann, 1963.

HOROWITZ, David. *Shakespeare, an existential view*, Tavistock, 1965, reprinted by permission of Tavistock Publications.

HOUSE, Edward M. *The intimate papers of Colonel House*, Ernest Benn, 1926.

HOUSMAN, A. E. *A Shropshire lad*, 1896.

HROMADKA, Joseph. *Thoughts of a Czech pastor*, SCM Press, 1970, reprinted by permission of SCM Press Ltd.

HUDSON, W. H. *A shepherd's life*, Methuen, 1910.

HULME, T. E. *Speculations*, Kegan Paul, 1924.

JAMES, Henry. *A little tour in France*, OUP, 1984.

JOHNSON, Martin. *Modern art and scientific thought*, Urbana, 1971.

JOHNSON, Paul. *The offshore islanders*, Weidenfeld & Nicolson, 1972.

JONES, David. *Epoch and artist*, Faber, 1959, reprinted by permission of Faber & Faber Ltd.

KAROLYI, Michael. *Memoirs*, Jonathan Cape, 1956.

KEATS, John. 'On sitting down to read *King Lear* once again', 'Sonnet on Fame', 'Written on a blank page in Shakespeare's poems', *Poems*, Penguin Poetry Library, 1953; 'Ode to a nightingale', 'To Autumn', *New Oxford book of English verse*, OUP, 1972.

KESEY, Ken. *One flew over the cuckoo's nest*, Signet Classics, 1962, reprinted by permission of Sterling Lord Literistic Inc., copyright 1962 by Ken Kesey.

KÜNG, Hans. *The living church*, Sheed & Ward, 1963, reprinted by permission of Sheed & Ward Ltd.

LASH, Nicholas. *A matter of hope*, DLT, 1981, reprinted by permission of Darton, Longman, & Todd.

LAWRENCE, D. H. 'Rose of all the world', 'The ship of death', *Collected poems*, Heinemann, 1964, reproduced with acknowledgments to Laurence Pollinger Ltd and the Estate of Frieda Lawrence Ravagli.

LILAR, Susanne. *Aspects of love in western society*, Thames & Hudson, 1965, reprinted by permission of Thames & Hudson Ltd.

LOWELL, Robert. 'Waking early Sunday morning', *Near the ocean*, Faber, reprinted by permission of Faber & Faber Ltd.

LOWRY, Malcolm. *Under the volcano*, Jonathan Cape, 1947, reprinted by permission of Peters, Fraser & Dunlop on behalf of the Malcolm Lowry Estate.

LYSAGHT, Sidney Royse. 'The penalty of love'.

MACHOVEC, M. *A Marxist looks at Jesus*, DLT, 1976, reprinted by permission of Darton, Longman & Todd.

MACINTYRE, Alasdair. *After virtue*, Duckworth, 1981, reprinted by permission of Duckworth.

MACMURRAY, John. *Search for reality in religion*, Allen & Unwin, 1965, reprinted by permission of HarperCollins Publishers Ltd; *Persons in relation*, Faber, 1957, reprinted by permission of Humanities Press International, Inc., Atlantic Highlands, NJ.

MARVELL, Andrew. 'The garden', *New Oxford book of English verse*, OUP, 1972.

MASTERS, Edgar Lee. 'Isaiah Beethoven', *Spoon river anthology*, Werner Laurie, 1915.

MATTIESSEN, F. O. *From the heart of Europe*, OUP, 1948.

MAUGHAM, Somerset. *Of human bondage*, Heinemann, 1915.

MARX, Karl. *Grundrisse*, 1857.

MAZLISH, B. see BRONOWSKI, J.

McLELLAN, David, see MARX, K.

McLOGHLEN, Diana. 'Hutton roof', *The last headlands*, Windus & Hogarth Press, 1972, reprinted by permission of Random House UK Ltd.

MEREDITH, George. 'Modern love', *New Oxford book of English verse*, OUP, 1972.

MEW, Charlotte. 'Moorland night', *Collected poems and prose*, Virago in association with Carcanet, 1982, reprinted by permission of Carcanet Press Ltd.

MEYNELL, Alice. 'The unknown God', *The poems of Alice Meynell*, Burns Oates & Washbourne, 1924; 'Letter from a girl to her own old age'.

MOORE, Marianne. 'What are years?', *The complete poems of Marianne Moore*, Faber, 1969, reprinted by permission of Faber & Faber Ltd.

MORRIS, William. 'Hear a word, a word in season', *Poems by the way*, Longmans, 1896; *The earthly paradise: August*, 1868.

MUIR, Edwin. *An autobiography*, Hogarth Press, 1940, reprinted by permission of Random House UK Ltd; 'One foot in Eden', 'Nothing there but faith', 'October at Helbrunn', 'The heart could never speak', *Collected poems*, Faber, 1960, reprinted by permission of Faber & Faber Ltd.

MURDOCH, Iris. *The black prince*, Chatto & Windus, 1973; *The sacred and profane love machine*, Chatto & Windus, 1974, reprinted by permission of Random House UK Ltd. *The sovereignty of good*, RKP, 1970, reprinted by permission of Routledge & Kegan Paul.

NEEDHAM, Joseph. 'Cambridge summer', *History is on our side*, Allen & Unwin, 1946; *Time: the refreshing river*, Allen & Unwin, 1943, reprinted by permission of HarperCollins Publishers Ltd.

NEVINSON, H. W. 'A ballade of time', *Henry W. Nevinson*, Ernest Benn Ltd.

NICHOLSON, Norman. 'Egremont', *Selected poems 1940–1982*, Faber, 1966, reprinted by permission of Faber & Faber Ltd.

NOTT, Kathleen. *The emperor's clothes*, Heinemann, 1953.

O'CONNOR, Frank. 'From the Irish of Murrough O'Daly'.

PASTERNAK, Boris. *Dr Zhivago*, Collins Harvill, 1958, reprinted by permission of HarperCollins Ltd.

PATER, Walter. *The Renaissance*, Macmillan, 1912.

PEARSE, Innes, and CROCKER, Lucy. *The Peckham experiment*, Allen & Unwin Ltd, 1943.

PEARSE, Padraic. 'The fool', *Collected works*, New York, AMS Press, 1978.

PÉGUY, Charles. 'A prayer in confidence', *The mystery of Holy Innocents and other poems*, Harvill Press, 1956.

PETER OF CLUNY, in Radice, B. (ed.), *The letters of Abélard and Héloïse*, Penguin, 1974, reprinted by permission of Penguin Books Ltd.

PEVSNER, Nicholas. *The Englishness of English art*, Architectural Press, 1956, reprinted by permission of Butterworth-Heinemann Ltd.

PHILLIPS, Anthony. *God B.C.*

PICASSO, Pablo. Anon. translation of a speech given at Sheffield City Hall, 1950, private manuscript.

PLOWMAN, Max. 'On living near the grave of Father Tyrell'.

PORTER, Peter. 'Cat's fugue', *Collected poems*, 1983, copyright Peter Porter 1983, reprinted by permission of Oxford University Press.

POWYS, John Cowper. *Owen Glendower*, Bodley Head, 1941; *Wolf Solent*, Penguin, 1978; *Weymouth Sands*, John Lane, 1935.

PRESS, John. *The fire and the fountain*, OUP, 1955, reprinted by permission.

PROUST, Marcel. *Swann's way*, Random House, 1922.

QUILLER-COUCH, Arthur. 'Upon Eckington bridge', *Poems of today*, Sidgwick & Jackson, 1915.

RAINE, Kathleen. 'Parting', *Stone and flower*, Nicholson & Watson, 1943; 'Winter fire', *Collected poems*, Hamish Hamilton, 1956.

RATUSHINSKAYA, Irina. *No I'm not afraid*, Bloodaxe Books, reprinted by permission of Bloodaxe Books Ltd.

RAY, Gordon N. *Thackeray: the age of wisdom*, OUP, 1958, reprinted by permission of Oxford University Press.

READ, Herbert. *The contrary experience*, Faber, 1963, reprinted by permission of the author.

RICHARDS, I. A. *Principles of literary criticism*, Kegan Paul, 1925.

RIDLER, Anne. 'A waving hand', 'Nothing is lost', *New and selected poems*, Faber, 1988, reprinted by permission of Faber & Faber Ltd.

RIEU, E. V. 'The lost cat', *Cuckoo calling*, Methuen, 1933, reprinted by permission of R. Rieu.

ROBERTS, Michael. *The modern mind*, Faber, 1937.

ROETHKE, Theodore. 'The waking', 'The motion', *The collected poems of Theodore Roethke*, Faber, 1968, reprinted by permission of Faber & Faber Ltd.

ROOT, Howard. 'Beginning all over again', *Soundings*, CUP, 1962, reprinted by permission of Cambridge University Press.

ROSENBERG, H. *The tradition of the new*, Thames & Hudson, 1962, reprinted by permission of Thames & Hudson Ltd.

ROSENZWEIG, Franz. *The star of redemption*, RKP, 1971; 'Letter of Ilse Hahn, March 1920', in GLATZER, N. N., *Franz Rosenzweig: his life and thought*, Schocken Books, 1953.

ROSSETTI, Christina. 'Remember', *New Oxford book of English verse*, OUP, 1972.

RUSKIN, John. *The stones of Venice vol.2*, Everyman, Dent, 1907.

RUSSELL, John. *Henry Moore*, Penguin, 1973; *Francis Bacon*, Thames & Hudson, 1979, reprinted by permission of Thames & Hudson Ltd.

RUTHERFORD, Mark. *Deliverance*, T. Fisher Unwin, 1980.

SANDBURG, Carl. 'Grass', 'The long shadow of Lincoln, *Complete poems*, Harcourt Brace Jovanovich, New York, 1969.

SANTAYANA, George. *The last puritan*, Constable, 1935; *English liberty in America*; 'Dickens', *Selected works vol.1*, reprinted by permission of Cambridge University Press.

SASSOON, Siegfried. 'Invocation', 'Prehistoric burials', 'Because we two can never again come back', *Collected poems 1908–1956*, Faber & Faber, 1984, reprinted by permission of George Sassoon.

SAVAGE, D. S. 'February', *A time to mourn*, reproduced by permission of The Brynmill Press Ltd., Pockthorpe Cottage, Denton, nr Harleston, Norfolk, IP20 0AS, copyright The Brynmill Press Ltd.

SAVILLE, Maud. 'The night before the storm died', unpublished, used with permission.

SCHILLEBEECKX, E. *Jesus*, Collins, 1979.

SCOTT, Walter. 'Madge Wildfire's song', *New Oxford book of English verse*, OUP, 1972.

SCOVELL, E. J. 'Bloody cranesbill on the Downs', *Collected poems*, Carcanet, 1988, reprinted by permission of Carcanet Press Ltd.

SEDLEY, Sir Charles. 'Song', *New Oxford book of English verse*, OUP, 1972.

SEEBOHM, F. *The Oxford reformers*, Everyman, Dent.

SEXTON, Anne. 'The death notebooks', *Complete poems*, Houghton Mifflin, Boston, 1981.

SHAKESPEARE, William. 'Sonnet xxix', Sonnet xxx', 'Sonnet cxxix', 'Sonnet cvi', 'Sonnet xv', 'Sonnet lxv', 'Sonnet lxxiii', *The winter's tale*, *The merchant of Venice*, *Measure for measure*, *Henry VIII*, *The tempest*, *Cymbeline*.

SHOVE, Fredegond. 'The new ghost', *Poems*, CUP, 1956.

SILKIN, Jon. 'Death of a son', *Collected poems*, reprinted by permission of Jon Silkin and Routledge & Kegan Paul.

SIMPSON, Louis. 'Walt Whitman at Bear mountain', *Collected poems*, Paragon House Publishers, 1988.

SISSON, C. H. 'A letter to John Donne', *Collected poems, 1943–83*, Carcanet, 1984; 'The Usk', *In the Trojan ditch*, Carcanet, 1974, reprinted by permission of Carcanet Press Ltd.

SOLZHENITSYN, Alexander. *Matryona's home*, in Blake, P., and Hayward, M., (eds.), *Half-way to the moon*, Weidenfeld & Nicolson, 1964.

SOUTHERN, R. W. *Medieval Humanism and other studies*, Basil Blackwell, 1970, reprinted by permission.

SPENCER, Stanley. see COLLIS, M.

STEINER, George. *After Babel*, OUP, 1975, reprinted by permission of Oxford University Press. *Real presences*, Faber, 1989; *Language and silence*, Penguin, 1975, reprinted by permission of Faber & Faber Ltd.

STERN, Karl. *The flight from woman*, Allen & Unwin, 1966, reprinted by permission of HarperCollins Publishers Ltd.

STEVENS, Wallace. 'Sunday morning', *The collected poems of Wallace Stevens*, Faber, 1953, reprinted by permission of Faber & Faber Ltd.

STUBBS, Aelred. 'Martyr of Hope' in BIKO, Steve, *I write what I like*, Bowerdean Press, 1978, reprinted by permission of Bowerdean Press.

SWINBURNE, A. C. 'A leave-taking', *New Oxford book of English verse*, OUP, 1972; 'A Jacobite's exile 1746'; 'The triumph of time'.

TAWNEY, R. H. *Diary*.

TEILHARD DE CHARDIN, Pierre. *Le milieu divin*, Collins, 1960.

TENNYSON, Alfred. 'In the valley of Cauteretz', 'Ulysses', *New Oxford book of English verse*, OUP, 1972; 'The princess', 'In memoriam', *Poems*, OUP, 1913.

THACKERAY, W. M. *The history of Henry Esmond*, OUP, 1903.

THOMAS, Dylan. 'This bread I break', 'And death shall have no dominion', 'Poem in October', 'The conversation of prayer', *Collected poems 1934–53*, Dent, 1988, reprinted by permission of David Higham Associates.

THOMAS, R. S. 'Kneeling', *Selected poems 1946–1968*, Hart-Davis, MacGibbon Ltd, 1973; 'The woman', *Later poems*, Macmillan, 1983, reprinted by permission of Macmillan London Ltd.

TING, K. H. *No longer strangers*, Orbis, 1989, reprinted by permission of Orbis Books.

TOYNBEE, Arnold. *A study of history, vol.4*, OUP, 1939, reprinted by permission of Oxford University Press.

TRAHERNE, Thomas. *Centuries of meditation 4.72*.

TREECE, Henry. 'Invitation and warning', *Invitation and warning*, Faber, 1942.

TRILLING, Lionel. *The middle of the journey*, Secker & Warburg, 1948, reprinted by permission of Martin Secker & Warburg Ltd. 'Huckleberry Finn', *The liberal imagination*, Secker & Warburg, 1951, reprinted by permission of the author.

TWAIN, Mark. *Life on the Mississippi*, Penguin, 1984.

TYRELL, George. *The life of George Tyrell vol.2*, Edward Arnold, 1912.

VAN DER POST, Laurens. *The face beside the fire*, Hogarth Press, 1953, reprinted by permission of Random House UK Ltd.

VANZETTI, Bartolomeo. 'Speech before execution', quoted by Fast, Howard, in *The passion of Sacco and Vanzetti*, Bodley Head, 1954.

VON HÜGEL, Friedrich. *The mystical element in religion*, Dent, 1961; *Essays and addresses*, Dent, 1926.

WADDELL, Helen. *The wandering scholars*, Constable, 1934.

WATKINS, Vernon. 'Testimony', 'Cantata for the waking of Lazarus', 'The heron', *Collected poems*, Golgonooza, 1986, reprinted by permission of Golgonooza Press.

WEBER, Alfred. *Farewell to European history*, Kegan Paul, 1947.

WEIL, Simone. *Waiting on God*, Routledge & Kegan Paul, 1951; 'A note on social democracy', *Oppression and liberty*, RKP, 1958.

WHITE, Antonia. *The hound and the falcon*, London, 1965, reproduced by permission of Virago Press.

WHITE, Patrick. *Riders in the chariot*, Eyre & Spottiswoode, 1961,
    reproduced by permission of the Estate of Patrick White.
WHYTE, Lancelot L. *The next development in man*, Cresset Press, 1944.
WILLIAMSON, Henry. *Dandelion days*, Zenith, 1983.
WILSON, Angus. *The middle age of Mrs Eliot*, Secker & Warburg, 1958,
    reprinted by permission of Martin Secker & Warburg Ltd.
WILSON, Edmund. 'On "Finnegan's wake" ', *The wound and the bow*,
    Methuen, 1961.
WILSON, R. N. D. *'St Apollinare in Classe'*.
WOLFE, Thomas. *Look homeward, angel*, Penguin, 1984.
WOOLF, Virginia. *To the lighthouse*, Hogarth, 1990; *The waves*, Hogarth,
    1931.
WORDSWORTH, William. 'Intimations of immortality', *New Oxford book
    of English verse*, OUP, 1972.

YEATS, W. B. 'When you are old', 'Byzantium', 'The second coming',
    Oxford book of twentieth century English verse, OUP, 1973; 'Among
    schoolchildren', 'Easter 1916', *New Oxford book of English verse*, OUP,
    1972; 'The happiest of poets', *The poems*, Dent, 1990; 'A prayer for my
    daughter', *Collected poems*, Macmillan, 1928.
YOUNG, G. W. 'High hills', *Collected poems*, Methuen, 1936.

ZAEHNER, R. C. *Concordant discord*, OUP, 1970, copyright R. C. Zaehner
    1970, reproduced by permission of Curtis Brown Ltd, London.

Author Index